Collecting Autographs For Fun and Profit

Robert W. Pelton

BETTERWAY PUBLICATIONS, INC.
WHITE HALL, VIRGINIA

```
929.88   P393c  1987
Pelton, Robert W., 1934-
Collecting autographs for
  fun and profit.
```

Published by Betterway Publications, Inc.
Box 80
White Hall, VA 22987

Cover design by Deborah B. Chappell

Typography by Papercraft Printing & Design Co., Inc.

Copyright ©1987 by Robert W. Pelton

All rights reserved. No part of this book may be reproduced by any means, except by a reviewer who wishes to quote brief excerpts in connection with a review in a magazine or newspaper.

Library of Congress Cataloging-in-Publication Data

Pelton, Robert W.
    Collecting autographs for fun and profit.

    Includes index.
    1. Autographs—Collectors and collecting. I. Title.
Z41.P46   1987   929.8'8'075   87-14809
ISBN 0-932620-80-9 (pbk.)

Printed in the United States of America
0987654321

Dedication

Kristie Lynn, my best friend and sweetheart

and to

My two lovely daughters,
Kristie Kathleen and Martha Ruth,
who both have brought many new rays of sunshine
into my life

and to

Those thousands of notables
who so generously responded to my autograph requests,
thereby giving me an abiding faith
in the essential kindness of famous people

and, lastly, to

This marvelous nation of ours, with its unparalleled postal system—making our's one of the few countries where autograph collecting can be pursued so successfully.

I would like particularly to thank the following: Perez-Steele Galleries, Fort Washington, Pennsylvania, for use of their Hall of Fame art post cards; the National Baseball Hall of Fame and Museum in Cooperstown, New York for use of their plaque cards; T.C.G., T.C.M.A., Tops Chewing Gum, Inc., Dexter Press, and Grand Slam for the use of various baseball cards; the Manuscript Division of the New York Public Library; the Astor, Lenox, and Tilden Foundations for use of John Quincy Adams' poetic prayer; and Tom Hoy of the *Washington Star* for use of Mamie Eisenhower's photograph.

Contents

PART I. An Introduction to Autograph Collecting
1. A Brief History of Autograph Collecting............13
2. How to Write for Autographs and Replies to Expect..21
3. Address Sources and Forms of Salutation..........31
4. Suggested Categories for Specialization............35
5. Values of Autographs and What Affects Them......53
6. Some Anecdotes and Interesting Sidelights..........71

PART II. Baseball Autographs
7. Hall of Fame Members: Values....................83
8. Some Living Hall of Famers: Addresses..........107
9. Directory of Major League Baseball Parks.........115
10. Career Leaders and Record Holders: Addresses.....119
11. MVP's: Addresses 123
12. Old-Timers: Addresses...........................127

PART III. Getting Down to Business
13. Exhibiting and Lecturing........................135
14. Proper Care of Autographs......................139
15. Record-Keeping.................................145
16. Helpful Sources and Other Data.................149

APPENDIX: A Collector's Glossary..................151

INDEX..155

Sincerely,

James A. Michener
James A. Michener

Errol Flynn

Sincerely yours,
Whittaker Chambers

Harold H. Burton

Willie Mosconi

John F. Kennedy

Sincerely yours,
Walter P. Chrysler, Jr.

Bess W. Truman

Sincerely yours,

J. Edgar Hoover

C. de Gaulle

Richard Nixon

Adlai E. Stevenson

Pius PP. XII

Sam Rayburn
Speaker of the House of Representatives

Introduction

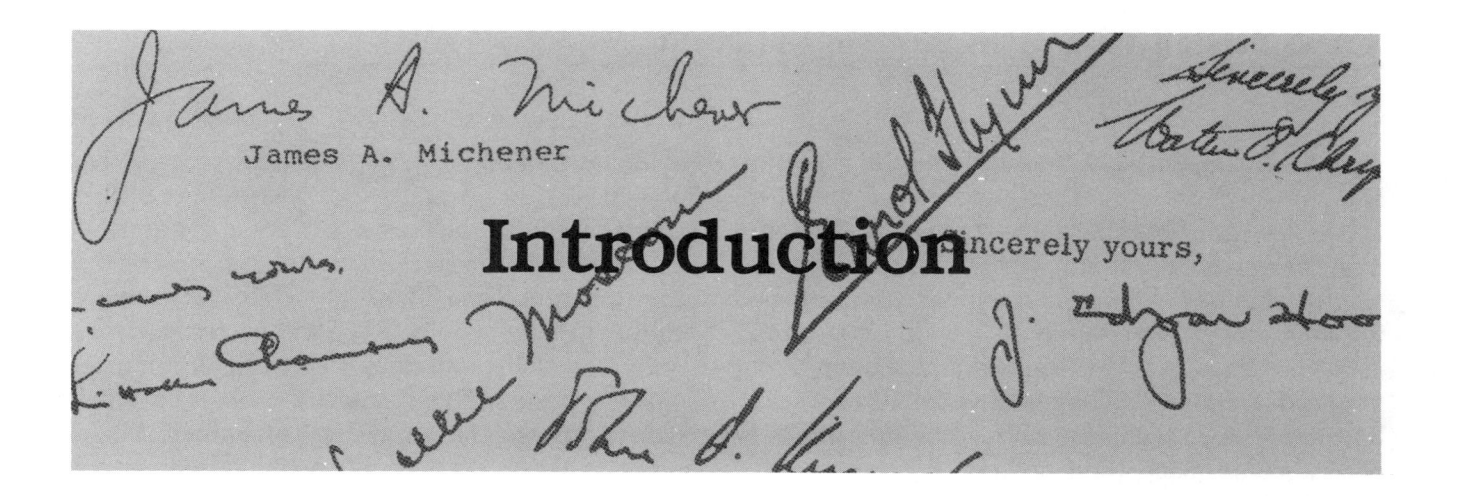

The popular hobby of autograph collecting consists of acquiring and preserving the signatures of notable people or people associated with particular events. When any person signs his or her name or makes their "mark" on anything, an autograph is produced. Anyone who takes the time to collect and preserve such evidence of human existence takes an active part in history as it's being made. The collector becomes, in a sense, a custodian of civilization, for autographs—and the letters, notes and photographs on which they appear—can provide a singular means of tracking the past and the present.

People collect all sorts of things: coins, buttons, stamps, baseball cards, you name it. Some may choose to concentrate on objects of nature—such as butterflies, rocks and mineral specimens or seashells—while others go after timely keepsakes of modern-day living—House and Senate passes, ashtrays, matchbooks, etc. Whatever category of treasure a collector pursues, he or she can't help but get caught up in the suspense and excitement of the hunt itself. This feeling is enhanced by a rewarding thrill of achievement whenever one or more items are added to a growing collection, like the time I obtained Tony Zale's autograph. This barrel-chested, tough-looking stranger simply walked up to me in a bus station and asked, "Do you know who I am?"

I responded with a puzzled look that said, "No, should I?"

He then offered me a meaty hand and introduced himself, saying "I'm Anthony Zalinski."

"Anthony Zalinski? Who's Anthony Zalinski?", I exclaimed.

Tony grinned big. "That's my real name," he replied. "But everybody knows me as Tony Zale, the middleweight boxer."

I recognized the name immediately at this point—Tony Zale, one of the roughest, toughest brawlers in ring history and arch foe of the famed Rocky Graziano. He still looked as though he could

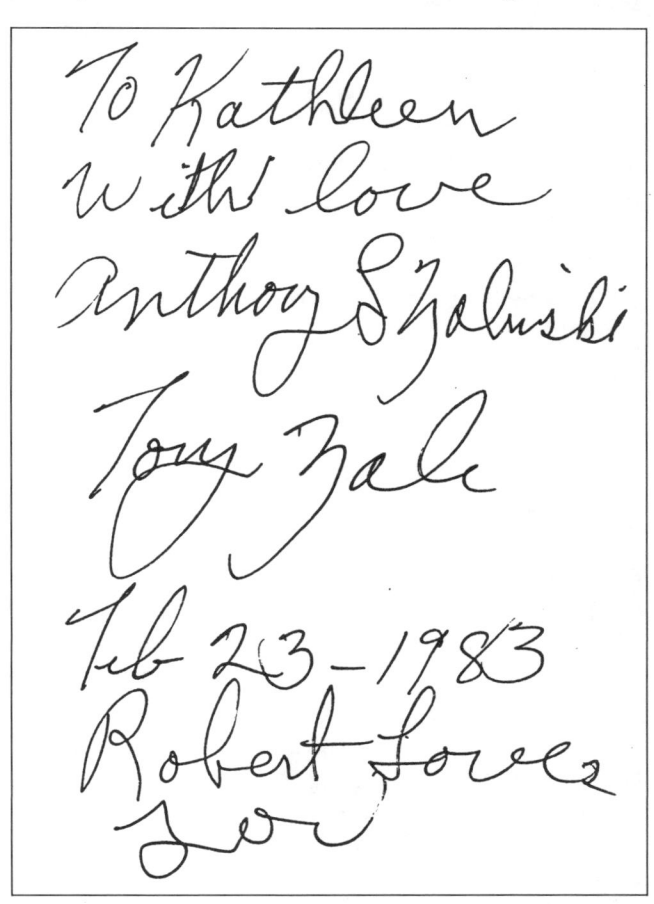

Tony Zale—former boxing great of years gone by. The author obtained this autograph for his daughter while waiting for a Greyhoud bus in Knoxville, Tennessee.

step in the ring with the best of them, too. Not only was Tony nice enough to provide me with his autograph, but I had the distinct pleasure of spending over an hour listening to him reminisce about some of his past fights—and expound on how he felt about today's boxers in his weight class, such as Marvelous Marvin Hagler and Sugar Ray Leonard. Of course, Tony believed neither would have even belonged in the ring with either himself or Graziano during their heyday.

Over the years autograph collecting is likely to prove to be one of the most gratifying of hobbies, both from personal and monetary standpoints. It is an exhilarating undertaking for the collector and stimulating to friends and acquaintances. Any autograph—whether it be that of George Wallace or George Washington—is a natural conversation piece and a fascinating fragment of history. This points to another virtue of the hobby: eventually it is likely to pay for itself. Many easily obtained autographs will have considerable value on the collectors' market one day, if and when the hobbyist decides to part with them. Even those seemingly least in demand when acquired may be worth much more than the cost of acquisition, provided the collector is prudent in his efforts. Going after the autographs of only contemporary personalities who achieve fleeting notoriety in the news columns will probably not result in a collection of any long-lasting distinction of interest or value.

Autographs can be traded as well as sold, and this is likely to happen when there are duplicates or when an individual's field of interest changes. Ordinarily, collectors will advertise the material they have available for trading in hobby magazines and newsletters or they will contact other hobbyists through membership in organizations such as the Manuscript Society. Sometimes they will list the items or categories that will be acceptable for exchange. Antique shops and dealers in old or rare books often handle autographs as a sideline, and they frequently are willing to trade items with collectors. There are also many reputable autograph dealers who can offer further trading opportunities. If a collector has material a dealer specifically wants or needs, an equitable exchange usually can be negotiated. However, few dealers are likely to be interested in an autographed photograph of the current second baseman of the New York Yankees, so be sure to use common sense in your dealings or you'll wind up just wasting everyone's time.

One unfortunate aspect of the autograph hobby is that it has suffered somewhat from abuse by the unscrupulous. There are collectors who are simply greedy people. They will pester celebrities with only their own potential profit in mind. For example, anyone can send a baseball or a color photograph to the great Hall of Famer, Mickey Mantle. Mickey is a kind-hearted gentleman who loves children. He never refuses a legitimate appeal for an autograph coming from a child or a teenager. Nor will he turn down one from parents writing for their children. In my case, I wanted a personalized signed color photograph for my stepson James and my daughter Kathleen. (Martha Ruth wasn't a part of our family at the time.) Mickey generously took a few minutes out of his busy schedule to honor this special request. Like many other celebrities, Mantle will honor all

Photograph of Mrs. Eisenhower which was obtained from the U.S. Army Photographic Agency and sent to her for signing. A simple L.S. by this First Lady sometimes comes on the market for between $30.00 and $40.00, but they are difficult to find.

reasonable petitions for autographs. A ball signed by him will be valued at $50.00 to $65.00 on the current market. His personally autographed photograph could bring as much as $18.00 to $40.00.

It's always a good idea to consider enclosing two photographs rather than only one when sending a request for autographs. Most notables will sign as many as two per request. It certainly won't cost more in postage to include an extra photo for signing, and you'd have two great collectors' items—both to keep, or one to keep for your personal collection and one for possible trade for an autograph you don't have. Unprincipled collectors, often dealers posing as legitimate hobbyists, will rush to sell photographs and letters like these as soon as they are received. These individuals lose out on the intellectual and emotional rewards but, more importantly, they give the hobby a bad name.

Even the more sincere and judicious collector, due to the nature of his pursuit, ends up taking advantage of the enormous generosity of the many celebrities who grant autographs. The true collector derives immense personal satisfaction from simply keeping and augmenting his collection, and from studying it, displaying it and talking about it. Eventually, if he does decide to sell all or part of his treasures—because the price is right or his tastes have changed or he's run out of storage space—the decision is not made hastily or without a wrench.

Autograph collecting is certainly one of the least costly hobbies in the collecting category. For mere pennies a day, and the investment of a little time and imagination, even the youngest beginner can accumulate an astonishing number of letters, signatures and autographed photographs from contemporary celebrities. To start, all one needs is a supply of postage stamps, stationery, some envelopes—and a list of notables. The results are sure to be astonishing and profitable as well.

Artist sketch of Los Angeles Dodger's Fernando Valenzuela. The author purchased this drawing from the artist—Randy Rustin of Joplin, Missouri—and sent it to Fernando for signing. It has a special significance, for this star pitcher is one of the most difficult autographs to obtain in modern day baseball. He even included a personal handwritten and signed letter with the autographed sketch! Fernando made an exception in this case. Why? Simply because he liked the original drawing. In fact, in his return letter to me, he asked if the artist would do a similar sketch for him. I, in turn, contacted Randy and told him of Fernando's request. He was extremely pleased and agreed to do so for the Dodger's pitching ace.

12 Collecting Autographs For Fun and Profit

Dr. Wernher von Braun, director of the United States space program and our nation's most famous space expert. A L.S. by this man can bring upwards of $45.00 on the collector's market!

The original seven astronauts. Sent to the author by Alan B Shepard shortly after the space program was initiated.

    I met and talked at length with Wally Schirra while attending a medical convention with my wife in 1985. Wally was there as a representative of a major drug company. He was standing in an Actifed booth autographing 8×10 color photographs of himself on request. I told Wally about the above photo of himself and the other astronauts. He recalled that NASA had issued a few of them early in the space program, and that even fewer had been sent out fully autographed. He advised me to take special care of mine because of its rarity. While we chatted, Wally also graciously signed photos of himself for my children, relatives and various friends. It was great fun to meet a celebrity of such stature and refreshing to find that he was so down to earth and personable.

1. A Brief History of Autograph Collecting

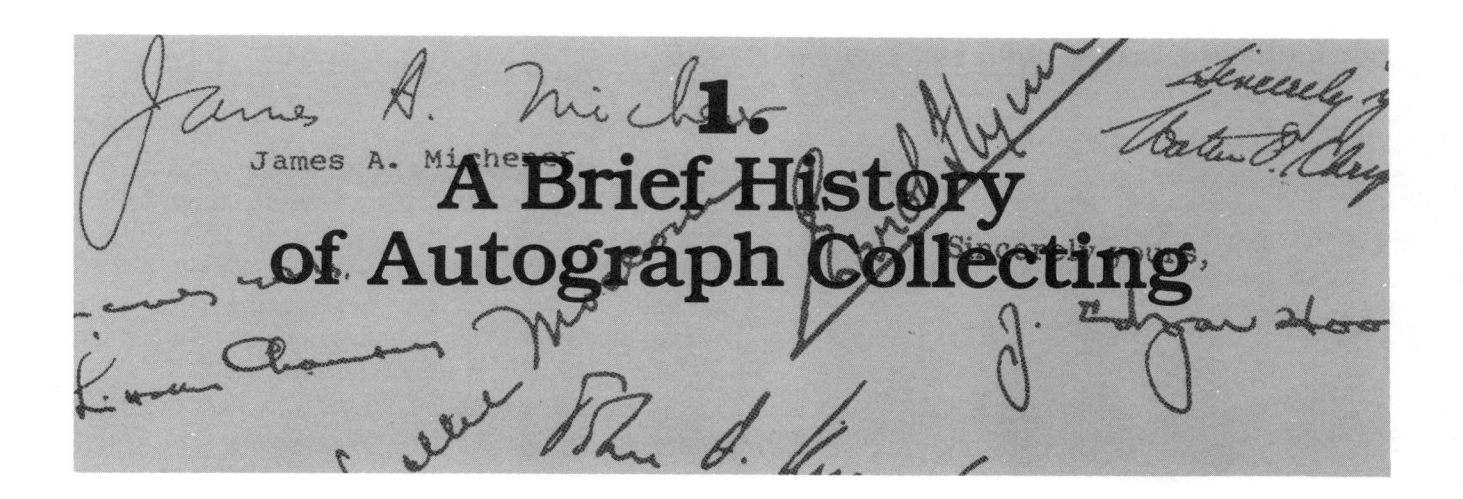

The term "autograph" literally means "self-written" and refers to a vast spectrum of materials, not just signatures. It encompasses such handwritten matter as diaries, letters, manuscripts, musical scores, charters and documents. The pursuit of autographs in all these various forms is an ancient hobby, its claims to antiquity having been established by thorough documentation. Historical evidence clearly indicates that almost as soon as people began to write, others started to collect and preserve their writings for posterity.

Looking back, autograph collecting seems to have followed the development pattern of writing materials in general. The oldest known surviving written records are the clay tablets and bricks of the ancient Chaldeans and Sumerians; their writing consisted of cuneiform characters engraved on tablets by square-ended, wedge-shaped pieces of bone. These tablets were then sent from one person or place to another as a commonplace form of communication.

Briefly, we know that in ancient Egypt rolls of papyrus, made from the fiber of the papyrus plant, were popular among early autograph collectors. Developed in the third millenium B.C., this was the first writing material to closely resemble paper. The words of the old Hebrew scholars have been preserved on thick rolls of this early stationery. Inscriptions on animal skins have been found that date from ancient times. None of the earliest of these leather specimens survive today, but many fine examples of later documents on parchment and vellum, which are treated animal skins, are treasured by museums and libraries throughout the world. Eventually, by the seventh century, papyrus was replaced almost entirely by these superior writing materials. Paper as we know it today has been traced back to China in A.D. 105. The art of paper-making was a closely-guarded secret of the Chinese, but the formula fell into the hands of the Arabs in the middle of the eighth century and then started spreading to western Europe around the middle of the 12th century.

Past civilizations are known to have made use of brass, copper, lead, bronze and other metals as common writing materials. The Bible refers to the use of "an iron pen and lead" (Job, 19:24) as well as bark. The ancient Romans used the inner bark, which they called liber, and from this we derive the word "library" as a place where books (libri) are stored.

Pens used by most ancient civilizations were usually in the form of hollow tubular stalks of grass, such as the papyrus reeds used by the Egyptians, or the hollow joints of bamboo stalks used by the Chinese. Around 250 B.C. the Chinese scholar Meng Tien is credited with having developed the camel's hair brush.

The quill pen, mentioned in records dating back to the seventh century C.E., was used when Thomas Jefferson signed the Declaration of Independence. He provided his own personal quill pen, the feather of which came from a goose raised at Monticello, Jefferson's Virginia home. Our Constitution and Bill of Rights were likewise inscribed with goose quill pens. The origin of metal pens is uncertain, but a bronze pen was found in the ruins of Pompeii in A.D. 79 and steel pens are known to have been first developed in England at the beginning of the 19th century. The first practical

14 Collecting Autographs For Fun and Profit

fountain pen—one with a built-in ink reservoir—was invented by Waterman in 1884.

From this brief sketch we can see that even in antiquity, there would have been a plentiful supply of autographic material. The earliest attempt at autograph collecting was undertaken initially by the libraries of the ancient world. Every Egyptian temple had its own library of volumna—the term the Romans used to refer to papyrus rolls—with specimens uncovered that date back to 2500 B.C. An intense competition is known to have existed between the great libraries of Alexandria and Pergamum in the second century B.C. Such flourishing libraries were not to be found in ancient Rome however, where all the libraries were private in the beginning, and stocked with war booty. Cicero and the two Plinys were three of the most notable Roman collectors, and one Roman emperor even specialized in compiling the writings of Chinese scholars. In China, it wasn't uncommon to find autographic materials used as wallpaper on the interiors of homes and temples.

Pliny, the Elder   *Pliny, the Younger*

Sixteenth-century Europeans were extremely earnest collectors. They assembled all the important writings they could garner through purchases or trade. Most noteworthy collections of the Renaissance years were destroyed by numerous wars, but some exceptionally good material has survived and can be found in museums and libraries.

Albums with blank pages were first produced in Germany late in the Middle Ages. These oblong, pocket-sized books were called alba amicorum. Similar to our modern-day autograph albums, they were in demand with traveling people and quickly gained in popularity when it became fashionable to collect the signatures of notables. The little autograph book was adopted during the sixteenth century by German university students, who commonly used it for collecting the inscriptions of campus friends and acquaintances. An entry written by John Milton appears in one of these albums. The British Museum owns a fine collection of alba amicorum, one dated as early as 1554.

The earliest known European lay signature, dated 1096, is that of the Cid, called "The flower of Spanish chivalry". Most people in higher stations of life were not able to write to any extent, and the kings of England, of that period, normally validated written material with a personal seal, unable as they were to sign even their own names. Old parchment deeds written in Latin during the reign of Edward II (1284-1327) are scarce, yet one can occasionally be picked up for around $375. Norman kings generally signed by making a cross. The first English king whose writing survives Edward III (1327-1377), although he wasn't the first literate king. There are specimens surviving from all subsequent English monarchs. A deed in mint condition, written in Latin and dated 1477, 16 years after Edward IV's conquest of England, sells for $175 on today's market. A document written and signed by Edward VII can be purchased for as little as $125.

The art of letter writing became more widespread throughout the world as literacy increased. Initially, it was quite expensive to write a letter, because of the prohibitive cost of paper. To have one delivered once it had been written was even more costly. It is difficult today to envision life without a decent postal system, yet, until relatively recent times, each piece of correspondence had to be hand-carried by a courier. Since the cost of this ancient delivery service was astronomical, receiving a letter was a rare event in those early days. Letters were sent only in cases of dire necessity. As a result, people who received letters generally saved them. It is to this practice that we owe the preservation of many outstanding examples of autographic material.

Countless official British government papers from as late as the eighteenth and nineteenth centuries were lost to future generations because

This beautiful poetic prayer was written by Representative John Quincy Adams of Massachusetts while he sat in the Second Session of the Twenty-fifth Congress. Benjamin Franklin

private citizens found it fashionable to keep such writings for themselves. Many shortsighted autograph collectors of that era were interested only in the signatures. They would cut these out and paste them in personal scrapbooks, often discarding the all-important body of the document. No consideration was given to the fact that future generations were thereby being deprived of valuable data and insights, or that future historical research would be seriously imparied. Today, most governments have passed statutes designed to preserve public records of this kind.

Early letters and diaries were equally significant historically, considering that at one time they were the only recorded first-hand accounts of great events. There wasn't always an Associated Press (AP) or a United Press International (UPI) on hand to provide coverage. No worldwide news service reported Columbus's journey to the New World. His letters are an important documentation of history. Beginning collectors are often pleasantly surprised at the large number of documents and letters of famous historical figures still on the market, frequently at reasonable prices too.

Letters do not have to be extremely old to be historically valuable or important. A letter from John Glenn, Neil Armstrong or Alan Shepard describing some phase of space flight would be a wonderful treasure to own. Another prize would be a letter from Wernher von Braun, America's top rocket authority, giving his expert opinion of Unidentified Flying Objects. A few lines from Albert Speer about his role in the building of Nazi Germany would be marvelous, as would a letter from Einstein explaining his theory of relativity. An eyewitness report of an earthquake tragedy or manned space-craft launching, well-written by even an unknown lay person could one day be of value.

Fortunately, many private collectors preserve such papers intact. Recognizing their literary or historical significance collectors will avoid mutilating them just for the sake of obtaining a signature of a distinguished personality. Collections of this sort going back to the eighteenth century are stored in the Bibliotheque Nationale in Paris and the British Museum in London. One outstanding American collection, owned by the New York Public Library, includes one of the finest complete sets of the Signers of the Declaration of Independence.

Great libraries in many European nations are given credit for preserving documents, letters and other autographic materials directly related to the history of their particular country. This is not the case in America, where all the honor belongs to private collectors, who eventually bequeath their magnificent collections to various institutions or, during their lifetimes, make generous gifts of their manuscript material. Libraries and historical societies in the United States have taken an interest in preserving historical records only since the early 1900's. The only exception has been an historical society in Massachusetts that began collecting manuscripts as far back as 1795. Most states now have at least one large historical society, and there are at least 240 historical society libraries situated throughout the country, all of which collect old manuscripts. The Wisconsin State Historical Society Library, for example, holds over 750,000 important items on the development of the American West.

Some institutions, such as the Rutherford B. Hayes Library and the Roosevelt Library, specialize in one particular field. Other institutions have highly specialized holdings within a vast general collection. American university libraries in particular house some of the most extensive specialized autograph collections in the world. The University of Virginia Library, for instance, possesses over four million manuscripts related to the history of the southeastern United States. Its collections of music and Chinese literature are outstanding. Yale is particularly noted for its Benjamin Franklin papers and its fabulous collections of Boswell-Johnson papers.

The University of Texas Library has over 3,800,000 documents and manuscripts in its huge collection. Its Mexican history material is the most comprehensive in the United States. Here too are extensive collections of English literature and American poetry.

North Carolina can boast of two marvelous collections! Duke University has over 2,700,000 manuscripts on Walt Whitman, English and American literature of the eighteenth and nineteenth centuries, Italian history and the American South. The collection at the University of North Carolina numbers over three million manuscripts. Specialized categories include Spanish Drama, French history of the Napoleonic era, Scandinavian literature and George Bernard Shaw.

The Library of Congress in Washington, D.C., has by far the largest and one of the most distinguished autograph collections in the world—30 million manuscripts. This great institution was created by Congress in 1800 and is run by a staff of over 3,000 persons.

In 1903, manuscript collections from the Historical Division of the Department of State were transferred to the Library of Congress. This included the papers of Benjamin Franklin, Alexander Hamilton and Presidents Washington, Jefferson, Madison and Monroe. The Presidential papers were purchased by Congress—$45,000 was paid for the papers of Washington; $20,000 each for those of Jefferson and James Monroe; $65,000 was paid to Dolly Madison for her husband's papers. Besides the personal papers of most of the Presidents, there are also those of other statesmen, scientists, military and literary figures. The library augments these holdings with historically valuable materials written by prominent Americans from all walks of life. For example, there are manuscript materials of important people in the field of aviation, that trace its development from the time of the Wright brothers and Octave Chanute to the present day.

Other fine American library manuscript collections are the outgrowth of the collecting zeal and generosity of farsighted and historically-minded private citizens. J. Pierpont Morgan, the financier, began by collecting the autographic materials of Presidents of the United States. He also spent years acquiring papers written by bishops of the Methodist and Episcopal churches. Morgan's interests continually expanded and he went on to collect medieval and Renaissance illuminated manuscripts as well as original author handwritten manuscripts. One of his more notable possessions was Verrazano's 1524 diary of a voyage to the New World. Other materials included: Pliny the Younger's sixth century letters; William Penn's 1684 will; the Franklin letters; and letters written by Edgar Allen Poe.

Another outstanding private library was founded early in the twentieth century by the railroad magnate Henry Huntington. Eventually it was deeded to the citizens of the United States with an $8 million trust fund for maintenance. More than two million manuscripts attest to this man's importance as a collector. Rare items include a manuscript copy of Chaucer's *The Canterbury Tales*. The original manuscript of Franklin's *Autobiography* is preserved in this library. Also housed here are: over 200 letters and documents of Abraham Lincoln and 68 letters written by Mary Todd Lincoln; 350 Thomas Jefferson letters; and 400 letters and documents written by Washington.

Franklin *Poe*

The British Museum Library originated in 1753 with the purchase of Sir Hans Sloane's collection of Harleian manuscripts, one of which was written by Shakespeare. Their treasures encompass the seventeenth century material of John Evelyn and Sir Robert Cotton's important document collection. The royal library of the English kings from the time of Henry VII was donated to the museum by George II. Included were the *Codex Alexandrinus*, a vellum manuscript of the Old and New Testaments in Greek which were done in the fifth century. Among the many priceless documents in this library are the beautifully illuminated Lindisfarne Gospels from the seventh century; the earliest known copies of the *Iliad* and the *Odyssey*; and an outstanding Aristotle manuscript, *On the Constitution of Athens*.

England boasts the famous Bodleian Library which was founded in 1602 at Oxford. Its entire collection numbers about 50,000 items, so it can't really rival American university libraries in quantity of material. However, it has some of the earliest surviving paper manuscripts—a copy of Euclid dated 888 and a Clarkianus of Plato done around 895.

18 Collecting Autographs For Fun and Profit

The John Rylands Library in Manchester, England is one of the most important in the world. It has a collection of over 100,000 charters and deeds as well as other priceless manuscript materials.

There are numerous outstanding European libraries with extensive manuscript collections, notably: the university library at Amsterdam (62,000 manuscripts); the Lenin State Library in Moscow (2,500,000 manuscripts); the National Library of Greece (200,000 manuscripts); and the National Central Library in Florence (800,000 documents and manuscripts).

King George II

The Vatican Apostolic Library in Rome is certainly worthy of special mention. It was founded in 1450 by Pope Nicholas V. Over 60,000 manuscripts encompass such rarities as Cicero's *Republic* from the third century; fourth and sixth century handwritten copies of Virgil; and original manuscripts from such men as Giovanni Boccaccio, St. Thomas Aquinas, Martin Luther, Michelangelo and Dante.

Major libraries generally have permanent exhibits of some of their treasures, and special displays of others on particular anniversaries. For instance, the British Museum exhibits a collection of literary material by English writers from Sir Thomas Wyatt to the present, including many corrected drafts. The Library of Congress permanently displays the rough draft of Jefferson's Declaration of Independence, the Constitution, and Lincoln's first and second drafts of the Gettysburg Address.

Thomas Aquinas

Giovanni Boccaccio

Martin Luther

Some libraries publish descriptions of their holdings. Among those available from the Library of Congress are: *List of manuscript Collections in the Library of Congress;* and *Guide to Archives and manuscripts in the United States.* A *Quarterly Journal* that lists current acquisitions is also published. For an up-to-date list of available publications, write to: manuscript Division, The Library of Congress, Washington, D.C. 20540.

Autograph collecting became commercialized when the first catalogs offering autographs for sale were published in France during the early 1800's. Of the initial catalogs issued in the United States, the following two are especially notable: "A Priced Catalogue of Autographs for Sale at the Great Central Fair for the U.S. Sanitary Commission", and "The Collector". The first of these, a fifty-page catalog, was published in Philadelphia in 1864 by Henry B. Ashmead. It contained such items for sale as: a George Washington letter sent from Valley Forge in April, 1778 ($15.00); Thomas Jefferson letters ($5.00 each); a Benedict Arnold letter date 1776 ($10.00); Audubon letters ($3.50 each). Autographic material to be bid on at auction included William Penn's 1682 deed from the Indians and the 1763-1768 Mason-Dixon diary.

The first American dealer to specialize in autographic materials was Charles De F. Burns, author of *The American Antiquarian.* Burns started his business back in 1882 and his publication was actually a catalog with a preface much like that found in "The Collector". Photocopies of this interesting catalog are available from the New York Public Library, Photographic Service, Fifth Avenue and Forty-Second Street, New York, New York 10018.

William Penn

Bejamin Perley Poore, an avid collector, wrote the first column on autograph collecting for Gleason's Pictorial. This magazine was published

The Collector, a combination magazine/catalog, has been published since 1887 by the firm of Walter R. Benjamin. It is the only one of the early catalogs still being published today. Their current address is provided in Chapter 16.

in Boston during the 1850's. Poore also wrote articles describing the handwriting characteristics of eminent persons. Alexander Hamilton, he declared, "wrote with a singularly neat hand". Robespierre, adjudged Poore, "wrote a perverse, crabbed hand, which he endeavored to render graceful and fair".

The Curiosity Cabinet was another early magazine advertising autographic materials. This one was published by William P. Brown from 1870 to 1877 in New York City. An issue dated April, 1877, listed a collection for sale "rich in American Colonial and Revolutionary heroes, the veterans of 1812, and Statesmen, Authors and Generals down to the present day, affording collectors an opportunity of adding to their treasure". One item of great interest was a letter signed by George Washington, dated 1776. The price was a mere $15.00. There were also handwritten letters of Charles Dickens and General Lafayette listed for a price of only $10.00 each.

Many of these older publications can still be found and purchased at reasonable prices. All it takes is a thorough search in stores specializing in used books and magazines.

In the United States today, untold thousands of collectors specialize in acquiring signatures alone, while others accumulate signed photographs and letters. Fewer than 2,000 collectors, including individuals and institutions, seriously gather important collections of manuscripts and letters in specific fields, such as science, history and literature. Nonetheless, the selling, buying and trading of autographic material is now big business, of international stature.

The first newspaper specializing in autograph collecting was published by S.H. Calhoun, Jr., in Nebraska City, Nebraska, from 1887 to 1888. It claimed, and probably correctly so at that particular time, to be the only newspaper of its type in the world "Devoted to the Interests of Autograph Collecting."

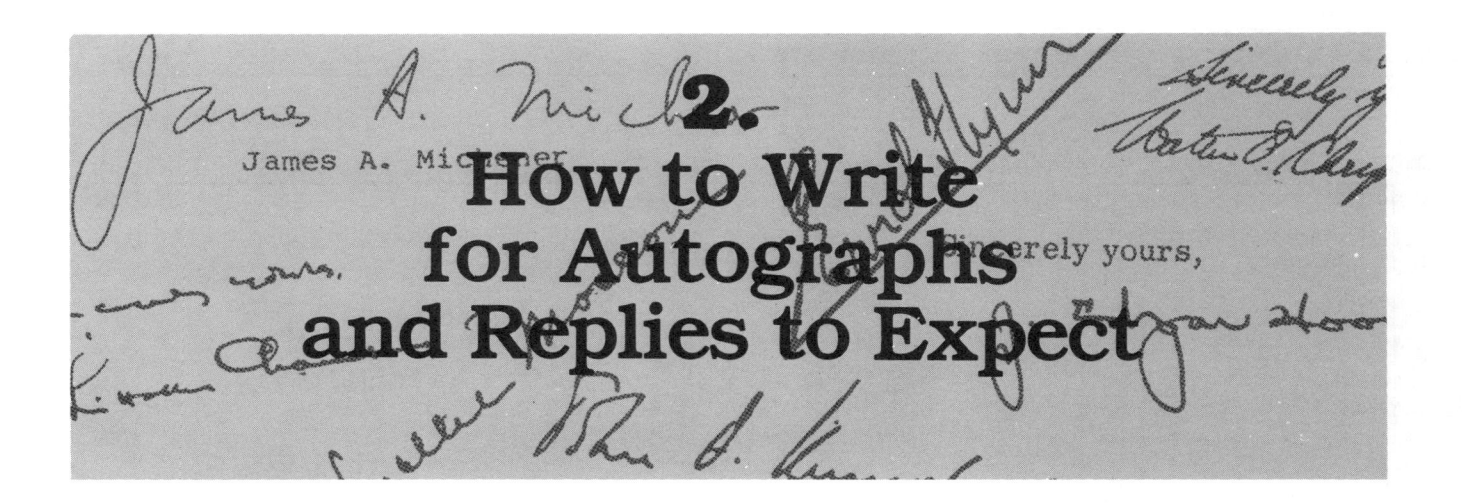

2. How to Write for Autographs and Replies to Expect

The first step in building a collection of your own is to invest in a supply of envelopes, writing paper, stamps and a packet of 3x5 unlined file cards, or some photographs. Even today, youngsters who are beginning as I did, with a severely limited amount of pocket money, can make a satisfactory start with just a modest amount of supplies, buying more as finances permit. A budding collector should always remember to be considerate. Requests should be mailed in the form of a short note or letter, with a file card or photograph enclosed for the requested signature, along with a self-addressed, stamped envelope for its return. When this method is followed, the autographs are easy to store or to combine in a nice display because they are all on cards or photographs of the same size.

In collecting signed photographs via the mail—postcard requests often do bring fruitful results, especially in the political arena—rules of common courtesy dictate that a stamped, self-addressed manila envelope be included with your request. Writing to a well-known celebrity and asking him/her to sign and then return your photograph can be an imposition. As a collector you are not only taking up some of the notable's time but you are also asking, as a total stranger, to be given something of value for nothing more than the price of postage and a small amount of effort. In the case of a truly important, world-renowned individual, you stand to gain a letter or a signed picture souvenir worth several dollars, perhaps. In effect, when responding to such requests, the celebrity is writing the autograph collector a check for that amount of money. It's only common courtesy that the famous individual shouldn't be put to any more trouble and expense than necessary. Usually, if a collector doesn't send a photograph for signing, the celebrity must purchase his own photographs to send out. Even if such photographs are sometimes regarded as part of the price of fame, the postage and return mailing envelopes are always—rightfully—the responsibility of the collector. In spite of the fact that numerous prominent personaliteis will honor simple postcard requests for autographed photographs, it is far better manners not to abuse their generosity by failing to provide return mailing.

Names in the news are one of the keys to successful collecting. Quite often a celebrity's hometown will be noted in a newspaper or magazine article about the individual. Periodicals dealing with specific fields—medicine, the arts, theater, science, sports, education, books, and so on—can be additional sources for tracking down famous people. Make it a habit to jot down names and addresses at once, whenever you come upon them, since newspapers get thrown away promptly in many homes, and magazines have a way of getting mislaid. Chapter 3 contains a list of address sources. These are primarily reference books found in most public libraries, that can be consulted for home addresses of well-known people in various fields. Revealing biographical details will often be included. Information is also given as to the correct forms of address to use when writing to officials in government, both in the United States and in foreign countries.

How should an autograph request be phrased? Be direct, concise and clear. There is no need to write a lengthy letter, or to be flowery, or to pay

> JAMES THURBER
>
> 29th March, 1961
>
> Dear Mr. Pelton,
>
> I never send out autographed photographs or any others. If I did I would get nothing else done.
>
> Best wishes,
>
> Sincerely yours
>
> *[signature]*
>
> James Thurber

A delightful and original response was that of the late James Thurber. He refused to send out any kind of autographic material to his fans under any circumstances. Instead, he sent the humorous letter above—and it was authentically signed by the great man.

false compliments. The above note shows the phrasing that has worked well for this author in countless instances, though it can be varied to suit the circumstances. For instance, a collector interested in art or music who would like to accumulate the autographs of the great recording artists, singers, composers, or musicians, might phrase a letter somewhat like the following, altering the request to suit the situation:

> As a student of music (modern art) and an autograph collector, I am combining my two interests by collecting the signatures (or signed photographs) of today's greatest musicians. I sincerely hope you will be kind enough to sign and return the enclosed photograph for my collection.
>
> Gratefully yours,

If the famous personality is not one whom the collector particularly admires, there is no need to be dishonest. When such is the case, a request may resemble the following:

> My hobby is collecting the autographs of the outstanding world leaders. Naturally, I would like to add your signature (or signed photograph) to my collection. I would be most grateful if you would send it to me in the enclosed self-addressed, stamped envelope.
>
> Cordially,

Requests phrased like the foregoing examples are suitable for collecting signed 3 by 5 cards or autographed photographs. To obtain a personal letter from a celebrity, it is usually necessary to write the person a letter that *merits* a comparable answer. Simply asking "Will you please write me a letter to add to my collection of letters from famous people" will not achieve the desired results. However, a letter questioning a celebrity about some aspect of his or her career, requesting his or her opinion on an issue or problem of concern, or showing an intelligent interest in their specialty may produce a personal response that can be a real treasure. General Dean, former prisoner of war during the Korean conflict, is a perfect example of this. See his letter of response on the next page.

Requests for autographs and signed photographs can be sent at any time during the year. In some circumstances they are more likely to produce successful results. For instance as explained in the next chapter, the time to get a President's autograph is during a campaign. A collector must send out letters to all the competing candidates. Each will be eager to respond to requests since they are politicians seeking favors from the voters. The best time for obtaining autographs of foreign dignitaries is usually at a time when they are visiting the United States. Newspaper items often carry information about where he or she is staying and for how long. The letter illustrated on page 27, from V.K. Krishna Menon of India, a notorious hate-America campaigner of many years' standing, was obtained under such circumstances. He had consistently ignored all my requests for an autograph—even a simple signature—sent to him in India. But he went to the trouble of writing a full-page letter in his own hand when the request came

---

> 403 N. Greenhill Road
> Mt. Juliet, Tenn. 37122
>
> Dear _____:
>
> As a long-time admirer of yours, I would like to ask a special favor. Would you please autograph the enclosed photo of yourself so I may add it to my collection? I appreciate your taking the time to do this for me.
>
> Cordially,
>
> Robert W. Pelton

1035 Park Hills Road
Berkeley 8, California
1 May 1961

Mr. Bob Pelton
1311 King Avenue
Pascagovia, Mississippi

Dear Bob:

    Thank you very much for your card which came in January. It arrived while I was on a trip, and in the accumulation of mail that I found upon my return it was overlooked. Hence my delay in acknowledgment.

    I regret to say that I did not receive any mail from you while I was a prisoner of the North Koreans. But that is not surprising as I only received about 5% of the mail that was addressed to me. In fact I received a higher percentage of the letters written by my daughter than any other. I imagine it was because it was so surprising to my Oriental captors that an Occidental daughter would show such filial devotion. Every time my letters were delivered to me my guards would mention the fact that they had no idea that an American daughter would ever show such devotion. At any rate I appreciate your having written me and I would have certainly enjoyed hearing from you, as the few letters I received were greatly treasured.

    Under separate cover I am sending you the photograph that you requested.

    With all best wishes, I am

        Sincerely,

        William F. Dean
        Major General, U.S.A.(Ret.)

The correspondence accompanying signed photographs or other autographic specimens provides valuable evidence of authenticity. This letter from General Dean is a good example. And the content is more interesting than most letters since he mentions specific things about his North Korean captors.

to him while he was visiting in America. I had a similar success a few years ago in the case of the King and Queen of Siam (Thailand). This gracious couple were kind enough to send me two small, signed photographs from upstate New York while they were on an official visit.

A good time to obtain an autograph without so much as an official request is around any of the major holidays, such as Christmas, New Year's and Easter. For example, send a Christmas card to any notable in the world whom you admire. Add the leaders of foreign nations to your Christmas card list, or send them special cards of greeting on any of their own country's major national holidays. The results will often be astonishing. People who make a practice of never giving out autographs of any kind generally do respond favorably on special occasions. They may send only a signed greeting card of some sort in return, rather than a photograph, but these unusual autographs will make a unique collection in themselves. They will certainly add variety to an otherwise standard collection of signatures and photographs. The official card from Ronald Reagan as Governor of California was sent in response to a Christmas card to him and Nancy.

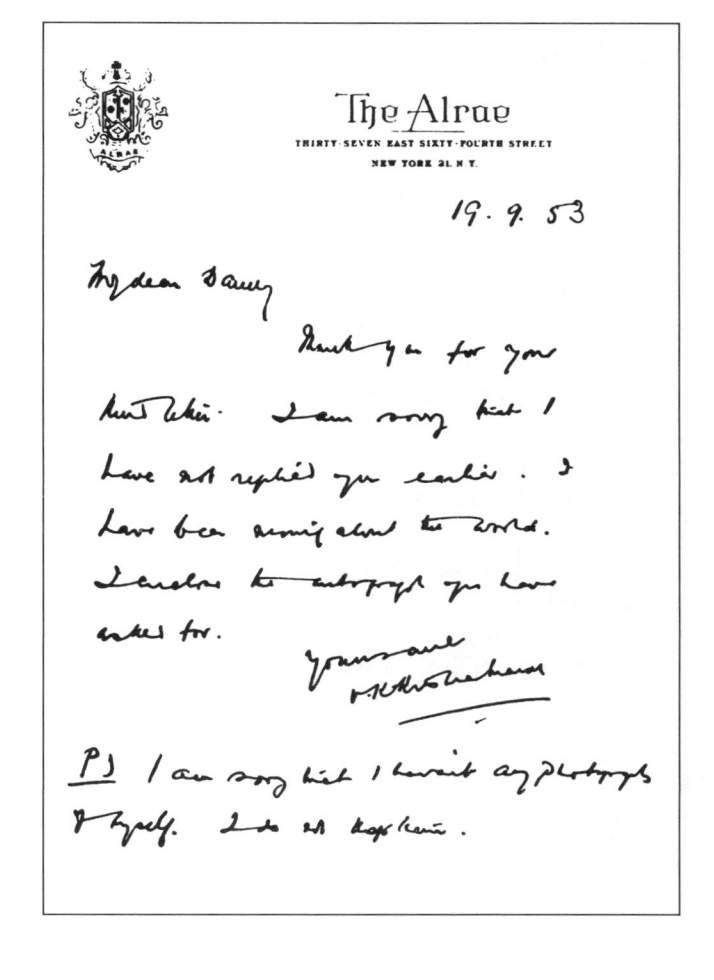

Replies to written request for autographs and signed photographs usually arrive within one to three weeks. Some, such as the foreign ones, may take longer, and a few of the signatures will probably not be original. A number of busy public figures have signed phtographs and autographed cards reproduced by the thousands to use in responding to ordinary requests. If an obvious reproduciton is received, simply return it to the sender with a courteous note explaining that you collect only authentic signatures. Inform the personality that you would appreciate it if he or she would sign the enclosed photograph personally. Be sure to always enclose postage and an envelope for the return mailing. The majority of these celebrities will almost always comply with this second request.

In most cases, a letter will accompany the return of an autographed photograph. This letter is generally signed by the notable's secretary, and says little more than that so-and-so was happy to sign the picture. Often the collector can't be sure that the secretary was not the one who actually signed the photograph. Secretarial signatures are most common on pictures of film stars, for instance. Some busy politicians turn to the "robot pen," too, so they won't have to be bothered signing for collectors. The chance of a signature being genuine is greater if the collector asks that the photograph be autographed to him or her personally—i.e., "To Robert with best wishes, Warren E. Burger."

Today, not only are photographic facsimile signatures put on photographs; printed facsimile signatures are often used on the letters accompanying signed photographs and on cards sent in answer to requests. Most copies of signatures are relatively easy top spot. Seldom are they good enough to fool an experienced collector. The "autographed" photographs that come in the picture holder of a new billfold are photographic facsimiles.

Printed facsimile of Lyndon Johnson's signature on standard letter his secretary sent to accompany signed photographs, even when the photograph was actually signed by the senator. Many other politicians utilize this same technique for responding to autograph requests.

These are so obviously reproduced photographically that even a child would recognize them. Another undisguised facsimile would be the signature of a sports star, that sometimes appears on cereal boxes as an endorsement of the product.

Some of the characteristics to check for when attempting to determine an autograph's authenticity, are given below. Use a magnifying glass!

Printed Facsimile	*Ink Signature*
No shading	Shaded
Dull	Shiny
No color variation	Variations in depth of color
No weight variations	Variations in weight of strokes

Always save any accompanying correspondence received with autographs or signed pictures. Keep them even if they are merely printed form letters or one-sentence notes signed by a secretary rather than by the celebrity. Store these notes and letters carefully. They will often be valuable proof of authenticity for photographs and other autographic items. Such letters and notes will be indispensable when all or part of a collection is being traded or sold.

By far, the majority of today's public officials and other notables will answer sincere requests for autographs. You'll always encounter a few who will ignore all requests or answer only if the request is repeated several times. Don't give up quickly or become discouraged. Write another letter in about three weeks, particularly if the autograph is an especially desirable one needed for your collection. Sooner or later, an answer of some kind will come, though perhaps only from a secretary or an aide. If nothing seems to get the desired results, take the time to write a more personal letter, explaining in detail why the individual's autograph is so important to obtain.

An honest show of interest in the notable's background, career, hobbies, writings, opinions, locality, education, philanthropies or talents is much more likely to generate a reply. A little biographical research at the local library may uncover a clue as to an interest shared with the celebrity or a favorite sport or hobby. In any case, even the most difficult men and women have been known

> OFFICE OF THE VICE PRESIDENT
> WASHINGTON
> February 16, 1961
>
> Dear Friend:
>
> Thank you so much for your cordial letter and your very kind and generous words.
>
> Mrs. Johnson and I are delighted to have the opportunity of autographing your inaugural program. I am sure President Kennedy would be happy to sign it, too, but I'd like to suggest that you write him directly at the White House. I believe it would be more satisfactory for him to receive the request directly from you, rather than getting it second-hand from me.
>
> It was good to hear from you, and I hope you will continue to share your thinking with me as we move forward into what I believe will be a dynamic, constructive period in our nation's life.
>
> Kindest regards and all good wishes.
>
> Sincerely,
>
> Lyndon B. Johnson

Johnson didn't use the standard printed form letter with a facsimile signature when he responded to the author's request for a special autograph on an inaugural program. He did sometimes make exceptions like this.

to respond readily to sincerity or a more thoughtful approach. A well-written letter of this sort quite often brings the most desired of all types of replies: a fully handwritten and signed letter (A.L.S.); or a typed letter signed (L.S.) by the eminent personage. A complete list of autograph abbreviations and terms is given in the glossary at the back of this book.

A number of famous people respond readily to all requests for autographs, yet they make it a practice *never* to send out photographs of themselves. Eleanor Roosevelt is a case in point. She always courteously answered requests for her autograph by sending out a small card containing her signature. This gracious lady would not have photographs made to autograph because she believed she was too unattractive. One day, while browsing in a used bookstore, I noticed a picture biography of Mrs. Roosevelt on a special-sale table. I purchased a copy of this inexpensive book, and studied the photographs carefully to choose those that seemed to me to be the most unusual and appealing, for I was a long-time admirer of this great woman. Finally, I settled on two of them. I cut these two out and mailed them to her with a letter asking that she sign both. Eleanor generously honored my request. Today, these autographed pictures are quite valuable since they are rare and one-of-a-kind collector's items.

28 Collecting Autographs For Fun and Profit

Financier Bernard Baruch and former Presidents Herbert Hoover and Harry Truman were others who consistently ignored requests for signed photographs. Truman's secretary responded with a note saying the former President didn't give out signed photographs. Baruch would not even bother answering. Herbert Hoover would send a personal card instead, as shown above, and to obtain even this would take at least four requests. I finally obtained two photographs of Hoover from the Army Photographic Agency and sent these to his suite in the Waldorf Astoria, with a polite note of request that he sign. Both the photographs were autographed on the first mailing and promptly returned! These photographs have an unusual feature—each was neatly inscribed in gold ink! They are quite valuable today.

Herbert Hoover would never sign and send out his own photographs to collectors. The only time this man would sign pictures was when the item was sent to him along with the request.

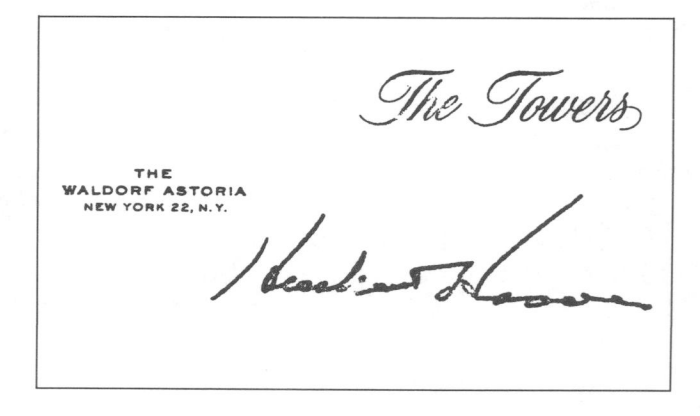

Very rare one-of-a-kind autographed photograph of Eleanor Roosevelt, a woman who wouldn't normally send her picture to collectors because she felt unattractive.

To obtain Mr. Truman's and Mr. Baruch's autographs, the same procedure was followed. A selection of photographs was submitted to them for signing. In both instances, the pictures were autographed and returned within a two-week period. Truman's photographs are particularly nice collector's items since they are in full color. And each is a one-of-a-kind autograph, not ever to be found on the market. They were obtained only because the author sent photographs along with the request.

A practice I utilized in obtaining Fidel Castro's autograph is a useful one to remember when writing to foreign personages. I wrote to Castro a few months after the Marxist revolution in Cuba. Many months passed before a reply was forthcoming. The envelope I received contained an unsigned 8 by 10 picture of the bearded one along with an official letter from one of the top ministers in the government informing me that Fidel was busy running the country. He was said to have no time to answer such requests. Also enclosed were three propaganda booklets on land reform and Castro's program for a Communist Cuba, written for grammar-school children. These souvenirs were of interest—and perhaps had some value—yet they certainly weren't comparable to an autographed photograph. I carefully rewrapped the photo, enclosed a self-addressed mailer for its return, to which I attached Cuban postage stamps, and sent the package to Dr. Juan A. Orta, Executive Director of the Prime Minister's Office, who had acknowledged my initial request. I also enclosed the following note:

Bernard Baruch didn't both answering autograph requests of the ordinary kind. However, he would autograph a photograph, but only when a collector went to the trouble of acquiring one and then sending it on to him at his home.

Dear Mr. Orta:

I am writing you in regard to your letter of February 15, 1960. I was quite disappointed to discover that Mr. Castro's signature was not on the enclosed photograph. Therefore, I am returning it in the hope that you will be kind enough to help me further in this matter. I do realize, as you so explicitly stated in your recent letter, that the Prime Minister is very busy and does not have the time to spare for this sort of thing, but I hope he can be induced to make an exception with my request. I have a large collection of signed photographs from personalities of importance in all walks of life. One part of this collection is devoted to world leaders. I have been successful in obtaining the autographs of most men in a position similar to that of Prime Minister Castro. As you can understand, his photograph would certainly be an important addition to this set, and it is absolutely necessary to bring my collection up to date. If you can be of any assistance to me in this matter, your favor would be much appreciated.

Thanking you for your time and your courtesy,

A few months later the photograph was returned—signed by Fidel Castro. I would like to point out that my request letter wasn't falsely complimentary, but it *was* courteous. The use of Cuban stamps on the return mailer was important. If nothing else brings positive results from an important foreign personage, the use of his nation's own stamps usually helps. People often admire persistence also, even if somewhat begrudgingly. Always remember, don't give up too easily when refused an autograph. Your persistence may pay dividends!

3. Address Sources and Forms of Salutation

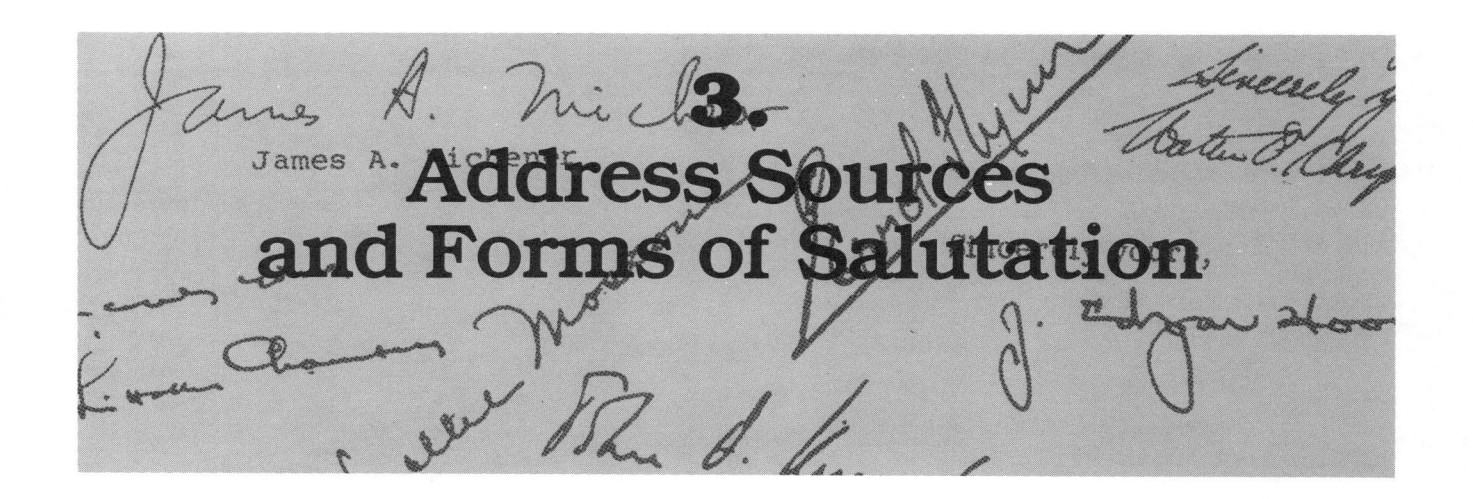

It's extremely important for budding collectors to know how certain celebrities, people in the news, politicians and others should be addressed when making autograph requests.

Most notables in the following categories will respond favorably to requests for autographed photographs from hobbyists. The collector will seldom have to purchase these photographs from another source and then spend the extra postage and time necessary to properly package and mail them. Most famous personages normally keep photographs of themselves on hand, and are happy to send the sincere collector at least a 5x7. Some will even respond with an 8x10. John L. Lewis, President of the United Mine Workers, used to send 11 by 14 photographs, mounted and ready for framing. When submitting a request for an autograph, the following forms of address should always be used:

U.S. GOVERNMENT OFFICIALS

The President of the United States
Envelope Address:
The President (or the President and Mrs. _____)
The White House
Washington, D.C. 20500

Salutation:
Mr. President; Dear Mr. President; Dear Sir; or Dear Mr. President and Mrs. _____

The Vice-President of the United States
Envelope Address:
Same as above except substitute Vice-President in place of President

Salutation:
Same as above except substitute Vice-President in place of President.

Presidential Staff Members
Envelope Address:
Mr. (Mrs., Miss, Ms) Full Name
Title (Special Assistant to the President, Press Secretary, or other exact title)
The White House
Washington, D.C. 20500

Salutation:
Dear Mr. (Mrs., Miss, Ms) Last Name.

Cabinet Members
Envelope Address:
The Honorable (or Mr., Mrs., Miss, Ms, Secretary and Mrs. _____)
Secretary of (Name of Department)
Department of (Name of Department)
Washington, D.C. 20500

Salutation:
Dear Mr. Secretary; Dear Sir; Dear Madam Secretary; Dear Mr. and Mrs. _____; Dear Madam Secretary and Mr. _____.

United States Senators
Envelope Address:
The Honorable _____ (or Senator _____, Senator and Mrs. _____)
United States Senate
Washington, D.C. 20510

Salutation:
Dear Senator _____; Dear Senator and Mrs. _____; Dear Mr. and Mrs. _____.

32 Collecting Autographs For Fun and Profit

United States Representatives
Envelope Address:
The Honorable _____ (or Representative _____,
Representative and Mrs. _____)
United States House of Representatives
Washington, D.C. 20515

Salutation:
Dear Representative _____; Dear Representative and Mrs. _____; Dear Mr. and Mrs. _____.

Members of the Supreme Court
Envelope Address:
The Chief Justice of the United States (or The Honorable _____)
The Supreme Court of the United States
Washington, D.C. 20543

In the 1966 "off-year" California elections, Ronald Reagan thrashed the incumbent Democratic Governor Pat Brown by almost a million votes, and went on to become not only a powerful force in the Republican Party, but President of the United States as well. This specimen was obtained while Mr. Reagan was running for Governor.

The Honorable _____ (or Mr. Justice _____, Mrs. Justice _____, Madam Justice _____)
Associate Justice of the Supreme Court of the United States
Washington, D.C. 20543

Salutation:
Dear Mr. Chief Justice; Dear Sir.

Dear Mr. Justice; Dear Madam Justice; Dear Sir; Dear Madam.

State Governors
Envelope Address:
The Honorable _____
Governor of _____
State House
Official Address

Salutation:
Dear Governor _____; Dear Sir; Dear Madam.

Political autographs, especially those of House and Senate members, are an example of a sizable specialized category of collecting. They are almost effortless to acquire and sincere mail requests are usually answered promptly. The eloquent Illinois Senator, Everett M. Dirksen, was one of the most famous politicians of his day.

Address Sources and Forms of Salutation

General Benjamin O. Davis, Jr., was the first Black general in the history of the United States Air Force. He is a West Point graduate and a World War II combat pilot. His father was the first Negro general in the United States Army.

Military Leaders

A vice-admiral, and a rear admiral are both addressed as "Dear Admiral" in the salutation. Likewise, a lieutenant general, major general, or brigadier general are also addressed as "Dear General" in the salutation. All mail will be forwarded to the officer's present duty station.

Envelope Address:
Admiral _____, USN (or USCG)
The Pentagon
Washington, D.C. 20001
or
General _____, USA (or USMC, USAF)
The Pentagon,
Washington, D.C. 20001

Salutation:
Dear Admiral _____; Dear Sir.
or
Dear General _____; Dear Sir.

Heads of Foreign Governments

More formality is observed when addressing foreign dignitaries and officials than is common in the United States. It is always proper to address any foreign official in the same basic format given for foreign presidents, substituting, of course, the proper title. "The Right Honorable" instead of "His Excellency" is always considered to be correct for important British officials. When the ruler of a nation happens to be a royal personage, always address the envelope formally and respectfully.

Royalty

Envelope Address:
His (or Her) Majesty
King (or Queen) _____
Name of City
Name of Country

Salutation:
Your Majesty

Foreign Presidents

Envelope Address:
His Excellency
Full Name
President of _____
Address

Salutation:
Your Excellency.

Foreign Ambassadors to the United States

Use a title preceding the individual's name *only* if he or she has the right to such a title. For example, Lord, Baron, Dr., etc. Never address these dignitaries with Mr. Mrs., or Ms, as it is considered to be in poor taste and bad manners.

Envelope Address:
His (or Her) Excellency
Person's Full Name
Ambassador of _____
Address

Salutation:
Excellency; Your Excellency.

Dignitaries of the United Nations

Envelope Address:
His Excellency
Full Name
Secretary-General of the United Nations
New York, N.Y. 10016

Salutation:
Dear Mr. Secretary-General.

34   Collecting Autographs For Fun and Profit

The head of a nation's mission to the United Nations usually carries the personal rank of Ambassador. When the chief of a foreign mission to the U.N. doesn't have the ambassadorial title and status, he or she must be addressed as "The Honorable" rather than His or Her Excellency.

Envelope Address:
His (or Her) Excellency
Full Name
Representative of _____ to the United Nations
New York, N.Y. 10016

The Honorable _____
Representative of the United States to the United Nations
New York, N.Y. 10016

Salutation:
Excellency; Your Excellency;
Dear Mr. Ambassador; Dear Mrs. Ambassador; Dear Ambassador _____.

Dear Mr. Ambassador, Dear Mrs. Ambassador, Dear Ambassador _____.

AUTOGRAPH ADDRESS SOURCES FOR COLLECTORS

Each of the following reference books are excellent sources of addresses for autograph collectors. Smaller libraries may not have every book listed. Larger libraries will have a multitude of additional reference works that will be equally informative.

American Men of Science: These volumes cover the biological and physical sciences.
American Men of Science: These volumes cover the social and behavioral sciences.
Celebrity Register, The: Billed as "An irreverent compendium of American quotable notables." Also covers "international personalities best known in America."
Contemporary Authors: An excellent biographical guide to American authors and their books.
Directory of American Scholars: Four volumes loaded with important data on various American scholars.
International Who's Who, The.
International Year Book and Statesmen's Who's Who, The.
Who's Who.
Who's Who in America.
Who's Who in American Art: Includes sculptors, painters, cartoonists, illustrators, etc.
Who's Who in American Education.
Who's Who in Music: Billed as "a complete presentation of the contemporary music scene."
Who's Who in the Theater.
Who's Who of American Women: Also includes Canadian women.
World Who's Who in Commerce and Industry.

Tingfu F. Tsiang, Ambassador Extraordinary and Plenipotentiary. He was the Permanent Representative of China to the United Nations. Note the signature. The name is signed both in Chinese and in English, making this a rare form of autographic material, because of this particular method of signing.

4. Suggested Categories for Specialization

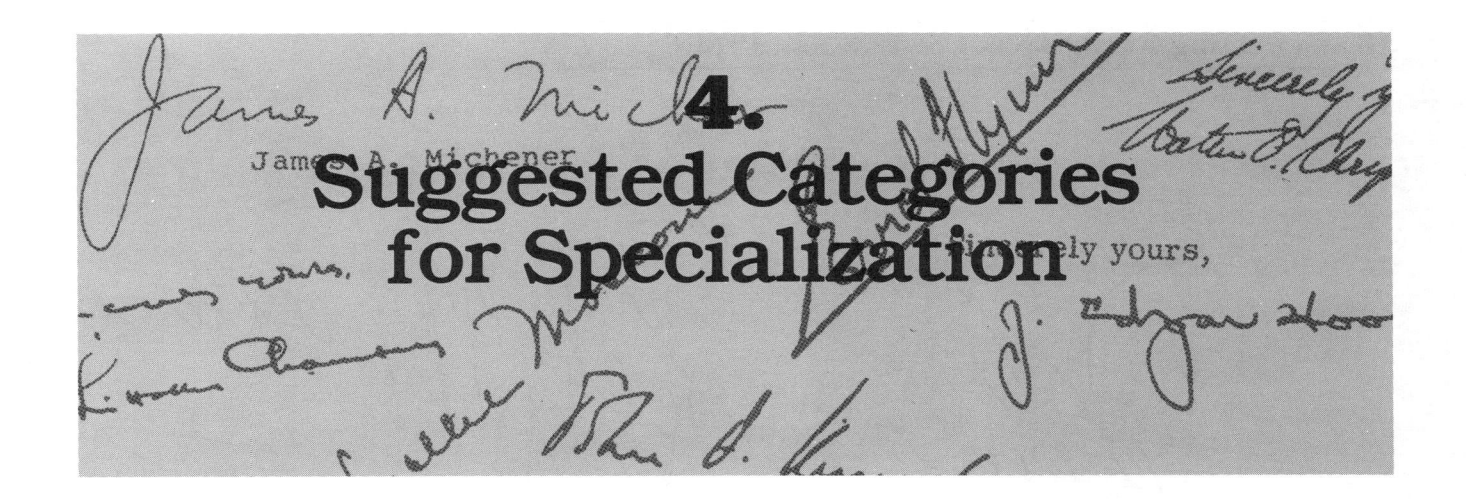

The field of autograph collecting is vast. Even when specializing, the possibilities are staggering. Let's consider the Congress of the United States as an example. In undertaking to collect all the current Senators and members of the House of Representatives in a single year it would be necessary to correspond with well over six hundred personalities of various levels of importance. Few, if any, collectors achieve a complete set of the Congress for any given year. Therefore, as a memento or a collector's item, a complete set could gain in value considerably. Accumulating such a set will require a great deal of time and effort, as well as the expenditure of no small sum for postage, envelopes and stationery.

In selecting a specialty—even in making the decision to specialize—the collector is well advised to think the matter through carefully. Some decide not to specialize, but instead try to gather autographs of the most noted personalities currently dominating major fields of endeavor. Such a project may sound fairly easy to the uninitiated, but it's not so effortless as it might appear at first.

A collection of this type, to be comprehensive, must include literally thousands of autographs. It would probably entail endless library research to select the names of notables in the categories with which the collector has no basic familiarity. Questions like the following would have to be asked: Is she nationally or internationally well known? Is he simiply a celebrity for the moment, or is his fame lasting? Exactly how important are her achievements? How old is he and will he be likely to go on to later accomplishments? Collecting the leading figures in various branches of expertise will require considerable common sense. The collector must use good judgement and apply more than a little serious thought, as well as expect to spend an appreciable amount of time and money.

Professional sports is a popular specialty category with beginners. The best practice is to stick with the top names in a field—the star player or athlete, the one whom people will not soon

One of the greatest black athletes of all time. This man won four gold medals in the 1936 Olympic games in Berlin. Jesse, now deceased, always responded quickly to autograph requests with this kind of action photograph.

35

36   Collecting Autographs For Fun and Profit

Joe Louis and Rocky Marciano, two of the greatest heavyweight champions the boxing world has ever seen.

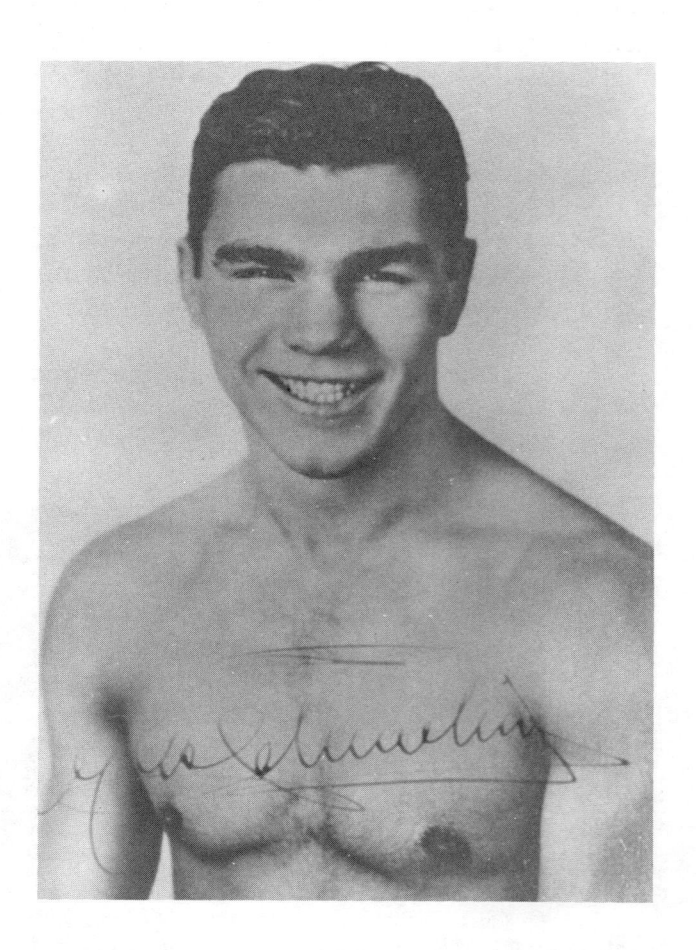

A simple signature of Max Schmeling, former heavyweight champion who once defeated Joe Louis, is worth at least $15.00 on today's autograph market.

Suggested Categories For Specialization 37

forget—to insure the possibility that the value of the collection will keep rising over the years. The autographs of contemporary sports figures the likes of Mickey Mantle, Willie Mays, Nolan Ryan, Cassius Clay (Muhammad Ali), Willie Hoppe, Jack Kemp, Wilt Chamberlain, and Gordie Howe, who turn into legends, may one day be worth a tidy sum.

Although many outstanding baseball Hall of Famers are now dead—Jackie Robinson, Ty Cobb, Rogers Hornsby, Walter Johnson, Eddie Plank, Casey Stengel, Kid Nichols, Clark Griffith—quite a number of the old-timers are still alive. They all answer autograph requests willingly. These men are part of the grand history of baseball. Even school-children have heard of the feats of Babe Ruth, Lou Gehrig, Pie Traynor, Mel Ott, Lloyd Waner, and numerous others. Their autographs are constantly increasing in value.

Boxers in all weight categories are excellent sources of 8x10 signed photographs. The most worthwhile to collect are the champions in each class. Heavyweight champions like Joe Louis, Larry Holmes, Max Schmeling, Jim Braddock, Joe Frazier, and Rocky Marciano are the most popular. Signatures alone from Jim Jeffries and Gene Tunney are valued at around $15.00 and up. Signed photographs of the following are worth at least $25.00 apiece: Jersey Joe Walcott, Jack Sharkey, and Floyd Patterson. Jack Dempsey's signed photograph brings about $35.00, while one of Muhammad Ali is valued at around $40.00 and up. Sugar Ray Leonard, a welterweight and middleweight champion, is generous about sending out signed photographs. They are worth at least $15.00, while one of Tommy Hearns can be purchased for $10.00. And former middleweight champion Sugar Ray Robinson's signed photographs bring a minimum of $25.00 on the collector's market. Here, as in all other collecting categories, those most in demand rate a higher price, whether buying or selling.

The autographed photographs of wrestlers are worth accumulating only if the collector is a dedicated wrestling fan who would find personal satisfaction in acquiring them. Such material has little trade or resale value, and is regarded as trash by most collectors.

It is surprisingly easy to obtain autographed pictures from veteran professional golfers the caliber of Bobby Jones, Doug Ford, Jim Demaret, Ben Hogan, and Arnold Palmer. Palmer's signed photograph is worth at least $20.00. Golfing autographic material always seems to have excellent resale or trade value. The minimum a top golfer's signed photograph usually brings is about $10.00 on the collector's market. Even a signature of Walter Hagen is worth more than this amount. Apparently the public never really forgets the great personalities in this field, and such autographs always make an exciting addition to any collection. The signatures and photographs of professional basketball players are equally easy to obtain. Simply write to the coach, club owner, or any individual player.

Film and rock stars are glamorous figures and are quick to achieve international fame. More young people are interested in a signed photograph of Clint Eastwood or Michael Jackson, for example, than that of Ronald Reagan or Jonas Salk, simply because thre is more awareness that Eastwood and Jackson exist. However, *most* autographs in this category are worthless as resale items. They have little or no lasting value on the market or for most serious collectors unless one of two things happen: either the particular personality becomes notorious and controversial, as did Fatty Arbuckle, or he/she achieves marked success in another field, as did Ronald Reagan. In general, it is pointless to collect any but the big names in the film or pop music categories. Don't bother with hopeful starlets and the like. Most film stars send photographs signed by a private secretary or use photographic facsimiles. None of these are worth anything to a collector—not even for trading purposes.

38   Collecting Autographs For Fun and Profit

Zsa Zsa Gabor

The majority of autographs from television personalities are also worthless, unless the intention is to use them as current items and temporary eye-catchers when exhibiting a collection. Into this relatively valueless class fall such people as the actors and actresses who star in daytime soap operas, or the hosts of giveaway shows (Monte Hall, Bob Barker, etc.). There have been a few television notables who may be considered more desirable to collect—such as Johnny Carson, Milton Berle, Ed Sullivan and Arthur Godfrey—because they may have an unusual or interesting background, or their success has endured. Gypsy Rose Lee, an internationally known stripper at one time, is an excellent example of a TV personality with a unique background. A Christmas card signed by Gypsy sells for at least $25.00

The fine arts offer many collecting possibilities. Musicians, writers, sculptors, painters and composers are all popular specialty categories. Possibilities include Marian Anderson, Gore Vidal, Grandma Moses, Erskine Caldwell and Robert Casadesus. The legitimate theatre has a wide assortment of personalities, including some of the most brilliant minds in the world, as well as some of the most celebrated eccentrics. Well worth

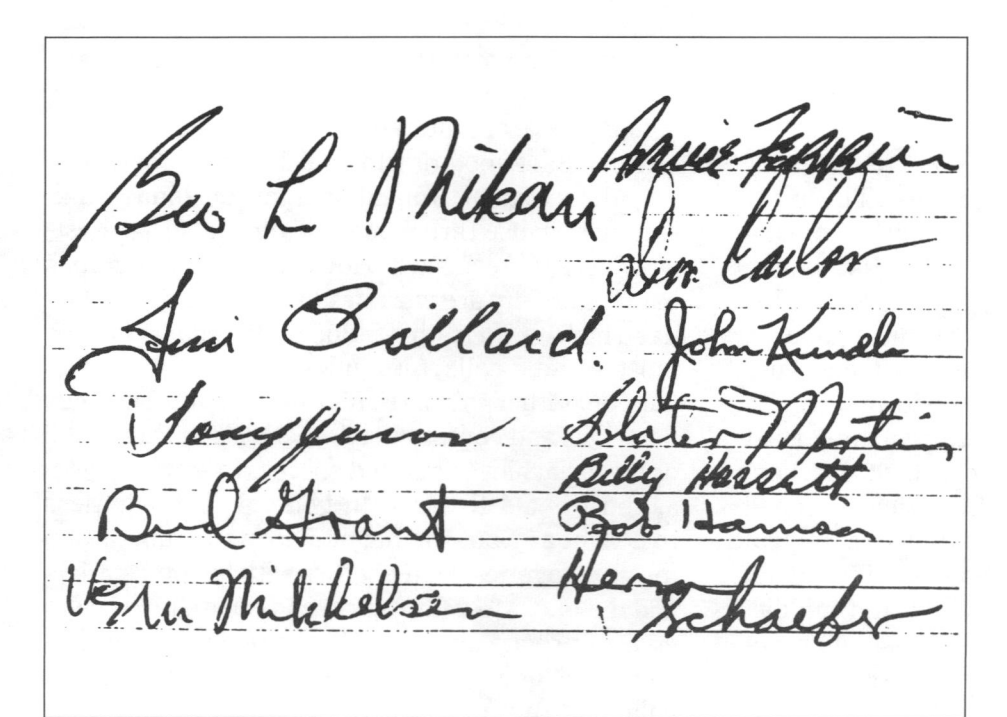

The Minneapolis Lakers, NBA Champs in 1949-1950. Hall of Famer George Mikan, basketball's greatest professional player of the first half of the century, sent this card to the author.

considering are names such as Richard Burton, Geraldine Page, Mary Martin, Ruth Gordon, and Richard Chamberlain, etc. The demand for all types of autographic material, including signed photographs, from these creative people and others in the related arts is always high.

Cartoonists the caliber of Chester Gould, Jimmy Hatlo, Walt Kelly, or Hank Ketchum are an especially amusing category. A collector may be lucky and manage to obtain a signed preliminary cartoon layout rather than the usual autographed photograph. Walt Kelly sometimes would send one of his rough drafts in place of a picture of himself. Such unique items are much more valuable because they are rarer than the ordinary autographs, and they also add variety and a nice humorous touch to a collection.

At least 75 percent of all senators and representatives will respond to autograph requests with a signed 8x10 photograph. Others will send smaller pictures, or they'll reply with colorful autographed brochure that will include backgorund information about themselves. The latter makes for interesting collectibles.

The Harlem Globetrotters of 1949, one of the finest basketball teams ever assembled. Marques Haynes, the greatest dribbler in the world, sent this card to the author.

An exciting and worthwhile collection could be made of the governors of all fifty states. Many of these politicians will send collectors an authentically signed 8x10 photograph accompanied by a personal letter. On special request, a governor will send a signed folder, about 5x7 in size, featuring his picture on the cover superimposed over an official map, with details about himself and his particular state. A complete collection of these souvenir pamphlets is likely to grow in value over the years. It is particularly desirable to try to acquire an 8x10 photograph of any governor who has made a national name for himself, like Ronald Reagan. Other excellent collectibles would be the former Governor of Arkansas, Orville Faubus and George Wallace of Alabama.

Supreme Court Justices always graciously honor sincere requests for autographs. The photographs these men and women sign and send to collectors may vary considerably. Former Associate Justice Douglas made a practice of responding with a 5x7 light weight paper photograph. Former Associate Justice Tom Clark used to send a beautiful 11x14 photograph of himself dressed in courtroom attire. Former Chief Justice Earl Warren sent either an 8x10 full-face picture or a 5x7 sheet containing a photograph and facsimile signature of each Associate Justice. Warren always signed the sheet next to his own picture. Upon request, Warren and most of the other Associate Justices would pass the sheet around for all the other court members to sign also.

Front of Visitor's Pass

Back of Visitor's Pass

If asked to do so, Senators and members of the House of Representatives will also send a special visitor's pass along with their signed photograph. This pass often bears a stamped signature, but the sender will personally autograph it when requested by a collector. Such passes make a unique specialty.

Suggested Categories For Specialization 41

Members of the SUPREME COURT of the UNITED STATES, October 14, 1958

EARL WARREN, CHIEF JUSTICE OF THE UNITED STATES, was born in Los Angeles, California, on March 19, 1891. He was appointed by President Eisenhower on September 30, 1953, during a recess of the Senate as Chief Justice of the United States and took the oaths of office and his seat October 5, 1953. He was nominated by President Eisenhower on January 11, 1954, as Chief Justice of the United States, was confirmed by the Senate on March 1, 1954, and took the oaths of office on March 20, 1954.

HUGO L. BLACK, ASSOCIATE JUSTICE, was born in Clay County, Alabama, February 27, 1886. He was nominated by President Roosevelt, August 12, 1937, as an Associate Justice, and took his seat October 4, 1937.

FELIX FRANKFURTER, ASSOCIATE JUSTICE, was born in Vienna, Austria, November 15, 1882, and was brought to the United States in 1894. He was nominated from Massachusetts by President Roosevelt, January 5, 1939, as an Associate Justice, and took his seat January 30, 1939.

WILLIAM O. DOUGLAS, ASSOCIATE JUSTICE, was born in Maine, Minnesota, October 16, 1898. He was nominated from the State of Connecticut as an Associate Justice by President Roosevelt, March 20, 1939, and took his seat April 17, 1939.

TOM C. CLARK, ASSOCIATE JUSTICE, was born in Dallas, Texas, September 23, 1899. He was nominated from Texas as an Associate Justice by President Truman on August 2, 1949, and took his seat October 3, 1949.

JOHN M. HARLAN, ASSOCIATE JUSTICE, was born in Chicago, Illinois, May 20, 1899. He was nominated from New York as an Associate Justice by President Eisenhower, January 10, 1955, and took his seat March 28, 1955.

WM. J. BRENNAN, JR., ASSOCIATE JUSTICE, was born in Newark, New Jersey, April 25, 1906. He was appointed from New Jersey as an Associate Justice of the Supreme Court by President Eisenhower on October 15, 1956, during a recess of the Senate and took the oaths of office and his seat on October 16, 1956. He was nominated by President Eisenhower on January 14, 1957 as an Associate Justice of the Supreme Court, was confirmed by the Senate on March 19, 1957, and took the oaths of office on March 22, 1957.

CHARLES E. WHITTAKER, ASSOCIATE JUSTICE, was born in Doniphan County, Kansas, February 22, 1901. He was nominated from Missouri by President Eisenhower, March 2, 1957, as an Associate Justice, and took his seat March 25, 1957.

POTTER STEWART, ASSOCIATE JUSTICE, was born in Jackson, Michigan, January 23, 1915. He was appointed from Ohio as an Associate Justice of the Supreme Court by President Eisenhower on October 14, 1958, during a recess of the Senate and took the oaths of office and his seat on that day. He was nominated by President Eisenhower on January 17, 1959, as an Associate Justice of the Supreme Court, was confirmed by the Senate on May 5, 1959, and took the oaths of office on May 15, 1959.

Sent to the author while Earl Warren, former Governor of California, sat as Chief Justice of the Supreme Court. Chief Justice Warren personally handed this sheet to each member of the court for autographing. The signatures to the left are authentically signed by each Associate Justice.

42 Collecting Autographs For Fun and Profit

J. Edgar Hoover, the man who set up and directed the Federal Bureau of Investigation for many years. Hoover was always willing to personally answer questions in his letters and he never refused to send a signed photograph on request.

J. Edgar Hoover, the famed director of the Federal Bureau of Investigation (F.B.I.) for so many years, made a point of answering all autograph requests personally. The signed photographs he would send ranged in size from a small 3x5 to a striking 14x17 portrait. There was never any way of knowing in advance which photograph any given request would generate. Hoover also responded with personal letters and answered any questions about the organization he headed, or about any matter of national interest. He always took the time to write an accompanying letter with each signed photograph. Hoover's signature alone on an official agency card brings about $15.00 on the collector's market.

The Presidential Cabinet appointees, who are assigned supervisory posts over each major section of the executive branch of our government, are terrific collector's items for beginners. They are logical additions to a political collection or one composed of personalities in the national spotlight. Some collectors make it a practice to obtain a complete set of the President's so-called "official family" for each new administration. The monetary value of a single Cabinet member's signed photograph, however, is not very high. It will be less that that of a heavyweight champion, a member of baseball's Hall of Fame, or a news-making artist the stature of Salvador Dali, unless the appointee subsequently earns some greater distinction. The value is enhanced also if a collector makes it a practice to obtain autographs from all the Cabinet members under different administrations over a period of many years.

Only under the most unusual circumstances is it possible to obtain a signed photograph of a President while he is in office, but this is relatively easy to accomplish while the man is actively campaigning for the office. While a Presidential autograph may be rare, it's not impossible to get. With a stroke of luck, I managed it by acting fast when newly-elected President John F. Kennedy finished selecting his ten Cabinet members. The New York

Nelson Rockefeller, a man who wanted to be President but who never quite made it with the voters. Instead, he was known best as one of New York's outstanding governors.

Suggested Categories For Specialization   43

This unique photograph was sent to Postmaster General Day with a request that he personally have it signed by all other Cabinet appointees and finally the President. A bold request? Yes! And one the author really didn't dare hope would get results. But it worked and may again for an enterprising collector.

The letter from the White House which accompanied the photograph of President John F. Kennedy and all of his initial Cabinet appointees. This letter is important as a collectible, but even more significant, it authenticates the signatures on the photograph by both words and the date.

THE WHITE HOUSE
WASHINGTON

July 26, 1961

Dear Mr. Pelton:

I am happy to send you the enclosed picture which the President and Cabinet Members have signed for you. The picture comes with their very best wishes.

Sincerely,

Priscilla Wear
Office of the President

Mr. Bob Pelton
1311 King Ave.
Pascagoula, Miss.

Enclosure

Times carried a photo layout containing a large picture of J.F.K. in the middle, surrounded by smaller pictures of his new Cabinet. I put in an order for an 8x10 copy of the original. Then I carefully framed the photograph on a white matte board with 2" wide borders. This provided both space and a suitable surface for signing, especially since the photograph itself was a high gloss finish.

My original intention was to send the photograph to each Cabinet member in turn. I planned to include a polite letter asking the particular member to sign his name on the matte border alongside his picture, and then to return the photograph in the enclosed self-addressed, stamped manila envelope. This would total ten mailings, plus the careful preparation of ten stamped mailers for the returns. As a final step, after all ten Cabinet members had finally autographed the photograph, it was to be mailed to President Kennedy. Hopefully, when the President realized how many months of effort had gone into this project, he would make an exception and add his signature to the others.

The matted photograph was protectively packaged, but prior to sealing the large envelope addressed to Postmaster General J. Edward Day, this postscript was added to the enclosed letter:

> P.S. If you can possibly find the time in your busy schedule, would you mind passing this picture on to all the other members of the Cabinet and then to President Kennedy for his signature? Perhaps you could do this most easily during a Cabinet meeting.

I didn't really expect Mr. Day to do any more than affix his own signature and return the photograph. Imagine my pleasant surprise when six months later, the photograph sent to the Postmaster General was returned. It had been signed by the entire Cabinet and President Kennedy as well. This was good fortune beyond any collector's wildest dreams! In addition, the photograph was accompanied by a personal letter from the White House. Today, these autographic items would bring from $1,000 to $1,500 if they were for sale.

One further bit of advice in the matter of presidential autographs. In any national electon year, try making a careful appraisal of all the men who aspire to head their party's ticket. Send a request to each one while he is in the midst of the campaign for the nomination. In 1964, Nelson Rockefeller, William Scranton, and Barry Goldwater were the major contenders for the Republican Party nomination. George Romney and Richard Nixon were considered to be the dark horses. On the Democratic side, Lyndon Johnson was believed to be a sure thing, but several men were being mentioned for the second spot on the ticket, among them Robert Kennedy and Hubert Humphrey. In 1980, Jimmy Carter was the incumbent President, but he was challenged by Edward M. "Ted" Kennedy and Edmund Brown, Jr. for the nomination of the Democratic Party. Ronald Reagan was the Republican favorite but many others were trying. These included John Anderson, Howard Baker, George Bush, John Connolly, Robert Dole, and Gerald Ford.

Richard M. Nixon

Requests for an autographed photograph were sent to all the hopefuls of both parties, and each responded favorably. No matter who won the race, my collection now included authentic signed photographs of the next President of the United States. And, as an additional bonus, there were the autographed photographs of the other political notables, one or more of whom, in years to come, might be our President.

An autographed photograph of the Vice-President, on the other hand, is usually easy to acquire and generally worth from $10.00 to $15.00 even while the person is still in office. A farsighted collector will always try to obtain this kind of autographic material because there's always the chance that the current Vice-President may become the next President. If and when this takes place, pictures and autographs will no longer be given out freely. The Presidency of Lyndon Johnson is a good case in point, as is that of Richard Nixon.

A letter, note or signed photograph from an outstanding scientist, especially Nobel Prize winners, is always worth many times more than one from the average congressman or military leader. Top names in the scientific fields rank equally with the top celebrities in the fine arts, as far as autograph collecting is concerned. There is a never-ending demand for material of this sort. Consider the current market value of a letter or a signed photograph from Albert Einstein, Dr. Albert Schweitzer, or others of comparable fame. Signed photographs or letters from astronauts and the scientists involved in the space program also make a timely sideline for any collector. Such a specialized collection will continue to grow in size, significance, and value with each passing year. A prize catch would certainly be a signed picture of all seven members of the original astronaut team. The author received his by writing in 1961 to Alan B. Shepard, Jr. Today, it is possible to get a complete set of 8x10 full color photographs authentically signed by each member of the team, but this will take a great deal of time and effort since at last count, they numbered over sixty.

Signed photographs of hundreds of generals and admirals in our armed forces are available for the asking. Almost all the top military notables send out at the very least an 8x10 picture. A few respond with larger ones. For example, General Nathan Twining, former Air Force Chief of Staff, would answer autograph requests with an 11x14 full color signed photograph mounted on heavy cardboard, along with a short personal note to the collector. Nothing will be lost in specifying, courteously, the size that is preferred for a particular collection. If the officer has photographs in different sizes, he will usually take the time to honor the specific request. This specialty category is vast and it's probably best to begin with only the top echelon in each branch of the service—the Marine Corps, Coast Guard, Navy, Army and Air

Former Vice President Hubert H. Humphrey sent the author this Christmas card in response to one sent his family. It is rarer and more valuable than the usual signed photograph Humphrey autographed for collectors. The typed letter (L.S.) accompanying most of his autographed photographs presently markets for around $20.00. His SP goes for $25.00 and up.

46 Collecting Autographs For Fun and Profit

This mailing envelope is inscribed in the hand of the famed Dr. Albert Schweitzer. It was sent to the author from Lambarene, Gabon, in response to a request that he autograph a book. He did, and enclosed a signed photograph as a bonus.

Suggested Categories For Specialization 47

Above, Dr. Fritz A. Lipmann, the renowned biochemist who shared the 1953 Nobel Prize for medicine and physiology. Right, Dr. James A. Van Allen, outstanding physicist and discoverer of the Van Allen radiation belts circling the earth.

Force. A few short years ago, top names such as Eisenhower, Bradley and MacArthur could be obtained easily. Today they are all wonderful collector's items, and each may be quite expensive to purchase from a dealer's catalog.

Autographs of royalty and prominent national leaders make an impressive specialty collection. So do foreign diplomats. Customarily, diplomats may respond with a signed, official embassy card, a signed sheet of embassy stationery, an autographed 5x7 photograph, or all of these items together. A larger photograph is seldom sent, even in reply to a specific request. This field alone is a goldmine for beginning collectors as they often can obtain at least three autographs of different types. Ambassador Louis Rakotomalala of the Malagasy Republic used to send a series of tiny 1x1 photographs all signed in his native language. Along with these unique photographs was an official note with his name and address printed in English. The Chinese and Japanese seem to enjoy signing both in English and in their own native script.

All national leaders of foreign countries and most royal personages will take the time to acknowledge autograph requests, but none of these people are prompt in doing so. The autographs of royalty are by far the most difficult to obtain. Persistence usually brings results however. Far too many autograph seekers tend to give up after one or two failures.

The late Konrad Adenauer, former Chancellor of the Federal Republic of Germany, was one of the few national leaders who would send a signed photograph in response to the first request. Bechara El-Khoury, former President of Lebanon, never sent anything other than small cards. Prince Rainier of Monaco and King Hussein of Jordan always replied promptly with a signed photograph. These were exceptions, for responses seldom ever come from foreign leaders in less than three months. A wait of six months or even longer is not uncommon. The prize is worth the long wait,

48 Collecting Autographs For Fun and Profit

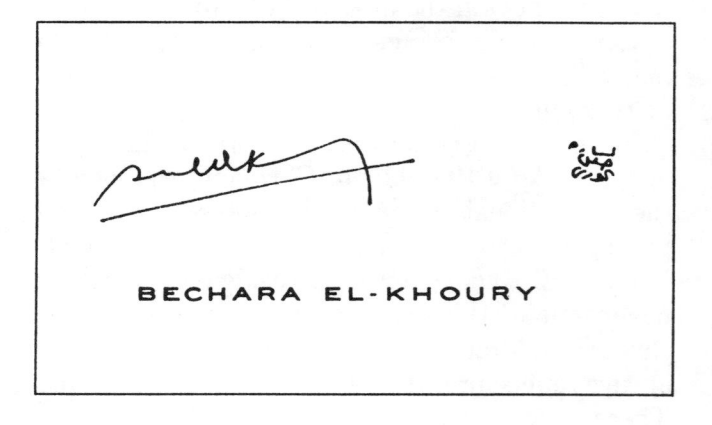

however, and such outstanding autographs are certainly worth the extra effort it takes. These signed photographs and other autographic material can be the highlight of any collection. They usually arrive accompanied by an authentically signed letter from the dignitary himself.

An ordinary postcard often brings fruitful results from foreign leaders, but a sincere letter is a much more dignified and respectful approach for such high-ranking personages. This can consist of the usual polite, concise appeal for the person's signed photograph. Use the example on the next page or a similar format when writing to a foreign leader, or use you own ingenuity—but foremost, keep the letter simple and to the point. If no reply is forthcoming and it is necessary to write again, add a few words in explanation of your interest in the career of the foreign leader or in the county itself. This usually brings the desired results!

Nine different letters requesting an autographed photograph were required to finally get results from President Ahmed Sekou Toure, first leader of the People's Revolutionary Republic of Guinea.

General of the Army Omar N. Bradley, former Chairman of the Joint Chiefs of Staff. This man is one of the nation's best known World War II leaders. His signature alone is offered by dealers at an asking price of $10.00 to $15.00.

> 4D3 North Greenhill Road
> Mt. Juliet, Tenn. 37122
>
> Dear _____:
>
> As a long-time admirer of yours and of your nation's progress in world affairs, I would like to have your autographed photo to add to my collection of "Great World Leaders." I hope you will be able to take a moment from your busy schedule to fill this request.
>
> Sincerely, an admirer
> Robert W. Pelton

Postal rates for foreign mailings vary considerably according to the nation. Remember too, most countries have both a Head of State and a Premier or Prime Minister. The names of these dignitaries can be found easily and quickly in any almanac.

Under one roof at the United Nations in New York City are hundreds, perhaps thousands, of notables from all over the world. The variety of autographic material received in response to requests can be astounding. It could be an extremely large or a minute-sized photograph. It may be an official embassy card signed, or even a folder describing the particular dignitary's native land. Some United Nations' representatives send out pamphlets explaining the role of the international organization. Others mail collectors packages of propaganda espousing a radical cause. Many of the photographs received are inscribed entirely in a foreign language. Some come in a combination of English and the writer's native national script. Whether they are legible to the collector doesn't really make much difference. Who the signer is can almost always be determined because the name and country are customarily stamped on the back of the photograph, in English.

PURCHASING PHOTOGRAPHS

All is not lost when, in spite of all efforts, it has proved impossible to obtain an autographed photograph of a praticularly important personality. There is another approach. Purchase a photograph from one of the major news agencies and mail it to the notable for signing. The extra work and expense involved may result in acquiring a rare collector's item. The value to a dedicated collector, especially for trading purposes at a later date, will almost always increase. And it certainly will be a better item to add to a collection than would be one of the stereotyped photographs so often sent out in answer to run-of-the-mill requests.

Photographs of notables appearing in a current newspaper can usually be ordered from one of the major wire services. The cost of such a print is admittedly high for the collector who normally bears only the price of stationery, envelopes, postage, and return mailers for his or her autographed photographs, but for an unusual picture specimen the investment of a few dollars will be well worthwhile. This type of specialty collecting can be fantastically satisfying and certainly profitable in the long run. Most of the pictures used in newspapers come from either United Press International (UPI) or the Associated Press (AP). They will carry the identifying letters of the service at the bottom of the picture. Call your local reference librarian for the address of each service.

Photographs of numerous famous Americans that are suitable for autographing can easily be purchased for even more reasonable prices. The U.S. Army Photographic Agency (address below) maintains a comprehensive historical collection of pictures covering the period during and after World War II. These include combat scenes and photos of prominent personages. The photographs are indexed by subject matter, geographical location and the names of individuals. For example, a photograph of former President Herbert Hoover accepting a gift of Japanese art books on behalf of Stanford University was obtained from this source. So was a unique photograph of Eisenhower and Bradley in Europe during World War II. When writing for information regarding available photographs, be sure to include as many possible details about the desired subject matter as possible. The agency replies with a descriptive list of what they have in the area of your interest. It's never possible to know in advance what any photographs will actually be like. A photograph from this source, when autographed by the person or persons involved, has a higher than usual value. It may be the only autographed one of its kind in the world.

Photographs of military or government notables prior to World War II are also available at reasonable prices. These can be ordered from the National Archives. Collectors can write to the following sources:

U.S. Army Photographic Agency, The Pentagon, Washington, D.C. 20301.

National Archives, Photographic Records Division, Pennsylvania Avenue at 8th Street, Washington, D.C. 20004.

COLLECTING AUTOGRAPHED BOOKS AS A SPECIALTY

Collecting autographed books can be an intersting sideline, or it can be a full-fledged hobby in itself. A signed book normally has many times the value of a signed photograph or a letter from the same notable. The cost involved in purchasing a book and then sending it off for autographing quite often turns out to be a blue chip investment for the collector. I have in my possession personally signed books from such personages as: Harry S. Truman, Pearl S. Buck, Alger Hiss, Wernher von Braun, Albert Schweitzer, James Byrnes, Dean Acheson, Bertrand Russell, and Billy Graham.

Stores specializing in old or used books often have a few autographed books in stock. Sometimes these are first editions or limited editions. Autographed copies of recent books can occasionally be found if the collector takes the time to browse through the material in stores handling secondhand books. Antique shops also are a decent source for discovering old autographed books, but these are so often overpriced. Flea markets and antique

Ralph J. Bunche was at one time the American member of the United Nations Secretariat. This man won the Nobel Peace Prize in 1953 for his tireless efforts in that area of worldwide concern.

auctions are excellent sources as well. I once picked up a signed copy of Ulysses S. Grant's autobiography for a mere $20.00 at a weekly antique auction in Kingston, Tennessee. It was buried in a box of old childrens' books and went unnoticed by all other bidders. Later, in checking current autograph values, the identical signed book was found to be listed in a dealer's catalog for $250.

It is no more difficult to get a book signed than it is to obtain an autographed photograph. In many cases, it actually turns out to be easier! In fact, a notable who consistently refuses to honor ordinary autograph requests, never seems to turn one down when it involves his or her book. First, find the author's address, using one of the reference sources listed in Chapter 16. Then, write a polite accompanying letter to the author. This need not be lengthy, but since it does request a valuable favor, a sentence or two about the letter writer's interest in the book will not go amiss. Some expression of sincere interest in the author or in the book is only common courtesy.

There are certain precautions and taboos to be aware of when mailing a book for autographing. A volume usually travels safely to its destination when sent in a special bookmailer. This is the best insurance against damage. A bookmailer is no more than a thickly padded envelope manufactured in a variety of dimensions to fit books of any size or shape. A book certainly cost more to mail, but the amount is relatively insignificant considering the time, effort, and money invested in obtaining it in the first place, and its potential value after it has been autographed.

Purchase *two* bookmailers for each book to be sent out for signing. One should be somewhat larger than the other since it must accomodate the book itself and the return mailer. Never fail to enclose a stamped, self-addressed bookmailer for the return of the book. An oversight of this magnitude is an inexcusable imposition on the author of the particular book.

According to postal regulations, the accompanying letter can be handled in either of two ways: (1) Put the letter inside the bookmailer with the book. Add an extra stamp to the outside of the bookmailer. Write on the front portion, "Letter Enclosed"; or (2) put the accompanying letter into a regular envelope addressed to the author and bearing the usual postage stamp. Glue or tape this envelope on the outside of the bookmailer. It will be necessary to have the book and its self-addressed return mailer weighed at the post office to determine the amount of postage required for its return. Then, have it weighed again, after placing it inside, the larger bookmailer, to determine the amount needed to send the package on its way.

A book sent to a foreign country for signing normally takes anywhere from six months to a year before it is returned. Books sent within the continental United States are generally returned within two weeks to three months.

Sinclair Lewis   *Frank Harris*

Andrew Carnegie   *Mozart*

Alexander Graham Bell

Benj. Disraeli

Lachn. McIntosh   *Rembrandt*

Eugene O'Neill   *W M Thackeray*

Wilbur Wright   *Orville Wright*

Noah Webster   *Gromyko*

M B Eddy

Enrico Caruso   *von Hindenburg*

G Washington

L da Vinci   *Lee de Forest*

P T Barnum

Benito Mussolini   *Oscar Wilde*

5. Values of Autographs and What Affects Them

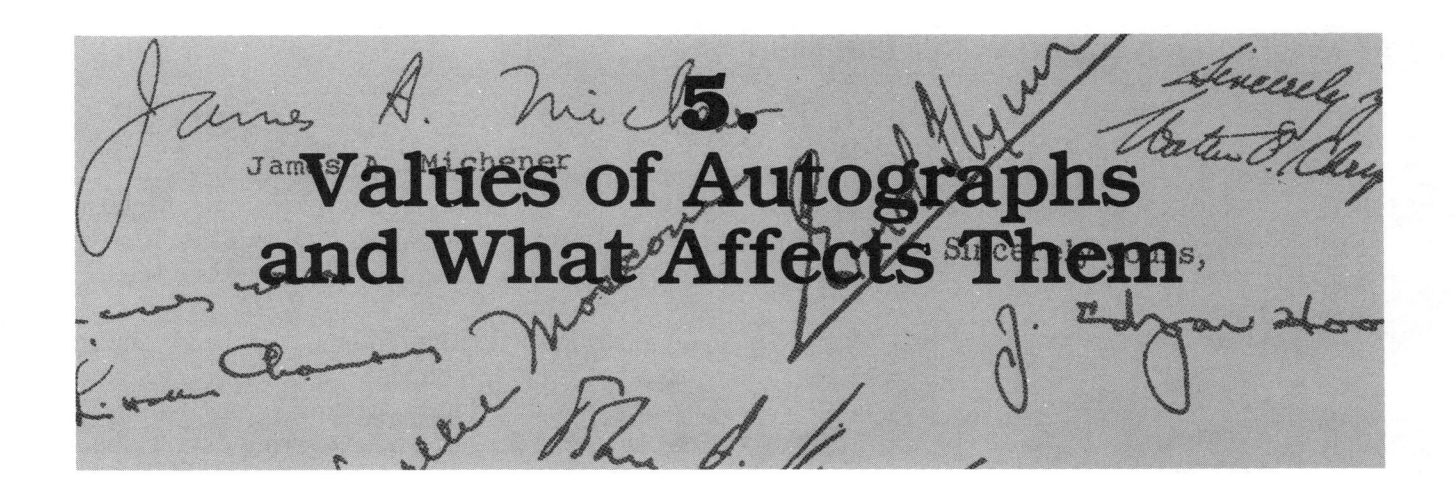

Whenever a letter or a document is sold for thousands of dollars, the news media tends to play up the fact. A great deal of publicity accompanies the sale of a Benjamin Franklin A.L.S. for $2,750; a Martin Luther A.L.S. for $6,000; a Button Gwinnett A.L.S. for $51,000; or a copy of Lincoln's Gettysburg Address for $54,000. Such high prices naturally scare many people away from the hobby. Some see collecting autographs as interesting, but not an avocation they could possibly afford to undertake. Little do they realize these high prices are the exceptions—not the rule. They must be compared to the average prices listed in dealer catalogs, and they must be contrasted to the amounts brough in at auction sales for the majority of autographic items.

Autograph prices more often than not do fall well within the average person's means. Documents signed by Morton or Hart, both Signers of the Declaration of Independence, are plentiful. Often they can be picked up for around $50.00 or less. Reasonably priced and readily available Signers include McKean, Carroll, Rodney, Huntington, Walton, Ellery, Rutledge, Clymer and Bartlett. I.O.U.'s signed by Robert Morris, another Signer, are still easy to find. They often cost less than a signed photogrpah of Lyndon Baines Johnson which, by the way, can be obtained for around $50.00 to $75.00. An A.D.S. by Oliver Wolcott will bring $100.00, whereas an A.L.S. by him goes for about $500.00. Higher prices—$1,000 or more—apply for an A.D.S. of George Wythe. A prize A.L.S. of Richard Henry Lee sometimes comes on the market for $1500 and up.

As a further example, a person unfamiliar with the autograph market will doubtless be amazed to find that material from the pens of such men as Henry Wadsworth Longfellow, Dwight Eisenhower, Jefferson Davis and Johannes Brahms sell for between $150.00 and $250.00. A Louis Pasteur signature can be obtained for less than $90.00. New collectors are constantly surprised by some of the prices found in dealer catalogs, as evidenced by the following: under $100—Richard Rodgers, Moshe Dayan, William Wordsworth, Queen Victoria, Richard E. Perry, John Penn, Ogden Nash, Daniel Webster, Frederick VIII, Buffalo Bill, Hendrik Willem Van Loon and Henry IV; under $50—Alexandre Dumas, Richard Haliburton, Thomas Huxley, Theodore Dreiser, Carlos Romulo, John Burroughs, Oliver Wolcott, Jr., Dean Rusk, the Three Stooges and Louis-Philippe; under $25—Norman Rockwell, Charles Evans Hughes, Eddie Cantor, Ben Hogan, Tom Dooley, Linus Pauling, Henry Wallace, Jonas Salk, Albert Sabin, Francois Duvalier, Lowell Thomas, William Gladstone, Robert Kennedy, Schuyler Colfax and Bruno Walter.

The prices of autographs, like those of any other collectible, are governed by several factors. They are:

- Identity of the writer
- Condition of the material
- Authenticity of the item
- Rarity of the item
- Current fads
- Date of the material
- Association of the item
- Length of the material
- Supply and Demand

Most of these categories are self-explanatory. For example, the content of a document or letter can be especially influential in determining its value. If a literary giant, a great historical figure and a scientist all write letters discussing major issues of the day, along with some simpler letters regarding a speech or acceptance of a dinner invitation, which one do you think would be of more value to a collector? Unquestionably it would depend upon the subject matter, even between two letters written by the same person. Inasmuch as length is generally related to content it, too, influences value. A letter discussing some matter in great detail is naturally worth much more than one consisting of only a sentence or two. Any letter in which famous people discuss their particular specialty adds more appeal for the collector. A Ludwig van Beethoven letter revealing something about how he wrote one of his symphonies, for example, would be more valuable than a letter accompanying a rent payment. A Salvador Dali note referring to his artistic theories would far exceed the value of one written in his youth before he had any claim to fame. Similarly, a letter from F. Scott Fitzgerald giving any details about his literary opinions or writing skills would outweigh in value a simple reply sent to an autograph seeker.

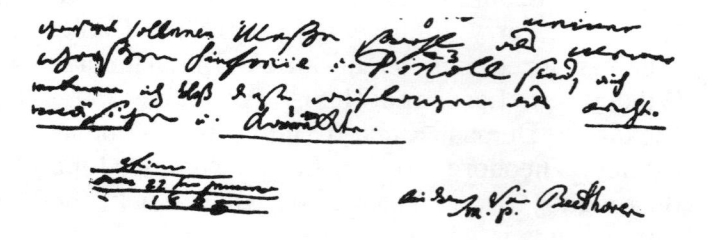

Age is not the sole reason for an extremely high price on certain autographic items. Material from America's Colonial period is valuable because of its scarcity, as is much of the material relating to the settling of the West. Wells Fargo communications with their fancy letterheads dating from between 1860 and 1872 on the other hand, are inexpensive. These exciting letters, handwritten on colorful stationery, covering details about official company business, often can be found for as little as $10.00 to $25.00 apiece. Pony Express letters are relatively common and they are often available at reasonable prices. American Express Company letters dating from the early 1900's can be obtained for less than $25.00. These letters may even be signed by the firm's president!

Likewise, many of the early Presidential documents are available to collectors for a few dollars. Our first Presidents for instance, were required by law to sign a special document before any American ship could leave our harbors. In later years a document was required before any whaling ship could set sail. These ornately embellished government forms were filled out for American whaling ships "bound for Atlantic Ocean Whaling." They are still relatively easy to obtain, and many dated during the late 1800's are available for less than $35.00.

The land grants signed by our early Presidents were numerous. The government made a practice of giving war veterans a land bonus in appreciation for having served their nation valiantly in a time of crisis. These grants varied from 100 to 15,000 acres for those who enlisted in the Revolutionary armies, with the amount of acreage dependent upon a soldier's rank and his length of military service. Land grants were also awarded to citizens as compensation for losses suffered during the Revolution.

Most early land grants were for land in Virginia and Ohio, with approximately 85,000 grants issued before 1833 for land in Ohio alone. Each grant had to be personally signed by the President. The result was a huge backlog of over 20,000, and on March 2, 1833, Congress finally authorized President Andrew Jackson to have a clerk sign the grants in his place. These grants were printed on parchment prior to 1833. Each had to be signed not only by the President but cosigned by the Secretary of State or the Land Commissioner as well. Many are now brittle, yellow with age, and deeply creased if they have been folded in storage. Some are soiled, and on others the ink is badly faded. All such blemishes will detract from their value. Bright, clear, fresh-looking documents of this kind will always command higher prices.

Early American insurance policies are highly informative documents, and many are still priced reasonably. They bear little resemblance to our modern printed legal forms. Originally, any citizen could underwrite a ship's cargo for a specific sum simply by signing an explicitly worded statement of guarantee. These fine documents give considerable insight into the beginnings of certain early American business enterprises. They date from a period when piracy was common, and are worded to cover that peril along with other hazards of traveling on the high seas, such as fire, theft and enemy attack. During the 1850's, insurance policies were commonly written to cover whaling voyages. Excellent examples are those policies issued by the Union Mutual Marine Insurance of New Bedford. They were sold only to whaling vessels—"Wherever she may go on a whaling voyage." Old insurance policies of this type are still obtainable for less than $50.00.

In contrast to the relatively recent American material, European items dating as far back as the late Middle Ages can sometimes be purchased for a song. This is particularly true if the material was written by some obscure individual.

Association—to whom the letter was written—is of considerable importance in autograph valuation. A letter from William Faulkner to a contemporary literary figure is of greater value than one he wrote to a fan. A letter from Thomas Jefferson to John Hancock is much more desirable than one Jefferson wrote to a friend who had no particular claim to fame. And a letter from Nixon's Attorney General, John Mitchell, to his wife Martha would sell for far more than one written to another Cabinet Official or notable with no lasting distinction. A letter from George Washington to his wife, Martha, would far outweigh one penned to a little known politician of his day.

There are instances, however, when the identity of neither the writer nor the recipient matters. Letters and diaries from the Revolutionary War or the Civil War period do not need to be written by heroic high-ranking officers to have interest and value on today's market. A Hessian diary was sold a few years ago for close to $9,000. The author was Private Johannes Rubin, a German who fought with the British forces in the Colonies. His lengthy account spanned from 1776 to 1783. Material of this type always induces spirited bidding at an auction from both dealers and collectors. The more detailed the reporting of great events or battles, and the more legibly the diary is written, the more it will escalate in value.

One Civil War diary covering a period of six months in 1863 was recently listed at $35.00. Another diary spanning a three month period in 1864 sold for the same price. Both were in excellent condition. Numerous handwritten letters from obscure soldiers who fought during the Civil War were also offered recently for a mere $20.00 each. They were dated 1863 and 1864 and were of special interest because of the content: some requested clothing, while others mentioned deserting; a few mentioned General Lee and General Meade, telling how the Confederates made a stand but then had to retreat to safer ground. This type of material is always a good investment, for interest in it never wanes. A plentiful supply of autographic materials from Civil War generals can still be purchased reasonably even today, and are listed in various dealer catalogs. Some of these are:

Union Generals

C.C. Augur: A.L.S. $28.50
William W. Averell: A.L.S. $22.50
Francis C. Barlow: A.L.S. $250.00
Daniel Butterfield: Sig. $15.00
Darius N. Couch: A.L.S. $30.00
Jacob D. Cox: A.L.S. $30.00
Samuel W. Crawford: A.L.S. $50.00
George W. Cullum: Sig. $10.00
S.R. Curtis: A.D.S. $75.00
Henry E. Davies: L.S. $75.00
William R. Franklin: Sig. $12.50
Winfield Scott Hancock: Sig. $12.50
James A. Hardie: Sig. $12.50
Herman Haupt: A.L.S. $30.00
Joseph Hooker: Sig. $23.50
Rufus King: L.S. $28.50
George B. McClellan: Sig. $12.00

George G. Meade: Sig. $16.50
W.T. Sherman: Sig. $22.50
James S. Wadsworth: Sig. $16.50

Sherman   *Robert E. Lee*

Confederate Generals

J. Patton Anderson: A.L.S. $50.00
Turner Ashby: D.S. (rare) $275.00
William B. Bate: Sig. $18.00
P.G.T. Beauregard: A.L.S. $750.00
    D.S. $375.00
Braxton Bragg: D.S. $225.00
Robert Hall Chilton: A.L.S. $175.00
Joseph E. Johnston: Sig. $20.00
William Edmonson Jones: D.S. $35.00
    A.D.S. $35.00
G.W.C. "Custis" Lee: Sig. $17.50
Robert E. Lee: A.L.S. $3500.00
James Longstreet: Sig. $18.00
John Bankhead Magruder: Sig. $17.50
William "Little Billy" Mahone: Sig. $18.50
J.C. Pemberton: Sig. $17.50
Gideon J. Pillow: Sig. $17.50
M.W. Ranson: Sig. $16.50
Clement Hoffman Stone: D.S. $150.00
John G. Walker: A.N.S. $25.00
Joseph Wheeler: Sig. $10.00
    A.N.S. $20.00
John H. Winder: Sig. $30.00

Two rare items relating to President Lincoln's assassination are written in the hand of Albert Daggett, an obscure clerk in the State Department. On April 15, 1865, Albert wrote one letter to his fiancée, Julie Trenier, and the other to his mother. He gave an eyewitness account of the tragic event. A number of years ago, the Lincoln National Life Foundation obtained the letter written to the mother. At the time no one was even aware there was a second letter. The one to Julie Trenier was discovered later in some of her family effects, and was sold through a dealer for a mere $1250. The catalog listing described it as "one of the most complete, important, and contemporary coverages of the Lincoln assassination and following events ever to come on the market."

Wartime letters—from the Spanish-American War, World War I, World War II, the Korean War, and the Vietnam conflict—can be exceedingly interesting to collect. The "V" mail of World War II makes for an unusual specialty. In another quarter of a century, these modern items will be rare. Why? Because people today, when cleaning out old papers, believe them to be too common to be worth saving. Most of these letters will be lost to posterity, just as were the letters of the Revolution and Civil War.

Date is an influential factor in evaluating war autographic material. For example, in the case of Civil War items, anything written between 1861 and 1865 is worth immeasurably more than items from the same person at an earlier or later date. Increased valuation is always attached to battlefield letters and other material written during a period of war. Those written before or after a war usually go down in price accordingly. Although a military discharge dated 1868 can be purchased for around $35.00, one dated during the Civil War will bring a much higher price. A few years ago the "Steam Log" for the *Octorora,* a Civil War gunboat, sold for a $65.00 price tag. It was dated 1861. This ship saw action at Vicksburg and covered territory from Pensacola to New Orleans. Had it not been for the date, such a log would have brought barely half that price.

Fads markedly affect autograph prices. At times a particular personality, especially a contemporary one, experiences a sudden surge in popularity. Thus, Elvis Presley autographs may be worth more on the market now than they will be in fifty or a hundred years. By then, Elvis may have been all but forgotten, for tastes change with the generations. Common sense helps the collector avoid being swept up in current short-lived enthusiasms. Instead, aim for items signed by persons who are likely to be of lasting interest. Good bets are classical composers, world leaders, scientists, explorers, members of baseball's Hall of Fame, statesmen, and so on. Heed the words of Thomas

Madigan in *Word Shadows of the Greats:*

> "Few values seem as permanently secure as those of the autograph letters and manuscripts of men who have written their names large upon the pages of history and literature."

At present, the autographic material of John F. Kennedy offers an outstanding example of this fad in action. The same is true of Elvis and the Beatles. Exorbitant prices are charged for anything even remotely relating to these people. The inflated prices, often bordering on the ridiculous, are due to their current popularity.

The price of modern autographic material, particularly that of distinguished living persons, is usually not high. There is always the possibility the market will become glutted because collectors can send their own requests to living notables. Often, after a celebrity's death, a mass of his or her autographic material saturates the market, largely due to the fact that the people who had the material were unwilling to part with it while the celebrity was alive, perhaps out of respect for a noted contemporary.

An autograph may be extremely rare one year and quite common the next, as the demand for it is met. As the law of supply and demand suggests, if the market is saturated with the autographic material of a particular personality, prices will drop accordingly. A similar devaluation occurs when a dealer is overstocked or in need of cash and puts a large quantity of material on the market at reduced prices. Sometimes a great abundance of long-scarce material returns to the market in the settlement of a collector's estate, causing prices to fall also. Specialty material of the type held by libraries and historical societies seldom ever return to the market for dispersal, so the price for similar material tends to remain high.

After the typewriter came into popular usage, fewer letters were written fully in the hand of the signer. A L.S. by a President while he was in office became more common than an A.L.S. Therefore an A.L.S. from a later period commands the higher price. This holds true even if the L.S. has important historical contents or is quite lengthy. Here, not only does rarity play a part in pricing, sentiment also has an effect.

APPROXIMATE PRICES OF VARIOUS AUTOGRAPHIC MATERIALS

The remainder of this chapter is devoted to a general survey of recent prices of autographic materials. A sampling covering numerous categories will be presented, including information regarding scarcity and a description of certain specific autographs of interest. Naturally, the prices given are subject to fluctuation and change. And, remember, the price of a particular item is always influenced by its date, length, condition, content, association, and other factors, as previously discussed.

Foreign Writers

There are numerous rarities in this category of collecting, but there are also many autographs that will be readily available. The items include A.L.S., L.S., pages of prose, signed books, manuscript poems, simple signatures, and various documents. Here, again, it must be stressed that the list given is only a brief sampling. In a few instances, an individual is listed who is not a literary celebrity primarily, but one who did considerable writing in a particular specialty—for example, Charles Darwin.

Among the rarer items in the foreign literary category are specimens from the following British writers: Sir Walter Raleigh, Chaucer, Milton, Sir Philip Sidney, Lovelace, Bunyan, Herrick, and Suckling. Until less than 35 years ago, no autographic material of Chaucer's was thought to be in existence. If an A.L.S. (handwritten and signed letter) by Shakespeare were ever to appear on the market, it would command a minimum price of one million dollars—and possibly much, much more. Most authorities acknowledge only six existing Shakespearean documents of undisputed authenticity: the deed to his home; a lawsuit deposition; his home mortgage papers; and three signed sheets of his will. A possible seventh specimen appears on the title page of a book sitting in the Folger Shakespeare Memorial Library in Washington, D.C. After thorough testing, the signature appeared to be authentic, but authorities concluded that absolute identification could not possibly be established for a signature standing alone. The fate of the original Shakespearean manuscripts—his numerous plays and poems—is a continuing puzzle. The noted playwright seems to have placed as little value on them as, apparently, did the people to whom he entrusted them for publication. Isn't the same true of writers today?

Material from the pens of Frenchmen Corbiere, Rabelais, Molière, André Chénier, Corneille, Rimbaud, Laforgue, Racihe and Balzac are also scarce. No autographs of François Villon are known to exist. If a letter of this man were to be uncovered, it would probably bring a minimum price of around $15,000. A thirteen-page Baudelaire A.L.S.. recently sold for around $1,500. One Nietzsche A.L.S. brought a price of about $900, and another went for $300. A Goethe A.M.S. went for over $3,000 and an A.L.S. for about $2,300.

Letters written by Anatole France, Chateaubriand, Guizot, Romain Rolland, Lamartine and Jules Verne are relatively plentiful, as are those of Tennyson, Rossetti, George Meredith and Leigh Hunt. Letters written by Thomas Hardy and Robert Browning are fairly common and are usually dull reading. Charles Lamb, George Bernard Shaw and William Cowper, on the other hand, often wrote more interesting letters. Examples of material from other foreign writers are given below:

William Blake: A.L.S. $3,000 up
Robert Burns: Unsigned ms poems, $300 to $2,000; A.L.S. $500 up
Sir Richard Burton: A.L.S. $75.00 to $150
Lord Byron: A.L.S. discussing poetry. $1,000 to $1,500 up; A.L.S. routine matters. $150 up
Samuel T. Coleridge: A.L.S. $30.00 to $50.00
Marie Corelli: Sig. $10.00 to $20.00
Dinah M. Craik: A.L.S. $25.00 to $50.00
Samuel R. Crockett: A.L.S. $15.00 to $35.00

Percy Shelley *Thomas Gray*

Charles Darwin: A.L.S. $70.00 to $150; Signed ms. page from Origin of Species. $1,500 to $3,000; Signed ms. page from Descent of Man. $150 to $300
Charles Dickens: A.N.S. $100 up
John Donne: A.L.S. $3,000 to $4,000 up
John Dryden: A.L.S. $500 to $3000 up; Signed receipts. $200 up
T.S. Eliot: L.S. $150 to $300
St. John Ervine: T.L.S. $35.00 to $75.00
Edward Fitzgerald: A.L.S. $75.00 to $125
Edward M. Forster: A.L.S. $75.00 to $125
Sigmund Freud: A.L.S. $350 to $500 up
Oliver Goldsmith: A.L.S. $4,000 to $6,000 up
Thomas Gray: Unsigned ms pages. $100 to $200
Victor Hugo: A.L.S. $50.00 to $100 up
Ben Jonson: Signed books. $1,000 to $4,000 up
John Keats: A.L.S. $3,000 to $5,000 up
Rudyard Kipling: Sig. $20.00 to $40.00
Charles Lamb: A.L.S. $200 to $400
David Livingstone: A.L.S. $75.00 to $125 up
Francis Turner Palgrave: A.L.S. $10.00 to $25.00
Alexander Pope: Signed receipts: $100 up; A.L.S. $200 to $400
Theodore Reik: A.L.S. $20.00 to $35.00
George Sand: A.N.S. $35.00 to $75.00; A.L.S. $50.00 to $100
William Sharp: A.L.S. $25.00 to $50.00
Sir Walter Scott: A.L.S. $50.00 to $100
Percy Shelley: Check. $100 to $200
Tennyson: Sig. $40.00 to $60.00
Paul Verlaine: A.L.S. $100 to $300
William Butler Yeats: A.L.S. $100 to 300

American Writers

A good deal of autographic material is available in this category. Some of the rarer or more unique specimens are priced higher than the considerably older material from foreign writers. For instance, the original corrected manuscript for Tennessee Williams' *The Glass Menagerie*, dating from the 1940's, sold for $6,000.

The value of the original "Star-Spangled Banner" manuscript, one of the highest-priced pieces of American poetry, stems almost entirely from its historical rather than its literary significance. This manuscript is presently owned by the Maryland Historical Society. It is an excellent example of the fluctuation in price that a unique item may experience. The manuscript was originally owned by Judge Joseph Nicholson, one of Francis Scott Key's brothers-in-law, who had obtained it from the

Values of Autographs and What Affects Them 59

Francis Scott Key

Key's first draft of the National Anthem was lost at the type shop that set it in a handbill. A few days later he wrote the above copy from memory.

author. On September 15, 1814, the Judge took Key's poem to the Baltimore *American* where it was subsequently published as the "Defense of Fort McHenry", in a plain, unornamented handbill. The first draft was lost and Key inscribed another copy from memory. In 1907, the Nicholson family sold this manuscript for $2,500. In 1934, the same poem was purchased for $24,000 at an auction. Nearly 20 years later the Maryland Historical Society was able to obtain it for about the same price. There are two other known copies in existence. If the reputed lost fourth draft were ever to be located, it would command well over $50,000 as of today.

Among the more readily available and inexpensive American literary material, the following names appear: Theodore Dreiser, Julia Ward Howe, James Russell Lowell, Harriet Beecher Stowe, Booth Tarkington, Washington Irving, Robert Frost, Louisa May Alcott, William Cullen Bryant, Eugene Field, Sinclair Lewis, Kate Douglas Wiggin, James Fenimore Cooper, George Bancroft, Hamlin Garland, John Greenleaf Whittier, and John Burroughs.

In the following list of American writers, as with the previous foreign writers, there are a few individuals who were not literary primarily. These people wrote about their particular specialities:

John James Audubon: A.L.S. $500 to $900
Edgar Rice Burroughs: Sig. $35.00 to $40.00
Dane Coolidge: A.L.S. $35.00 to $60.00
George Cooper: A.Ms.S. $25.00 to $50.00
Thomas Costain: A.L.S. $25.00 to $50.00; A.D.S. $20.00 to $45.00

Marion F. Crawford: A.L.S. $35.00 to $75.00
Emily Dickinson: A.L.S. $300 to $500 up
Ralph Waldo Emerson: Sig. $30.00 to $60.00; A.L.S. $50.00 up
William Faulkner: *Pylon* signed. $300 to $400
Edna Ferber: L.S. $25.00 to $50.00
Clyde Fitch: A.L.S. $35.00 to $75.00 up
Robert Frost: *Selected Poems* signed. $75.00 to $150
Earle Stanley Gardner: SP. $15.00 to $25.00
Asa Gray: A.L.S. discussing botany. $50.00 to $100; A.L.S. routine matters. $10.00 to $20.00
Zane Grey: Sig. $15.00 to $25.00; SP. $40.00 to $75.00
Ernest Hemingway: A.N.S. $50.00 to $250

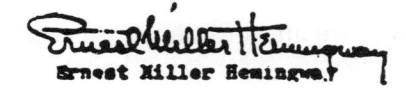

Oliver Wendell Holmes: A.L.S. $50.00 up
Julia Ward Howe: Sig. $25.00 to $40.00
Jack London: A.L.S. $250 to $350
Henry Wadsworth Longfellow: Sig. $10.00 up; A.L.S. $15.00 up
James Russell Lowell: A.L.S. $15.00 to $25.00
Edwin Markham: D.S. $40.00 to $75.00
Herman Melville: A.L.S. $350 to $500 up
H.L. Mencken: A.L.S. $75.00 to $150; SP. $75.00 to $125
Frank Norris: A.Ms.S page from McTeague. $50.00 to $100 up
Thomas Paine: A.L.S. $125 to $250 up
Edgar Allen Poe: A.L.S. $1200 to $2000; A two page A.L.S. brought $5,600 at auction a few years ago.

Emily Post: Sig $7.50 to $15.00
James Whitcomb Riley: A.Q.S. $60.00 to $90.00
Carl Sandburg: L.S. $35.00 to $60.00
William Saroyan: *My Name is Aram* signed. $35.00 to $75.00

Samuel Sewell (Colonial diarist): A.D.S. $60.00 to $100 up

James W. Riley *Walt Whitman*

Values of Autographs and What Affects Them 61

Henry David Thoreau: A.Ms.S page from journal. $350 up
Mark Twain: A.L.S. $250 to $500 up; Sig. (Twain and Clemens) $300 to $600 up

Gore Vidal: *Creation* signed. $50.00 to $75.00
Kurt Vonnegut: SP. $15.00 to $25.00
Walt Whitman: A.L.S. discussing *Leaves of Grass*. $750 to $1000 up; A.L.S. routine matters. $75.00 to $150 up; Sig. $15.00 to $25.00
Kate Douglas Wiggin: A.L.S. $15.00 to $25.00
Thorton Wilder: Book signed. $50.00 to $75.00

By no means a rarity, and still relatively inexpensive, are autographic items from the pens of Artemas Ward, Nathaniel Hawthorne, Horatio Alger, Vachel Lindsay, Elinor Wylie, Joel Barlow, Noah Webster, Ambrose Bierce, Sara Teasdale, Richard Hovey and Timothy Dwight.

Erskine Caldwell created a sensation some years ago with the publication of God's Little Acre. *Today, his signature will bring from $10.00 to $20.00. A meaty A.L.S. may be worth up to $100 or more.*

Some rarer and more expensive American literary materials are those of John Cotton, O. Henry, Thomas Wolfe, Joyce Kilmer, Charles Brockden Brown, Joseph Rodman Drake, Stephen Foster, Anne Bradstreet, Sidney Lanier, Royall Tyler, Stephen Crane, Alan Seeger and Jonathan Edwards.

The Theater

Autographs of even the greatest of stage actors and actresses usually don't command high prices because they're in plentiful supply. A.L.S. from Julia Marlowe, Adelaide Ristori, Ellen Terry, Fanny Davenport, Lily Langtry and Helen Faucit are among the most abundant ones. Those of Peg Woffington, Lola Montez, Gaby Deslys, Clair Morris, Eleanor Duse and Laura Keens are scarce. Below are some current values:

John Barrymore: L.S. $25.00 to $50.00
Sarah Bernhardt: A.L.S. $20.00 to $50.00
Edwin Booth: A.L.S. $25.00 to $50.00
Maurice Chevalier: Sig. $15.00 to $65.00
Sir Noel Coward: SP. $25.00 to $60.00
Jane Cowl: A.L.S. $25.00 to $45.00
   D.S. $20.00 to $40.00
Lotta Crabtree: A.L.S. $7.50 to $15.00
Charlotte Cushman: A.L.S. $35.00 to $55.00
Gaby Deslys: A.L.S. $10.00 to $25.00
Douglas Fairbanks, Sr: SP. $15.00 to $25.00
Helen Hayes: SP. $6.00 to $10.00

Marie Jansen:: A.L.S. $6.00 to $10.00 up
Al Jolson: Sig. $6.00 to $10.00
Charles Kean: A.L.S. $18.00 to $30.00
Fanny Kemble: A.L.S. $10.00 to $20.00
Lillie Langtry: SP. $75.00 to $150
Gertrude Lawrence: Sig. $5.00 to $10.00
Mary Mannering: Sig. on 1902 card. $10.00 to $20.00
Julia Marlowe: A.L.S. $35.00 to $60.00
   Sig. $10.00 to $20.00
Cathleen Nesbit: A.L.S. $15.00 to $30.00
Anna Pavlova: L.S. $200 to $400
Mary Pickford: SP. $6.00 to $15.00
Sarah Siddons: A.L.S. $50.00 to $100
Peg Woffington: A.L.S. $200 up

Film Stars

The autographs of movie stars do not generally command high prices as they are relatively easy to obtain. Most often, with few exceptions, their value wanes since many stars are soon forgotten by their fickle fans. Here are a few current values:

Abbott and Costello: Sig. together. $50.00 to $110
Charlie Chaplin: Sig. $35.00 to $75.00
Errol Flynn: Sig. $35.00 to $60.00
Lillian Gish: SP. $20.00 to $40.00
Oliver Hardy: D.S. $200 to $350
Jean Harlow: Sig. $10.00 to $15.00
Charles Laughton: D.S. $50.00 to $100
Marilyn Monroe: SP. $250 to $400
Paul Newman: D.S. $30.00 to $65.00
Anthony Quinn: SP. $15.00 to $30.00
Mack Sennett: Sig. $40.00 to $75.00
Sylvester Stallone: SP. $10.00 to $20.00
Gloria Swanson: Signed autobiography. $25.00 to $50.00
Sharon Tate: SP. $75.00 to $150
Shirley Temple: SP as a child. $35.00 to $75.00
Franchot Tone: Sig. $10.00 to $25.00
John Wayne: Sig. $25.00 to $100

Composers and Musicians

This is one category of autograph collecting that has always been of great international interest. The field of music—singers, composers, instrumentalists and conductors—will never be restricted by national boundaries. Autographic materials from composers of the seventeenth and eighteenth centuries are extremely scarce. Prices become astronomical when some unsigned scrap of Mozart or Bach music is offered for sale. A small Mozart document dated 1789 brought well over $4,000, even though it was in poor condition, and one of his A.L.S. brought approximately $5,000. Seven pages of Bach's sheet music sold for $2,800. Four of his A.M.S. brought in $1,200 to close to $10,000 apiece.

Signed musical fragments written by Schubert or Beethoven are valued at from $1,000 to $5,000. A Beethoven A.M.S. and a Brahms A.M.S. each sold for $10,000. An ordinary A.L.S. by Mendelsson is currently priced at $100 to $300—his letters are plentiful but always in great demand. However, a fragment of his music is quite rare and

Benny Goodman, widely known as "The King of Swing" during the era of teh Big Bands. Benny always promptly answered sincere requests for his autograph with a signed 5"x7" photo. These are valued today at from $15.00 to $35.00.

brings anywhere from $1,000 to $5,000 or more. An A.L.S. by German composer Hugo Wolf was recently offered for $1,000. One by Georges Bizet commanded a whopping $1,500. And a Claude Debussy A.L.S. brings about $875.

Music scraps signed by Verdi are available in the $150 to $300 price range, but A.L.S. by Verdi are fairly abundant and sell for a good deal less. Though musical fragments from Puccini, Leoncavallo and Pietro Mascagni are by no means common, they can be picked up for $100 to $300 apiece. Mascagni's SP brings a price of around $400. An A.L.S. by Giacomo Puccini commands $500 to $1,250. Signed musical autographs from Massenet, Saint-Saëns, Meyerbeer, Gounod and Offenbach are plentiful. These regularly sell for around $50.00 to $100. A scrap of music from the pen of Dvorsky

Values of Autographs and What Affects Them 63

After Cole Porter's death, his autograph automatically increased in value. This signed photograph was sent to the author in response to a request some years ago. A Cole Porter signature alone may bring as much as $55.00 on today's market.

is worth $75.00 and an A.L.S. by French opera soprano Emma Calve can be purchased for $60.00. Lastly, an A.L.S. by Hector Berlioz may bring as much as $500.

Signed musical specimens and A.L.S. from Rimski-Korsakov, Borodin and Tchaikovsky are rare and usually valued in the $300 to $500 range. A Chopin A.L.S. is also a scarce item. One can sometimes be acquired for between $450 and $750. His signed music is also difficult to locate. Edvard Grieg specimens are more common. They are worth only $100 to $200. A musical A.Ms.S. dated 1892 by violinist Eugene Ysaye, sells for $135. And an A.L.S. of Rudolph Frimi, Bohemian composer, is worth as much as $350.

A few bars of handwritten music, a sheet of printed music, or the title page of a song signed by any of the following can be readily purchased at the prices given:

$7.50 to $15.00 each:

Charles N. Allen—British violinist
Johann D. Behrens—Norwegian musician
Louis Gesensway—American violinist
Francis Korbay—Hungarian pianist
Mischa Levitski—Soviet pianist
George Washington Morgan—British composer
Flor Peeters—Belgian composer
Paul A. Reim—German composer
Frederick P. Search—American cellist
Fernando Tanara—Italian conductor
Camilla Urso—French violinist
Carl Zirrahn—German conductor

$10.00 to $20.00 each:

T. Adamowski—Polish violinist
Modest Altschuler—Soviet conductor
Felix Borowski—American composer
Richard Hoffman—British pianist
Erik Meyer-Helmund—Soviet composer
Victor de Sabata—Italian conductor

Varying prices for other materials:

Sir Thomas Beecham: Sig. $17.50
Irving Berlin: Sig. $25.00 to $35.00
Enrico Caruso: SP. $250 to $325
    Sig. $35.00 to $60.00
George M. Cohan: Sig. $10.00 to $20.00
Arthur Coquard: A.L.S. $15.00 to $25.00
Xavier Cugat: SP. $20.00 to $35.00
Percy A. Grainger: A.L.S. $100 to $150
Alexander Gretchaninoff: A.Ms.S. $100 to $150
Oscar Hammerstein: Sig. $10.00 to $20.00
W.C. Handy: SP. $50.00 to $75.00
Victor Herbert: A.Ms.S. $500 up
Rafael Joseffy: Ms.S. $50.00 to $75.00
Jerome Kern: A.Ms.S. $100 to $150
Fernando Paer: A.L.S. $50.00 to $75.00
Haydn Wood: A.Q.S. $25.00 to $50.00

Kings, Queens and Other Royalty

Autographic materials from royal personages are available at quite modest prices though, of course, the rarer specimens are priced accordingly. A Christmas card signed by Elizabeth II, Queen of Great Britain and Northern Ireland, can be obtained for around $200. A simple L.S. by Ferdinand III, Grand Duke of Tuscany, brings $75.00.

Perhaps the most expensive autograph in this class would be that of William the Conqueror—if if ever it were to come on the market. Only one is known to exist. This "signature" or mark in the form of a cross appeared on a document sold for $7,000 around 35 years ago. A L.S. by Elisabeth, Empress of Russia and wife of Alexander I, can be purchased for $100. And a L.S. by Elizabeth, Queen of Rumania (1843-1916), is obtainable for about the same price. This Queen even authored about 20 books while writing under the pseudoym of Carmen Sylva.

Some autographic material of other English rulers can be costly. The first Queen Elizabeth commands a stiff price—a D.S. may sell for $500 or more; an A.L.S. for $1,500 to $3,000. Materials from George V and George VI are the rarest of the kings bearing this name. A Christmas card signed by George V was offered a few years ago for the bargain price of only $3.00. So was one signed by Queen Mary.

The script of Louis XVII is among the rarest of the French kings. He was the little ten-year old uncrowned king who died in prison. The commonest examples of his handwriting are unsigned pages of notes taken from his schoolbooks. Even these sell for $300 to $500 per page. Francis II, youthful husband of Mary Stuart, father of Marie Louise who married Napoleon in 1810, is another of the few exceptions. His autographic material is quite rare, and prices are always extremely high. An A.L.S. can bring a $425 price tag. Below is a sampling of other rulers and their current prices:

Anne: D.S. $45.00 to $75.00 up
Charles I: D.S. $350 to $450 up
Charles II: D.S. $50.00 to $100 up
Charles IX: D.S. $50.00 to $150 up
Charles X: $15.00 to $50.00 up
Francis I: A.L.S. $50.00 to $150 up
    D.S. $50.00 to $150 up
    L.S. $500 to $750 up
Francis IV: L.S. $40.00 to $100 up
Francis V: L.S. $60.00 to $150 up
Frederick Augustus I: L.S. $75.00 to $150 up
Frederick the Great: L.S. $200 to $275 up
Frederick William I: L.S. $100 to $250 up
George III: D.S. $25.00 to $50.00 up
    A.L.S. $45.00 to $75.00 up
George IV: D.S. $15.00 to $50.00 up
    A.L.S. $30.00 to $50.00 up
Henry I: D.S. $1500 up
Henry II: A.L.S. $50.00 to $150 up
Henry III: D.S. $40.00 to $100 up
Henry IV: D.S. $40.00 to $100 up
Henry VII: D.S. $250 up
Henry VIII: D.S. $300 up
James I: D.S. $75.00 to $250 up
Louis XIII: D.S. $30.00 to $75.00 up
    A.L.S. $30.00 to $75.00 up
Louis XIV: D.S. $30.00 to $75.00 up
    A.L.S. $30.00 to $75.00 up

Louis

Louis XIV

Louis XV: D.S. $30.00 to $75.00 up
    A.L.S. $30.00 to $75.00 up
Louis XVI: D.S. $30.00 to $45.00 up
    A.L.S. $30.00 to $75.00 up
Louis XVIII: All forms. $15.00 to $50.00 up
Louise-Philippe: All forms. $15.00 to $50.00 up
Mary II: D.S. $45.00 to $75.00 up
Richard III: D.S. $750 up
Victoria: D.S. $40.00 to $100 up
    A.L.S. $40.00 to $100 up
William III: D.S. $45.00 to $75.00 up

Nazi Germany in World War II

Few autographs are available from any of Hitler's Nazi leadership. In fact, material from his henchmen isn't in great demand, except in a few instances where collectors have made a specialty of this area. A.L.S. or D.S. from the lesser-known Nazi leaders can easily be obtained for $25.00 to $100. Anything from the pen of Eva Braun, Hitler's mistress, would certainly be a prize, for no autographic material from this woman has yet come on the market.

The autographs of many of the top Nazi leaders—including Joseph Goebbels, Hess, Herman Goering, Wilhelm Joachim von Ribbentrop, Hans Frank, Alfred Rosenberg, Fritz Sauckel, Ernst Kaltenbrunner, Alfred Jodl, Julius Streicher and Frick—are scarce. This is not accidental. Once the outcome of the war seemed inevitable, most Nazi officials made it a point to burn all the letters and documents in their possession. A few current Nazi autograph prices follow:

Values of Autographs and What Affects Them 65

Dr. Joseph Goebbels: L.S. $250 to
    $500 up
Richard Heydrick: L.S. $175 to $300 up
Heinrich Himmler: D.S. $125 to $500 up
    L.S. $125 to $250 up
Adolph Hitler: D.S. Usually commissions or
    appointments. $50.00 to $150 up
    A.L.S. $1,000 to $1,500 up
    L.S. $300 to $500 up
    SP. $150 to $500 up
Wilhelm Keitel: D.S. $100 to $200 up
Robert Ley: D.S. $150 to $300 up
Albert Speer: L.S. $35.00 to $60.00
    SP. $25.00 to $50.00

Hitler

Sauckel

Kaltenbrunner

Streicher

Himmler

Goering

AMERICAN HISTORY

This broad classification naturally covers a wide variety of material. It is generally broken down into more limited categories. Among the scores of possible areas for specialization are: Early Colonial Governors, Explorers, the Wild West, American Financiers, Patriots of the Revolution, Revolutionary War Generals, Statesmen, the Gold Rush, Religious Leaders, Slavery, Pioneers, Naval History, Firearms and so on.

Autographs from men prominent during the American Revolution are still available today, some at quite reasonable prices. For example, William Moultrie's signature can be obtained for around $50.00 or less. He was known as the hero of Charleston and was captured by the British. Timothy Pickering's L.S. range in price from $150 to $250. An A.L.S by James Wood, Governor of Virginia and a colonel in the Revolution sometimes comes available for as little as $75.00. An A.L.S. by Henry Champion, a captain in the Revolution, can be picked up for $375. Ebenezer Cleaveland was the chaplain for the Massachusetts regiment of Artemas Ward. His A.L.S. is worth $500. A D.S. by James Beard, Commissioner of the Continental Navy, brings $125. Major Richard Clough Anderson was at Pulaski's side when the Polish general was killed. His A.D.S. can be purchased for a price of $375. Other items include: an A.L.S. by Colonel Charles T. Armand for $375; General Samuel H. Parsons D.S. for $60.00; General Otto H. Wiliams D.S. for between $50.00 and $75.00; General Edward Hand D.S. for $65.00; John Hancock D.S. for $950 or more; and an A.L.S. by the Marquis de Lafayette for around $325.

First Ladies:

In this category Martha Washington's autograph is one of the rarest. Her signature alone is worth at least $100 to $200; a nice A.L.S. brought $2,800 at an auction a few years ago. Mrs. Madison often wrote and signed religious poetry for autograph seekers of her day. These poems are presently available for as little as $50.00 to $100. The autographs of some of the lesser-known First Ladies are even scarcer than those of Martha Washington. Among this group are Anna Harrison, Rachel

Jackson, Sarah Polk and Eliza Monroe. An A.L.S. by Mrs. Jackson might sell for as much as $600 to $750. Margaret Taylor's A.L.S. can seldom be found on the market. Nor can the letters of Ida McKinley, Ellen Arthur, Martha Jefferson, Hannah Van Buren and Eliza Johnson.

More common are letters from Mary Lincoln, Abigail Adams and Lucretia Garfield. Florence Kling Harding's L.S. can be purchased for around $60.00. An A.N.S. by Grace Coolidge may go for as little as $50.00, whereas a mere signature sometimes brings close to $20.00. Letters from the pen of Mrs. Adams are available for $90.00 to $150. Eleanor Roosevelt's autographed book, *On My Own*, can be obtained for as little as $35.00; her L.S. for $55.00; and her signature for from $15.00 to $25.00. A L.S. by Mamie Eisenhower often sells for as much as $25.00 and up.

OTHER AUTOGRAPHIC AMERICANA

Prices for other categories of American autographs range all the way from a few dollars up to the hundreds and even thousands. The list below, arranged alphabetically, includes notable people from many fields of endeavor:

Ethan Allen: A.L.S. $1,000 to $3,000 up
Benedict Arnold: A.L.S. $500 to $1,500 up
William Bainbridge: A.L.S. $200 to $350 up
Henry Ward Beecher: Sig. $10.00 to $20.00 up
Alexander Graham Bell: L.S. $150 to $350 up
    Sig. $75.00 to $125 up
Buffalo Bill: A.L.S. $30.00 to $100 up
William Bonney (Billy the Kid): A.Q.S. $15.00 to $25.00 up
    Sig. $5.00 to $10.00 up
Daniel Boone: A.L.S. $1,000 up
    Signed surveys. $500 to $800 up
Aaron Burr: A.LS. $100 to $300 up
James F. Byrnes: SP. $10.00 to $25.00 up
Al Capone: SP. $300 to $500 up.
Sam Colt: A.L.S. $250 to $400 up
David Crockett: A.L.S. $750 to $2,00 up
    Franked sig. $300 to $500 up
George Custer: A.L.S. $300 to $500 up
Jefferson Davis: Sig. $10.00 to $15.00
Stephen Decatur: A.L.S. $75.00 to $200 up
George Dewey: A.L.S. $15.00 to $25.00 up
Thomas Dewey: Sig. $5.00 to $10.00 up
John Dillinger: A.L.S. $350 to $500 up
Walt Disney: Sig. $100 to $200
Dr. Tom Dooley: A.L.S. $6.00 to $12.00 up
William O. Douglas: Sig. $10.00 to $20.00
Amelia Earhart: Sig. $50.00 to $100 up
Thomas Edison: SP. $50.00 to $150 up
    A.N.S. $75.00 to $100 up
    Signed check. $75.00 to $150 up
David Farragut: A.L.S. $75.00 to $300 up
    Sig. $10.00 to $25.00 up
Benjamin Franklin: A.L.S. $3,000 to $5,000 up
    A.D.S. $1,000 to $2,000 up
    D.S. $1,500 to $2,500 up
Richard Gatling: A.N.S. $50.00 to $100 up
Charles Goodyear: A.L.S. $50.00 to $100 up
Horace Greeley: Sig. $15.00 to $25.00
Nathan Hale: A.L.S. $2,000 to $3,500 up
    A.N.S. $300 up
Averill Harriman: Sig. $6.00 to $10.00 up
    SP. $10.00 to $25.00 up
Oliver Wendell Holmes: A.Ms.S. $750 to $1,500 up
Patrick Henry: A.L.S. $750 to $1,500 up
Edward M. House: Sig. $7.00 to $15.00 up
Sam Houston: A.L.S. $1,500 to $2,500 up
    A.Ms.S. $3,000 up
J. Edgar Hoover: SP. $20.00 to $45.00 up
Stonewall Jackson: A.L.S. $1,600 up
John Paul Jones: A.L.S. $1,000 to $3,000 up
Alvin Karpis: L.S. $100 to $150 up
    Sig. $15.00 to $25.00 up

Values of Autographs and What Affects Them 67

Helen Keller: SP. $20.00 to $35.00 up
Owen Lattimore: SP. $10.00 to $25.00
Meriwether Lewis: A.D.S. $750 up
Henry Cabot Lodge: Sig. $7.00 up
    L.S. $10.00 up
Douglas MacArthur: Sig. $50.00 to $75.00 up
Robert A. Millikan: D.S. $150 to $250 up
Martha Mitchell: L.S. $75.00 to $150 up
William H. Moody: L.S. $40.00 to $75.00 up
Walter Mondale: SP. $10.00 to $25.00 up
John S. Mosby: Sig. $7.50 to $15.00 up
Annie Oakley: Sig. $75.00 to $150 up
Lee Harvey Oswald: A.N.S. $500 to $750 up
    A.L.S. $1600 up
Pawnee Bill: Sig. $15.00 to $25.00 up
    A.L.S. $30.00 to $50.00 up
Robert E. Peary: A.L.S. discussing North Pole. $100 to $300 up
    A.L.S. Routine matters. $25.00 to $50.00 up
    A.D.S. $100 to $250 up
    Sig. $10.00 to $25.00 up
John Penn: D.S. $25.00 to $75.00 up
Thomas Penn: D.S. $25.00 to $75.00 up
William Penn: A.L.S. $500 to $1,000 up
    D.S. $200 to $300 up
Oliver Hazard Perry: A.L.S. $100 to $200 up
    D.S. $55.00 to $100 up
John J. Pershing: A.L.S. $50.00 to $150 up
Melvin Purvis: Signed check. $25.00 to $75.00 up
Sally Rand: SP. $15.00 to $25.00 up
Paul Revere: A.D.S. $1,600 up
    Receipts. $100 to $250 up
William Pickney: A.L.S. $125 to $250 up
Eddie Rickenbacker: Sig. $8.00 to $16.00
Hyman Rickover: A.L.S. $75.00 to $150 up
    L.S. $50.00 to $125 up
Norman Rockwell: A.L.S. $20.00 to $45.00 up
    L.S. $8.00 to $15.00 up
Caesar Rodney: A.L.S. $50.00 to $75.00 up
Will Rogers: Sig. $20.00 to $50.00 up
Dean Rusk: L.S. $20.00 to $40.00 up
Paul A. Samuelson: SP. $25.00 to $40.00 up
Arthur Schlesinger: A.L.S. $15.00 to $45.00
Winfield Scott: A.L.S. $75.00 to $125 up
William H. Seward: Sig. $10.00 to $20.00 up
William Shockley: SP. $12.00 to $22.00 up
Sitting Bull: Sig. $15.00 to $50.00 up
Peter Stuyvesant: Land grants. $800 up
Daniel Webster: A.L.S. $60.00 to $100 up
Noah Webster: Sig. $75.00 to $110 up
Gideon Welles: D.S. $35.00 to $50.00 up
    Sig. $10.00 to $20.00 up
Orville Wright: D.S. $150 to $300 up
Brigham Young: Sig. $75.00 to $215 up

The collector on a limited budget whose interest lies in military material will find many autographic specimens are still readily available from generals, admirals, and others who served between the War of 1812 and the Civil War. An A.L.S. by Admiral George Henry Preble can be purchased for about $75.00 or less. His L.S. goes for less than $50.00. Captain George C. Reed, Commander of the *Constitution* in 1826 brings less than $100 for a L.S. Most A.L.S. and L.S. from this historical period can be obtained at reasonable prices—from $15.00 to $50.00, and often for a good deal less. Usually, material from the naval leaders of the Civil War is also inexpensive. In fact, Admiral David D. Porter's signature can be purchased for less than $20.00. Material from World War I and II military leaders ranges from $5.00 to $25.00 in price, according to the stature of the individual.

The name of radio newscaster Lowell Thomas was a household word in America some years ago. Lowell's signature alone is valued at over $15.00 on today's market. An autographed photo as shown above commands a respectable minimum of $35.00.

Signed photographs of many of these men are also available. A General Jonathan Wainwright A.L.S. goes for between $75.00 and $100.

Autographic material from the Colonial governors of the Virginia colony following Captain John Smith is extremely rare. Seldom found on the market are autographs of Sir Thomas Dale, Sir William Berkeley and Sir Thomas Gates. When any are offered for sale, however, they are reasonably priced except for those of Smith himself, which generally command from $2,000 to $6,000.

Material from such Colonial governors of New York as Peter Minuit, Wouter Van Twiller and Willem Kieft, like that of Peter Stuyvesant, are rarities in all forms except D.S. Later New York governors—Robert Hunter, William Tryon, Lord Bellomont, James DeLancey—are much more common. A D.S. by any of these men will cost between $25.00 and $50.00.

D.S. by most of the later Massachusetts governors are available for only $10.00 to $20.00 apiece. These would include William Shirley, Thomas Hutchinson and Francis Bernard. Material from the earlier Massachusetts governors is rare—a Carver A.L.S. might bring as much as $1,600 or more; one form Winthrop, Endicott or Bradford usually sells for at least $1,500. And an A.D.S. by Roger Wolcott, Colonial governor of Connecticut may go for $125.

Autographic materials from some members of the Continental Congress are still reasonably priced. For example, an A.L.S by Turbutt Wright may be found for only $50.00. An A.L.S. by Pennsylvania member Tench Coxe is available for as little as $40.00. This man's A.D.S. dated 1775, can be picked up for a mere $20.00. Lastly, a signature of Massachusetts member Thomas Cushing can be found listed for a paltry $25.00.

Lincoln material, among the most avidly sought by both dealers and collectors, usually stays in the higher price brackets. Few people of average income can afford the rarer Lincoln items. Prices for a few of these may be of interest.

Fourteen Lincoln A.L.S. written to Joshua Fry Speed, an intimate friend, were sold in 1952 for $35,000. Three of Mary Todd Lincoln's A.L.S. were sold along with them for $2,000. At this time, Lincoln's cut signatures were selling for from $10.00 to $15.00. Today they go for at least $150 and up.

The earliest document known to have been prepared by Lincoln was dated in 1833 and it sold for $1,000. Part of his math book used as a teenager brought $3,600. In it was the first known specimen of Lincoln's handwriting:

"Abraham Lincoln is my name
    And with my pen I wrote the same.
I wrote in both haste and speed
    And left it here for fools to read."

In 1956, an A.L.S. from Lincoln to General Ulysses S. Grant concerning a Union victory was auctioned off for $2,700. It read as follows:

City Point, April 2,
8:15 PM 1865

Lieut. General Grant

Allow me to tender to you and all with you, the nations grateful thanks for this additional, and magnificent success—At your kind suggestion, I think I will visit you tomorrow.

A. Lincoln

In 1963, $3,500 bought a two-page Lincoln A.L.S. regarding his possible Presidential nomination. An A.M.S. went for $16,000. It was Lincoln's address congratulating the Army of the Potomac. A printed copy of the Emancipation Proclamation signed by Lincoln, Seward and Nicolay was purchased for $9,500. Twenty-three other Lincoln letters and documents were also auctioned. The lowest price paid for a document was $90.00. The highest price paid for one of his letters was $4,250.

Only a few areas of specialization have thus far been mentioned. These give but a hint of the tremendous mass of available autographic materials of all types. They range from past centuries to more recent decades, right on up to the present. It would be impossible to list in these pages every great personage whose autograph is worth collecting. It would also be difficult to relate more than the smallest fraction of the fascinating anecdotes associated with collecting. And it would be impractical to set price guidelines for every conceivable class of material.

National leaders, present and past, are notables about whom relatively little has been said so far. Autographs from some of them are rare. All contemporary leaders in the Orient, most communist-bloc nations, and English royalty are difficult to acquire. The only exceptions among Oriental autographs are those of people who serve as diplomats in Washington or at the United Nations. Sun Yat-sen's letters are extremely rare. Signatures of Chairman Mao Tse-tung seldom come into a dealer's hands. Rarely is anything from Chiang Kai-shek seen on the market. Autographic material from Lenin or Stalin is tremendously rare. A unique SP of Lenin sold for $85.00 in 1951, and few have come up for sale since then. DeGaulle of France was always difficult and often discourteous when approached personally for his autograph; it was next to impossible to obtain anything from him through the mail. The same holds true for Gandhi.

Stalin

DeGaulle

Gandhi

The autographs of Mexican presidents, on the other hand, are generally easy to acquire and are more moderately priced. An A.L.S. from Winston Churchill sells for between $300 and $500. This man's signature alone sometimes can be found in the $75.00 to $150 price range.

Any A.L.S. with interesting content from Napoleon is scarce, and such a letter would be costly. His rarest material contains the spelling of his name in the Italian form—Buonaparte. This is the name he initially used in all correspondence. French catalogs occasionally list a Napoleon D.S. for as little as $25.00; a routine A.L.S. for between $60.00 and $100. To go further back in centuries: the log book kept on the HMS Victory by Lord Nelson was sold a few years ago for a little over $1,000; an Oliver Cromwell A.D.S. sells for $100 or more; and an extremely rare Cromwell A.L.S. will cost $300 and up.

By contrast, simple signatures of any of the following can be purchased for $25.00, and sometimes a good deal less: Marshal Tito, Pierre Trudeau, Romulo Betancourt, Janós Kadar, Menechem Begin, Syngman Rhee, Francisco Franco, Haile Selassie, Helmut Schmidt, Indira Gandhi, Anthony Eden, Jawaharlal Nehru, Antonio de Oliveira Salazar, Pieter Willem Botha, Harold Wilson, Valery Giscard d'Estaing, Moise Tshombe, David Ben-Gurion, Jose Lopez Portillo, Habib Bourguiba, Anwar Sadat, Ferdinand Marcos, John Malcolm Fraser, Ahmed Sekou Torre and Mendes-France.

Religious leaders are another category to consider. Prices range from a dollar or so for the autographs of current religious leaders, to thousands of dollars for old and/or unique specimens. Autographic material from any of the following can readily be obtained for $5.00 to $20.00: Bishop Fulton Sheen, Billy Graham, W.A. "Billy" Sunday, Bishop Pike, Rabbi Stephen Wise, Cardinal Spellman, Jim Bakker, Oral Roberts, Norman Vincent Peale, Markarios III and Jimmy Swaggert.

A John Wesley A.L.S. could bring $225 to $300. One from Ignatius Loyola may sell for over $6,000. An A.L.S. of Margaret Fox, one of the founders of spiritualism, may be picked up for around $25.00. Not long ago, a Latin Bible illuminated on vellum, circa 1300, was purchased for $4,200. Various thirteenth-century treatises of

St. Augustine sold for well over $3,500. A 1554 Martin Luther A.Ms.S brought $11,000. Various A.L.S. by this same man went for prices from $1,750 to $6,500. Two sermons by Thomas Clap, first president of Yale, sold for $75.00.

The scientific field has been given scant mention, though a wide selection of exciting autographic material is always available in this category. The young beginner can accumulate many signed photographs, letters and signatures from living scientists simply by sending a request to chosen personalities. All dealers have cut signatures, photos and letters for sale at low prices. For instance, some types of autographic material from any of the following can be purchased for under $20.00: Louis Leakey, Linus Pauling, James Van Allen, Jonas Salk, Booker T. Washington, William Shockley, Julian S. Huxley, Harlow Shapley, Owen Lattimore, Arthur H. Compton, Albert Sabin and Hermann Oberth.

Not long ago, a single-page A.L.S. by Alfred Nobel was sold for $160, and a two-page Lavoisier A.L.S. brought $500. Seventy-two A.L.S. by Marconi were purchased as a group for $1,064. An A.L.S. by noted British scientist, Havelock Ellis, will usually sell for around $100 and up. In the exceptionally scarce class: a mere three lines and a signature on a Galileo document sold for around $2,500.

In conclusion, a further word of warning should be added in regard to collecting only the cheapest and most easily obtainable autographic material, of current and recent celebrities. A collector has the privilege of accumulating whatever is most appealing, whether his interest lies in collecting specimens of movie stars, wrestlers, rock singers, television emcees, big-game hunters, or minor politicos. I can't emphasize too strongly, however, that collections of this type are not at likely to rise appreciably in value as the years pass. When no other material other than a signature ever comes on the market from a well-known personality, there is only a small chance the specimen will increase in value. But here, as in other collecting hobbies, being content with second-rate items or those in constant oversupply is not the mark of a wise investor. Therefore, each collector must first decide whether he or she can afford to collect only for the sentimental appeal certain signatures, signed photographs and other materials may have, or whether the collection is to be one of lasting value, intended to appreciate handsomely in time.

"Satchmo" Louis Armstrong was always happy to send an autographed photo to his fans. He tried to respond promptly to each and every request. Armstrong's signed photos aren't a rarity, yet they will bring aroudn $12.50 and up on the collector's market because of their popularity.

6.
Some Anecdotes and Interesting Sidelights

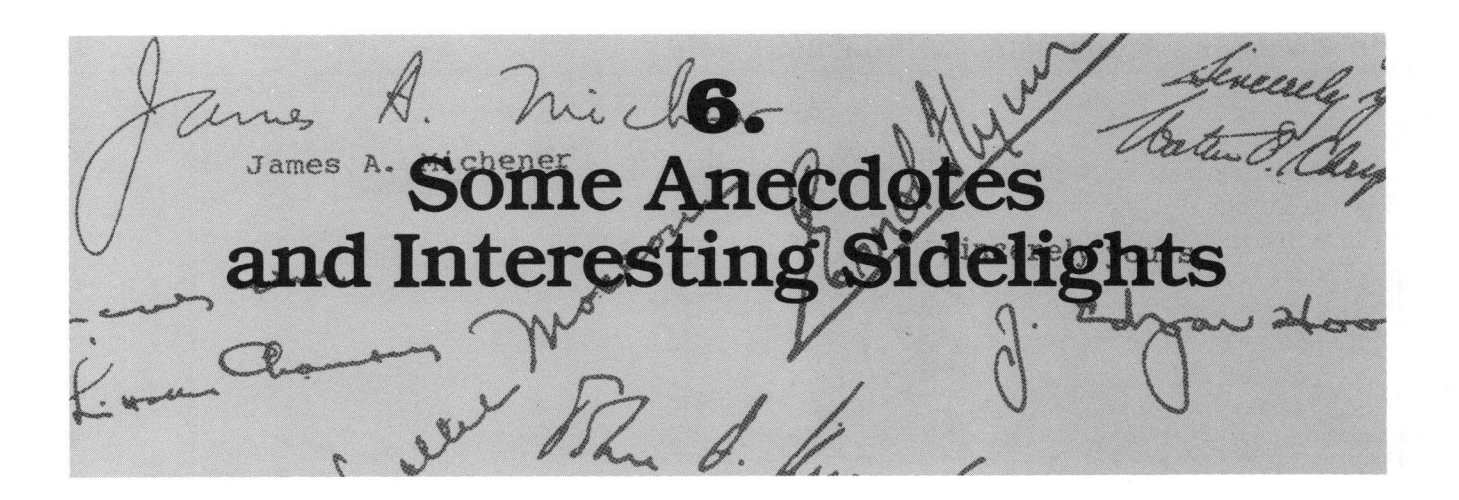

Throughout that long period of history when all letters were inscribed by hand, the task often fell to personal secretaries or aides. Quite frequently, the beginning collector may feel at a loss as to how to differentiate between a letter written entirely by a notable and one merely signed by that individual and penned by someone else. Many secretaries made it a practice to imitate the script for whomever they happened to be writing, thus adding to the confusion. However, when a letter was written by a secretary or an aide, the notable would usually affix his or her signature in a different color ink than was used in the body of the letter. Correspondence signed in this manner is quite easily identified.

During the course of the American Revolution, General George Washington had at least thirty-five aides handling his monumental letter-writing tasks. Later, some of these men became well known in their own right. A letter written by one of these aides and then signed by Washington can, in some instances, be worth considerably more than a letter written completely by the great military leader. Among his more prominent aides were Alexander Hamilton, James McHenry and Thomas Mifflin.

Presidential correspondence has always been burdensome. A number of our Chief Executives have resorted to using a rubber stamp for affixing their signatures; among them are Theodore and Franklin Roosevelt, Woodrow Wilson and Andrew Johnson. President Johnson was the only one in this group who truly required a rubber stamp! He was badly handicapped with a crippled right arm. Johnson's rubber stamped documents are commonly found in various dealer catalogs. They can be purchased for as little as $5.00 and up to $10.00 on today's collector's market.

A facsimile signature, usually an exact printed copy, can appear to be so authentic that even an expert will not always spot it at first glance. The majority of facsimiles, however, are not very successful and, therefore, are quite easily detected. Reproduced signatures of this kind are widely used on political solicitations, advertising mail and fund-raising letters. Four facsimile signatures used in recent years were of such superior quality as to be virtually undetectable by the naked eye, but when checked with a magnifying glass they were clearly reproductions. One signature was that of Dwight D. Eisenhower. It was sent out by the thousands on White House cards in response to requests for autographs during his Presidency. Another was on the card used by President and Mrs. Lyndon B. Johnson in answer to Christmas cards they received during the holiday period. A third was Jacqueline Kennedy's. After President Kennedy's untimely death, she made extensive use of a form letter with a printed facsimile signature to answer autograph requests and for replying to the many letters of condolence she received. The fourth is President Ronald Reagan. His excellent facsimile signature appears on numerous fund raising letters and appeals for support of his programs.

Autopen signatures have created a problem of disturbing proportions for autograph collectors. The Autopen is an electric machine that reproduces a script from an original signature recording. Plastic masters are simple to interchange, so that many individuals are able to share the same machine. One master can produce over 100,000 signatures without variance from the original! And one Autopen can sign as many as 3,000 signatures within an eight-hour period!

Autograph dealers and collectors generally try to avoid involvement in the authentication of signatures of this type. Some will undertake authentication only if they have more than one example of the person's writing on hand. The problem is that the use of the Autopen has become so common that an autograph buyer must be extremely wary when attempting to purchase material of this nature.

As collectors will discover, there is good reason to exercise caution. Each signature written by the Autopen fits precisely over any other. Authenticity cannot be determined unless the signature can be superimposed over another known to have been inscribed by the same person, since there is absolutely no deviation in the lines. Each specimen is an automatic precision reproduction of the original signature and is indistinguishable. The Autopen can even use a particular person's fountain pen if this is desirable. It's an established fact that no man or woman ever signs their name in exactly the same way twice, but Autopen signatures are always the same—as identical as a person's own fingerprints!

Sometimes confusion results when two or more people possess identical names but have no close physical or important historical relationship.

Some Anecdotes and Interesting Sidelights 73

For example, Thomas Lynch, Jr., a Signer of the Declaration of Independence, is one of the rarest and most sought after American autographs. Naturally, a collector couldn't help but get excited when stumbling upon a Lynch signature, but how that feeling would fizzle with the discovery that there was yet another Thomas Lynch—a New York merchant with no particular claim to fame! The same disappointment would surely result when uncovering a Nathan Hale signature (1755-1776), and then learning it was not that of the famed patriot. In addition to the man who proclaimed, "I regret that I have but one live to lose for my country," there were two other Nathan Hales: one was a Connecticut legislator (1742-1813); and the other, a nephew of the patriot, was editor of a Boston newspaper, the founder of a magazine and an active participant in New England railroad promotion.

Other famous names held by more than one person have been cause for confusion among autograph collectors and dealers. These include George Washington, John Brown, James Monroe, John Penn, Charles Dickens, Thomas Paine, William Bradford, James Madison, Winston Churchill, Rufus King, Caesar Rodney, Robert Morris, William Blount, Oliver Ellsworth, George Clinton, Henry Jackson, Israel Putnam, Francis Marion, and Anthony Wayne.

Pseudonyms can be another great source of perplexity to autograph collectors. Almost everyone knows certain famous pen names, such as that used by Samuel Langhorne Clemens who wrote under the name of Mark Twain. Other pseudonyms are not so widely recognized, nor are they restricted to the literary field. Many men corresponded under names different than their birth names in an effort to disguise their identity. This was a necessary deception at times while the Revolutionary War was being fought. For example, Alexander Hamilton is known to have used Camillus, Cato and Pacificus, as well as several other pseudonyms. Two excellent reference works on this subject will be found in chapter 16.

An individual's signature often varies in the course of his or her lifetime. Sometimes a signature is influenced merely by haste; at other times the writer is simply exhausted. Weakness, increasing age and illness show up in handwriting. Look at the signatures of Anthony Eden that follow

1951—Vigorous and strong

February 1953—Quite ill

One month later—Recovering

Barry Goldwater used the Autopen for signing his photographs during his unsuccessful Presidential bid in 1964. Prior to this time, and afterwards, autograph collectors would receive an authenticallly signed photograph on request.

74 Collecting Autographs For Fun and Profit

The signature of Lord Nelson, the British naval hero, varies for a most unusual reason. Nelson lost his right arm in the Battle of Santa Cruz de Tenerife in 1797. This man is one of the few notables in history to leave both right-handed and left-handed specimens of his script. He always signed his name "Horatio Nelson" before losing his arm. After his tragic loss, he signed "Nelson of Bronte." Which of the two signatures is rarer is a matter of constant dispute. Prices tend to vary extensively in the catalogs issued by different dealers.

A legitimate signature may be no more than a simple sign or mark. In the eleventh, twelfth, and thirteenth centuries, a mark was common in lieu of a written name, and would often denote the authorship of a letter or a document, for most people couldn't write. Literacy was the exception then, rather than the rule! Even kings couldn't write their own names! William the Conqueror made his mark by drawing a crude picture of a cross. Pizarro, the conqueror of Peru, signed documents by using a mark. Some Americn Indian chiefs signed documents with an "X"; others would sketch a crude, childlike picture of an animal.

Napoleon Bonaparte

Napoleon signed his name in a variety of ways. Apparently he used the Italian spelling (Buonaparte) primarily until February 29, 1796, and the French spelling (Bonaparte) thereafter. Signatures in the Italian spelling are the most coveted because of their extreme rarity. Here are a few examples:

Some Anecdotes and Interesting Sidelights 75

Meriwether Lewis

Enrico Caruso

Napoleon

Sam Houston

John Hancock

Picasso

Hitler

A paraph, which is nothing more than a flourish, can often serve as a valid means of identification for an individual. This is true not only when the paraph or flourish is part of the signature, but also when it stands alone, as it so often did in the case of a royal personage. Without the identifying flourish, which would always take precedence over the written signature, the signature itself was considered to be invalid. Among the notables whose signatures included a paraph were General George Clinton, the great Spanish artist Goya, Robert Fulton, Paderewski, Edgar Allen Poe, and Giuseppe Verdi. Others are shown above.

THE FRANKING PRIVILEGE

Franked letters, particularly those of President's wives have a special appeal to collectors interested in Americana. Most Presidential widows were, by special Act of Congress, granted the privilege of franking their mail (sending letters without any postage). The lady had only to sign her name on the envelope, in place of the postage stamp, with the word "FREE."

Some First Ladies Granted the Franking Privilege

A President's widow can use her own name for signing rather than her husband's once Congress grants authorization. Mary Lincoln's franked envelopes are quite popular with collectors. They're valued at well over $350 each when they can be found in dealer's catalogs. All autograph requests to Jacqueline Kennedy are answered with a printed facsimile of her signature on the envelope. It's highly doubtful whether *any* authentic franks of hers will ever exist unless she decides to write one as a special favor for an intimate friend.

While in office, a President isn't automatically given the franking privilege. It doesn't come with the job! When franking is allowed, it can be used only on official mail. However, if a President *is* granted the privilege, neither his wife nor other members of his immediate family are authorized to send letters out under his frank.

Many First Ladies have knowingly taken advantage of a good thing during the husband's term in office, ignoring the fact that such activity was clearly illegal. Dolly Madison was one of the chief culprits. She would send personal letters to friends bearing her husband's frank. Letters of this nature were also sent by Mary Lincoln and Abigail Adams. They can sometimes still be found listed for sale in dealer's catalogs.

A few incumbent Presidents were never given the franking privilege. Among the more recent of these were Harry Truman, Dwight Eisenhower, John Kennedy and Lyndon Johnson. However, former Presidents Truman and Eisenhower did receive this privilege after their terms in office.

SIGNERS OF THE DECLARATION OF INDEPENDENCE SETS

A few early autograph collectors were fortunate enough to accumulate complete sets of Signers of the Declaration of Independence. These include Israel Tefft, L.J. Cist, Elliott Danforth, William Sprague, and Dr. Thomas Addis Emmet. Autographic materials of a few of the Signers are virtually impossible to obtain today, but the majority are fairly accessible. In all, there are fewer than fifty complete sets of Signers in existence. And the majority of these are owned by insitutions.

Dr. Emmet was the crown prince of all Signer collectors—he actually acquired five complete sets, one of which is part of a complete set of autographs of members of the Old Congress. This Old Congress set and two of Emmet's Signer sets are now in the New York Public Library. Another is housed in the Historical Society of Pennsylvania. The fifth is owned by the Henry Huntington Library in San Marino, California. The following is a list of historical societies, colleges and universities, and libraries who possess complete Signer sets:

Historical Societies

Chicago Historical Society (1)
Historical Society of Pennsylvania (3)
Maine Historical Society (1)
New Jersey Historical Society (1)
State Historical Society of Wisconsin (1)
Western Reserve Historical Society (1)

Colleges and Universities

Amherst College, Amherst, Ma. (1)
Cornell University, Ithaca, N.Y. (1)
Haverford College, Haverford, Pa. (2)
St. John's Seminary, Camarillo, Ca. (1)
St. Mary's of the Lake Seminary, Mudelein, Il. (1)
University of Indiana, Bloomington, In. (1)
University of Pennsylvania, Philadelphia, Pa. (1)
West Chester State College, West Chester, Pa. (1)
Yale University, New Haven, Ct. (2)

Public and Private Libraries

Boston Public Library (1)
Henry Huntington Library (1)
Houghton Library, Harvard University (1)
John Work Garrett Library, Baltimore, Md. (1)
Library of Congress (1)
New York Public Library (4)
New York State Library (1)
Pierpont Morgan Library (2). This particular collection includes the handwritten will of Gwinnett.

The infamous John Wilkes Booth, an actor of some popularity, was the younger brother of Edwin Booth, one of the most famous theater personalities of his day. Although the rest of the Booth family were Union loyalists, John supported the South, becoming more fanatical as the war progressed. Both brothers were fairly prolific letter writers. Most people who received letters from John destroyed them after the assassination of Abraham Lincoln. Today, therefore, John's letters are extremely rare and are worth much more than those of his renowned brother. A revealing letter from Edwin concerning his brother's character would be worth far more than the many he wrote about theatrical engagements.

Five handwritten copies of Lincoln's Gettysburg Address are in existence today. The Library of Congress has two copies. The Illinois Historical Society has one. The fourth copy is privately owned. There is an interesting story connected with the fifth. In 1864, the historian George Bancroft asked his friend Lincoln to make this extra copy. It was to be auctioned during a benefit fair for military men and their families. Oddly enough, no one even offered a bid for this masterful document. It was subsequently given to Colonel Alexander Bliss, a man who happened to collect autographs as a hobby. This copy was purchased in 1949 for a record price of $54,000 by Oscar B. Cintas, former Ambassador to the United States from Cuba. His family later donated it to the United States Government. Ironically, this copy of the Gettysburg Address is the one found hanging in the Lincoln Room of the White House.

Black Hawk War discharges signed by Captain Abraham Lincoln are items of special rarity and interest to collectors. Sixty-seven are known to have existed at one time, and only five have been uncovered thus far. Lincoln commanded a company

78   Collecting Autographs For Fun and Profit

Mr. Lincoln's handwritten copy of the Gettysburg Address, made by him for the Soldirs' and Sailors' Fair in Baltimore, 1864. For its quiet depth of feeling and solemn beauty of expression this speech is rightly regarded as one of the great masterpieces of English prose.

> Four score and seven years ago our fathers brought forth on this continent, a new nation, conceived in Liberty, and dedicated to the proposition that all men are created equal.
>
> Now we are engaged in a great civil war, testing whether that nation, or any nation so conceived and so dedicated, can long endure. We are met on a great battlefield of that war. We have come to dedicate a portion of that field, as a final resting place for those who here gave their lives that that nation might live. It is altogether fitting and proper that we should do this.
>
> But, in a larger sense, we can not dedicate — we can not consecrate — we can not hallow — this ground. The brave men, living and dead, who struggled here, have consecrated it, far above our poor power to add or detract. The world will little note, nor long remember what we say here, but it can never forget what they did here. It is for us the living, rather, to be dedicated here to the unfinished work which they who fought here have thus far so nobly advanced. It is rather for us to be here dedicated to the great task remaining before us — that from these honored dead we take increased devotion to that cause for which they gave the last full measure of devotion — that we here highly resolve that these dead shall not have died in vain — that this nation, under God, shall have a new birth of freedom — and that government of the people, by the people, for the people, shall not perish from the earth.

Some Anecdotes and Interesting Sidelights

of sixty-seven men during the Black Hawk War. It was customary not to pay volunteer soldiers until their term of enlistment was completed. They might not receive any back pay until months after discharge. The official United States Army paymaster would make a tour through the area and try to locate the veterans. Four of the discharges found to date are official printed forms, on which Lincoln merely filled in the pertinent information and added his signature. The fifth Black Hawk War discharge, shown here, is the only one written entirely in Lincoln's own hand. It declares:

> I do hereby certify that Nathan Drake volunteered and served as a private in the company which I commanded—in the regiment commanded by Colonel Samuel M. Thompson—of the Brigade commanded by Brigadier General Samuel Whiteside—in an expedition directed against the Sac and Fox Indians—and that he was enrolled on the 29th day of April and discharged on the 8th day of June 1832—having served forty and two thirds days—given under my hand this 24th July 1832—
>
> A. Lincoln. Captain

A veteran in immediate need of cash didn't always have to wait those long months for his money. He could sign his discharge over to someone else, much as we now transfer the deed on a piece of property or a home. Nathan Drake assigned his claim to a local merchant. This handwritten note appears on the back of his discharge:

> For value received I assign all the benefit of the within discharge to John Taylor and hereby authorize the pay master to pay over to John Taylor, all the wages I may be entitled to receive for my services.
> Attest
> M. Mobley   Nathan Drake

Black Hawk War discharge fully handwritten by Abraham Lincoln when he was a Captain in the United States Army.

Nathan Drake's handwritten note on the reverse side of his Black Hawk War discharge. Courtesy of the Illinois Historical Society.

BE WARY OF FORGERIES

Varna Davis, wife of Jefferson Davis, President of the Confederacy, was adept at duplicating her husband's handwriting. She often wrote the body of his letters and then had Jefferson add his signature. Sometimes she even signed the letters for her husband. Later, he would be unable to tell whether he himself had written a particular letter entirely or even signed it—her imitation of his handwriting was so uncannily accurate. Such letters can still be found on today's market for as little as $75.00.

Such perfect imitations are rare, though they're the aim of all forgers. Of course, Varna Davis can't really be called a forger, since her intent was to be of secretarial assistance rather than to commit fraud. A professional forger, when producing an entire document, letter, or signature on a check—or merely attempting to alter or add to one—is generally inspired by greed or financial gain. Rarely does a forgery escape complete detection, but while the forged material is on the autograph market, it can create confusion among the experts and bring heartbreak to the uninitiated. Many forgeries are detected fairly easily through a slip-up in the forger's historical knowledge. The beginning collector should develop the habit of carefully checking the date of any item offered for sale. Always make certain it falls within the birth and death dates of the supposed writer. To detect a possible forgery, there are certain specific characteristics to check before making a purchase decision:

Erasures: Be wary of any indication of erasures or eradications of any kind.

Hesitation: Squared-off or forced-looking formations of letters and beginning blobs of ink.

Patching or Retraced Strokes: This may indicate the forger is trying to make the signature or script similar to the original. The handwriting may appear muddy or blotchy.

Roughness: Line edges will show a corrugated or wavery pattern. This may denote a forced copying of the signature.

Pen Lifts: Indicated by a variance in the stroke pressure. This changes the weight of the up and down strokes considerably, and makes the writing appear shaded.

Slant Changes: The slant sometimes changes normally, but this isn't common. There usually will not be an appreciable difference. If the signature isn't all the same slant, then question the seller thoroughly prior to making a purchase.

Ink Variation: Scrutinize the script

carefully for any difference in the type ink utilized by the writer.

In the business world today, check forgeries occur frequently. The authorities use computers for making comparisons that help to divulge the identity of a forger. There have been numerous cases of sheer stupidity on the part of citizens who have been taken in by a forger. Some cases actually border on the ridiculous! The FBI has enlarged one check from their case files for display purposes. It was drawn on "The East Bank of the Mississippi," in "Slippery Rock, Mississippi," and then endorsed by "U.R. Stuck." As silly as this may appear, the check was successfully cashed in a grocery store!

There are numerous ways in which autograph collectors can avoid being taken in by a forgery. The tremendous success experienced by counterfeiters isn't so much ingenuity on their part, as it is negligence on the part of collectors. Many cases on record could easily have been avoided had the buyer followed a few extremely simple precautionary rules:

Know Your Seller: It's easy to swallow a fast line from someone with a charming personality. This is especially true when purchasing a valuable autographic item.

Require Identification: Most businesses and individuals accept a driver's license, Social Security card, credit card, or even a fishing license, as valid identification. Entirely too much confidence is placed in these bits of paper. Courtney Townsend Taylor, a notorious forger who was finally snared by the FBI, had 57 fake draft cards. These were only a small part of his large stock which included Social Security cards, fishing licenses, etc.—all self made!

Require a Fingerprint: Whenever a stranger offers to sell autographic material of any importance, ask the person to place a thumbprint on your copy of the receipt. The seller shouldn't object unless he's of questionable character.

Ask Questions: Never be made to feel rushed by a fast talker! Freely ask questions about the material and the seller. The person trying to sell the autographic material shouldn't mind answering your questions if he or she is really legitimate.

Never Deal with a Child: A minor isn't legally responsible for any sale to an adult. Forgers often use children to do their selling. Don't be disarmed by a child's smile or sad tale of woe.

Best wishes,
Bob,
"Luke" Appling

Burleigh A. Grimes

Best wishes
Enos Slaughter
St Louis Cards

Best wishes to Bob
Ted Williams

Hank Greenberg

Ralph Kiner

Best Wishes
Johnny Mize

Red Ruffing

Joe Medwick

Bill T. Dickey

Joe DiMaggio

Carl Hubbell

Best Wishes
Sincerely,
Roy Campanella

7. Hall of Fame Members: Values

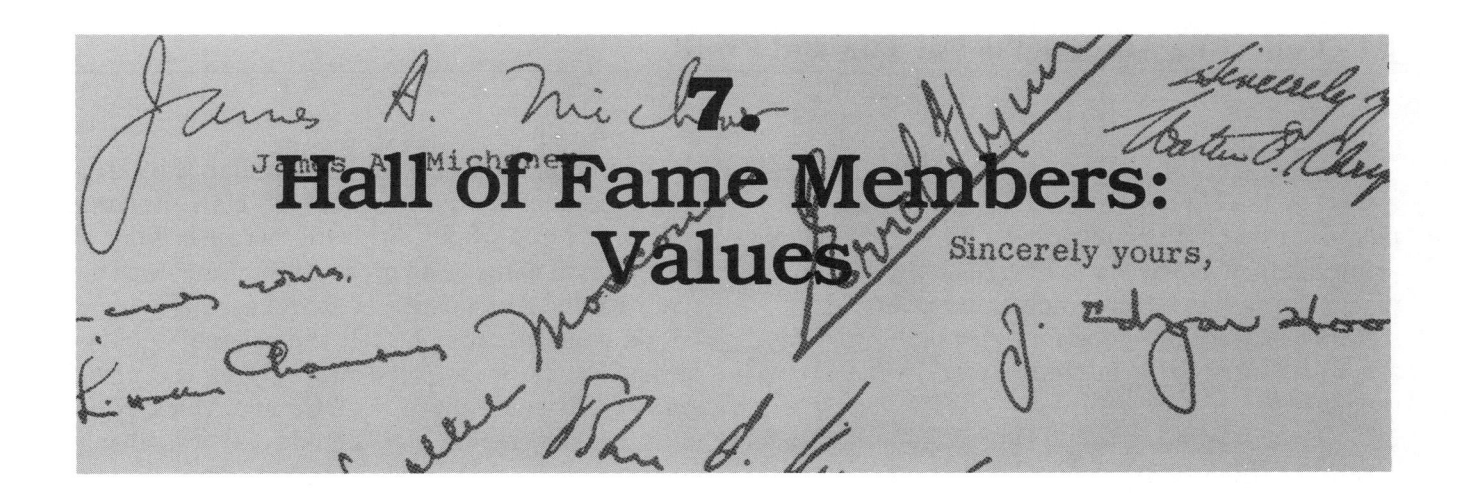

Albertype black and white Hall of Fame plaque cards were the first ones officially offered by the Baseball Hall of Fame in Cooperstown, New York. These plaques were sold from 1936 through 1952. Only 33 players out of the 62 inducted during this period could possibly have signed such cards, for the other 29 were already deceased prior to the cards being issued. Therefore, collectors should be wary of Albertype plaque cards signed by any player other than those listed below, when the words "Albertype Plaque Card" appear in the chart following their name. *All others are forgeries.* Note that one of the rarest finds would be that of George Wright since he died in 1937, only one short year after these plaques were issued initially. Any signed Albertype plaque card at all would be of great value, however—both as a collectible and monetarily.

Artvue black and white plaque cards were officially issued by the Hall of Fame from 1953 through 1963. Many more members of the Hall of Fame had died prior to this issue. Therefore, should a collector ever find an autograph of this type listed for sale by a dealer, check the player's name in this chapter to see whether or not he could possibly have signed such a card. Only 51 players out of a total of 94 inductees up to this time could have signed this type plaque card, as all the others were deceased before the issue date. "Artvue Plaque Card" will follow in the chart below, after the player's name, only if he could have signed one.

Some of the rarer Artvue plaque cards include those signed by Jesse Burkett, Kid Nichols and Ed Barrow—all of whom died in 1953, the issue year of these cards. Almost as rare are signings by Rabbit Maranville, Chief Bender and Hugh Duffy; they all died one year later, in 1954. Cy Young, Honus Wagner and Clark Griffith died in 1955, leaving a very short plaque-card-signing time period. The same observation applies to Al Simmons and Connie Mack, who died in 1956. Signed Artvue plaque cards are getting to be quite difficult to find, yet they are not nearly so rare as those issued under the Albertype logo. Seldom does an Albertype plaque ever come on the market.

Two kinds of yellow and brown plaque cards were officially issued by the Hall of Fame between 1964 and 1982. They are "Mike Roberts Color" and "Cuteich Color 3-D." Autographed cards of this kind are readily available through various autograph dealers. In addition, many are sold at baseball or sports card shows, that are popular throughout the nation. Prices will range from as low as one dollar and up, according to how popular the signer is at present and whether or not he is still living or deceased. Again, only those players with "Yellow Plaque Card" listed after their names could possibly have signed one of them. All others were deceased before the cards were issued. Collectors should be wary when finding a yellow-brown plaque card signed by Babe Ruth, Mickey Cochrane or any number of other players. They are out-and-out forgeries passed on by the unscrupulous. Those most difficult to obtain would include Paul Waner and Bill McKechnie, as both these men died in 1965, the year after these cards were first issued. Another rare find would be Jimmy Foxx because he lived only until 1967, three short years after these yellow plaque cards became available to collectors.

84 Collecting Autographs For Fun and Profit

Lastly, in 1981, Dexter Press was commissioned by the Hall of Fame to design a totally new plaque card. There is one in which the cards were printed up in a variety of bright colors. These plaques proved to be extremely unpopular with collectors and were not good for autographing. They are worth very little in comparison to the other types.

One sidelight regarding Hall of Famers is that several of them underwent name changes during the course of their careers. Maximilian Carnarius won't be found on the roster of Hall of Fame members but a Max Carey will, because this was Carey's real name. The great Al Simmons was actually named Aloysius Harry Szymanski! He changed his name because he felt the original couldn't be spelled or pronounced properly by the press. And would you believe this? Connie Mack's real name was Cornelius McGillicuddy? It was changed because he thought it sounded funny!

MEMBER OF BASEBALL'S HALL OF FAME (Their Values)	CUT SIGNATURE	3x5 CARD	ALBERTYPE PLACQUE	ARTVUE PLACQUE	PHOTOGRAPH	BASEBALL	BASEBALL CARD	OTHER (Their Values)
1936 INDUCTION								
Cobb, Tyrus Raymond "Ty" Active 1905-28. Deceased 1961	$18-$25	$35-$45	$100-$125	$50-$85	$60-$85	$85-$125	$75-$85	A.L.S.: $75 (recent) Centennial Baseball Stamp: $125 (recent)
Johnson, Walter Perry Active 1907-27. Deceased 1946	$50-$65	$90-$115	$100-$125		$75-$100	$110-$135	$75-$100	
Mathewson, Christopher "Christie" Active 1900-16. Deceased 1925	$100-$125	$190-$225			$195-$225	$125-$175	$175-$200	
Ruth, George Herman "Babe" Active 1914-35. Deceased 1948 *One recently sold for $300	$100-$125	$145-$175*	$225-$275		$225-250	$275-$350	$225-$350	
Wagner, John Peter "Honus" Active 1897-1917. Deceased 1955	$30-$45	$45-$60	$100-$125	$75-$100	$50-$75	$85-$110	$45-$65	A.N.S.: $100 (recent) Check: $75 (recent)
1937 INDUCTION								
Buckeley, Morgan G. First President of the National League, 1876. Deceased 1922	$140-$175	$210-$250			$325-$400	$550-$700	$325-$500	
Johnson, Byron Bancroft "Ban" Active 1900-27. Deceased 1931	$85-$110	$165-$200			$125-$175	$225-$300	$175-$225	
Lajoie, Napoleon "Larry" Active 1896-1916. Deceased 1959	$25-$35	$40-$50	$70-$125	$50-$65	$35-$45	$60-$85	$30-$45	A.L.S.: $75 (recent) Centennial Baseball Stamp: $65 (recent)

Hall of Fame Members: Values 85

MEMBER OF BASE-BALL'S HALL OF FAME (Their Values)	CUT SIGNA-TURE	3x5 CARD	ALBER-TYPE PLACQUE	ARTVUE PLACQUE	PHOTO-GRAPH	BASEBALL	BASEBALL CARD	OTHER (Their Values)
Mack, Cornelius Alexander "Connie" Active 1886-1950. Deceased 1956	$20-$35	$35-$50	$50-$75	$35-$50	$27-$40	$45-$75	$30-$45	A.L.S.: $50 (recent)
McGraw, John Joseph Active 1891-1932. Deceased 1934	$75-$100	$140-$175			$115-$150	$225-$300	$115-$150	
Speaker, Tristran E. "Tris" Active 1907-28. Deceased 1958	$20-$30	$30-$45	$60-$75	$45-$60	$40-$60	$60-$85	$35-$50	A.L.S.: $90 (recent) Centennial Baseball Stamp: $65 (recent)
Wright, George Active 1869-82. Deceased 1937	$85-$100	$165-$200	$300-$350		$220-$250	$375-$450	$220-$250	
Young, Denton True "Cy" Active 1890-1911. Deceased 1955 *One recently sold for $100	$25-$40	$40-$60	$65-$100	$50-$75	$40-$65*	$60-$85	$40-$65	Check: $45 (recent)
1938 INDUCTION								
Alexander, Grover Cleveland Active 1911-30. Deceased 1950	$45-$60	$70-$85	$115-$135		$115-$135	$115-$135	$100-$125	
Cartwright, Alexander Joy, Jr. Father of modern baseball, 1845 Deceased 1892.	$175-$200	$350-$425			$350-$425	$800-$1,000	$550-$700	
Chadwick, Henry Authored first baseball rule book in 1858. Deceased 1908	$225-$250	$335-$400			$335-$400	$650-$850	$335-$400	
1939 INDUCTION								
Anson, Adrian Constantine "Cap" Active 1876-98. Deceased 1922	$225-$260	$330-$375			$425-$500	$550-$700	$330-$375	
Collins, Edward Trowbridge Active 1906-30. Deceased 1951	$30-$45	$50-$75	$75-$100		$50-$80	$90-$125	$50-$80	L.S. $80 (recent)
Comiskey, Charles Albert Active 1883-1931. Deceased 1931	$65-$90	$115-$135			$110-$150	$115-$135	$115-$150	
Cummings, William Arthur "Candy" Active 1872-77. Deceased 1924	$225-$300	$325-$375			$275-$350	$550-$700	275-$350	
Ewing, William Buckingham "Buck" Active 1880-$1900. Invented the curve ball. Deceased 1906	$275-$350	$375-$425			$475-$550	$800-1,000 up	$325-$375	
Gehrig, Henry Louis "Lou" Active 1923-39. Deceased 1941	$85-$110	$175-$225	250-$300		$235-$275	$275-$350	$225-$275	

86 Collecting Autographs For Fun and Profit

MEMBER OF BASE-BALL'S HALL OF FAME (Their Values)	CUT SIGNA-TURE	3x5 CARD	ALBER-TYPE PLACQUE	ARTVUE PLACQUE	PHOTO-GRAPH	BASEBALL	BASEBALL CARD	OTHER (Their Values)
Keeler, William Henry "Willie" Active 1892-1910. Deceased 1923	$150-$175	$275-$325			$225-$275	$550-$750	$225-$300	
Radbourne, Charles G. "Old Hoss" Active 1881-91. Deceased 1897	*200-$250	$325-$375			$325-$375	$750-$1,000	$275-$350	
Sisler, George Harold Active 1915-30. Deceased 1973	$2-$3	$3.50-$5	$30-$45	$20-$25	$10-$15	$20-$40	$10-$15	A.L.S.: $25 (recent) L.S. : $20 (recent) Yellow Plaque: $10-$15
Spalding, Albert Goodwill Active 1871-91. Deceased 1915	$125-$150	$200-$250			$225-$275	$325-$375	$225-$275	

1940 INDUCTION
No one was inducted into the Hall of Fame this year.

1941 INDUCTION
No one was inducted into the Hall of Fame this year.

1942 INDUCTION

Hornsby, Rogers Active 1915-37. Deceased 1963	$15-$20	$30-$45	$75-$100	$50-$75	$45-$75	$65-$80	$30-$50	

1943 INDUCTION
No one was inducted into the Hall of Fame this year.

1944 INDUCTION

Landis, Kenesaw Mountain First Commissioner of Baseball. Active 1920-44. Deceased 1944	$30-$40	$70-$85	$65-$150		$45-$60	$70-$95	$35-$50	

1945 INDUCTION

Bresnahan, Roger Patrick Active 1897-1915. Deceased 1944	$90-$115	$165-$180			$165-$180	$275-$350	$125-$175	
Brouthers, Dennis "Dan" Active 1879-1904. Deceased 1932	$225-$250	$325-$350			$325-$375	$550-$750	$225-$275	
Clarke, Fred Clifford Active 1894-1915. Deceased 1960	$17-$25	$25-$35	$50-$75	$35-$50	$25-$40	$50-$75	$25-$50	A.L.S.: $100 (recent) Centennial Baseball Stamp: $50 (recent)

Hall of Fame Members: Values 87

MEMBER OF BASEBALL'S HALL OF FAME (Their Values)	CUT SIGNATURE	3x5 CARD	ALBERTYPE PLACQUE	ARTVUE PLACQUE	PHOTOGRAPH	BASEBALL	BASEBALL CARD	OTHER (Their Values)
Collins, James Joseph Active 1985-1908. Deceased 1943	$175-$200	$275-$325			$275-$325	$450-$625	$225-$275	
Delahanty, Edward James Active 1888-1903. Deceased 1903	$275-$325	$375-$425			$325-$375	$800-$1,100 up	$325-$400	
Duffy, Hugh Active 1888-1922. Deceased 1954	$35-$50	$70-$85	$115-$150	$90-$110	$75-$100	$125-$175	$75-$100	
Jennings, Hugh Ambrose "Hughey" Active 1891-1920. Deceased 1928	$125-$150	$200-$250			$150-$200	$325-$400	$150-$300	
Kelly, Michael Joseph "King" Active 1878-93. Deceased 1943	$125-$140	$200-$225			$175-$250	$350-$500	$175-$300	
O'Rourke, James Henry Active 1873-1904. Deceased 1919	$175-$225	$275-$325			$275-$325	$550-$750	$225-$300	
Robinson, Wilbert Active 1886-1931. Deceased 1934	$125-$150	$165-$180			$165-$180	$275-$325	$150-$300	
1946 INDUCTION								
Burkett, Jesse Cail Active 1890-1905. Deceased 1953	$60-$75	$110-$135	$135-$160	$110-$135	$110-$135	$125-$150 up	$115-$140	A.L.S.: $150 (recent)
Chance, Frank Leroy Active 1898-1914. Deceased 1924	$150-$175	$225-$250			$200-$235	$350-$500	$175-$250 up	
Chesbro, John Dwight Active 1899-1909. Deceased 1931	$140-$175	$225-$250			$175-$225	$325-$400	$175-$300 up	
Evers, John Joseph Active 1902-17. Deceased 1947	$75-$100	$135-$160	$150-$175		$140-$165	$250-$300	$150-$225 up	
Griffith, Clark Calvin "Cal" Active 1891-1955. Deceased 1955	$20-$30	$30-$40	$60-$75	$40-$75	$25-$40	$65-$85	$40-$65	A.L.S.: $75 (recent) Centennial Baseball Stamp: $75 (recent)
McCarthy, Thomas Francis Active 1884-96. Deceased 1922	$225-$250	$350-$380			$375-$425	$650-$1,000 up	$325-$400 up	
McGinnity, Joseph Jerome "Iron Man" Active 1899-1908. Deceased 1929	$225-$250	$335-$360			$375-$425	$650-$800	$335-$360 up	A.L.S.: $1,100 (recent)
Plank, Edward Steward "Eddie" Active 1901-17. Deceased 1926	$150-$175	$275-$300			$275-$310	$450-$600	$225-$300 up	
Tinker, Joseph Bert Active 1902-16. Deceased 1948	$80-$100	$135-$150	$145-$175		$135-$150	$175-$250	$125-$175 up	

88 Collecting Autographs For Fun and Profit

To Bob,
Good Luck
Napoleon Larry Lajoie

3-7-50

George Harold Sisler plaque

George Sisler

Frank Alexander

Hall of Fame Members: Values 89

MEMBER OF BASEBALL'S HALL OF FAME (Their Values)	CUT SIGNATURE	3x5 CARD	ALBERTYPE PLACQUE	ARTVUE PLACQUE	PHOTOGRAPH	BASEBALL	BASEBALL CARD	OTHER (Their Values)
Waddell, George Edward "Rube" Active 1897-1910. Deceased 1914	$225-$250	$375-$450			$325-$375	$800-$1,200 up	$275-$375 up	
Walsh, Edward Augustin "Eddie" Active 1904-17. Deceased 1959	$22-$28	$40-$55	$100-$150	$65-$90	$60-$85	$75-$125	$55-$95 up	Centennial Baseball Stamp: $65 (recent)
1947 INDUCTION								
Cochrane, Gordon Stanley "Mickey" Active 1925-38. Deceased 1962	$20-$35	$30-$40	$55-$75	$40-$55	$35-$50	$65-$90	$35-$55 up	A.N.S.: $65 (recent) Centennial Baseball Stamp: $18.50 (recent)
Frisch, Frank Francis "Frankie" Active 1919-37. Deceased 1973	$3-$4.50	$6-$10	$40-$55	$25-$35	$10-$15	$30-$50	$10-$25	Centennial Baseball Stamp: $40 (recent) Yellow Plaque: $12-$16
Grove, Robert Moses "Lefty" Active 1925-41. Deceased 1975	$2.50-$3.50	$6-$10	$25-$40	$17-$25	$8-$12	$20-$30	$8-$12	Centennial Baseball Stamp: $17.50 (recent) Yellow Plaque: $10-$15
Hubbell, Carl Owen Active 1928-43.	$1-$1.50	$2-$4	$20-$40	$14-$20	$4-$8	$15-$20	$4-$7 up	Perez-Steele Card: $10-$15 A.L.S.: $35 (recent) Centennial Baseball Stamp: $22.50 (recent) Yellow Plaque: $4-$7
1948 INDUCTION								
Pennock, Herbert Jeffers "Herb" Active 1912-34. Deceased 1948	$30-$45	$60-$75	$100-$125		$60-$75	$90-$115	$50-$65 up	
Traynor, Harold Joseph "Pie" Active 1920-39. Deceased 1972	$4-$8	$10-$15	$40-$50	$25-$30	$15-$20	$25-$40	$15-$30 up	Yellow Plaque: $15-$20

MEMBER OF BASEBALL'S HALL OF FAME (Their Values)	CUT SIGNATURE	3x5 CARD	ALBERTYPE PLACQUE	ARTVUE PLACQUE	PHOTOGRAPH	BASEBALL	BASEBALL CARD	OTHER (Their Values)
1949 INDUCTION								
Brown, Mordecai Peter Centennial Active 1903-16. Deceased 1948	$50-$65	$95-$100			$100-$125	$125-$150	$75-$100	
Gehringer, Charles Leonard "Charlie" Active 1924-42	$1-$2	$2-$3	$25-$30	$12-$17	$3-$5	$14-$18	$6-$10 up	Yellow Plaque: $3-$5 Perez-Steele Card: $10-$15
Nichols, Charles Augustus "Kid" Active 1890-1906. Deceased 1953	$20-$25	$35-$45	$90-$125	$65-$85	$35-$50	$65-$90	$35-$75 up	A.N.S.: $75 (recent) Centennial Baseball Stamp: $85 (recent)
1950 INDUCTION								
No one was inducted into the Hall of Fame this year.								
1951 INDUCTION								
Foxx, James Emory "Jimmy" Active 1925-45. Deceased 1967	$15-$20	$25-$35	$55-$75	$40-$50	$25-$35	$65-$80	$25-$40 up	Yellow Plaque: $35-$45 Centennial Baseball Stamp: $25 (recent)
Ott, Melvin Thomas "Mel" Active 1926-47. Deceased 1958	$20-$25	$30-$35	$60-$80	$45-$50	$35-$40	$60-$75	$35-$50 up	Check: $50 (recent) Centennial Baseball Stamp: $50 (recent)
1952 INDUCTION								
Heilman, Harry Edwin Active 1914-32. Deceased 1951	$40-$50	$85-$100			$85-$100	$135-$150	$85-$100 up	
Waner, Paul Glee Active 1926-45. Deceased 1965	$10-$13	$25-$30	$50-$75	$35-$40	$30-$45	$40-$50	$25-$50 up	Yellow Plaque: $20-$25
1953 INDUCTION								
Barrow, Edward Grant Active 1903-45. Deceased 1953	$25-$30	$35-$45		$50-$75	$45-$50	$60-$75	$60-$90 up	
Bender, Charles Albert "Chief" Active 1903-25. Deceased 1954	$30-$35	$45-$50		$65-$80	$60-$75	$90-$115	$65-$90 up	

Hall of Fame Members: Values 91

MEMBER OF BASE-BALL'S HALL OF FAME (Their Values)	CUT SIGNA-TURE	3x5 CARD	ALBER-TYPE PLACQUE	ARTVUE PLACQUE	PHOTO-GRAPH	BASEBALL	BASEBALL CARD	OTHER (Their Values)
Connolly, Thomas Henry Active 1898-1953. Deceased 1961	$30-$35	$40-$45		$50-$75	$30-$35	$65-$80	$35-$50 up	
Dean, Jay Hanna "Dizzy" Active 1930-47. Deceased 1974	$3-$5	$6-$10		$25-$35	$10-$15	$40-$50	$20-$35 up	A.L.S.: $45 (recent) Yellow Plaque: $10-$15
Clem, William J. Active 1905-51. Deceased 1951	$50-$55	$95-$110			$95-$110	$125-$150		
Simmons, Aloysius Harry "Al" Active 1924-44. Deceased 1956	$25-$30	$40-$45		$65-$80	$35-$50	$60-$90	$35-$65 up	
Wallace, Roderick John "Bobby" Active 1894-1918. Deceased 1960	$22-$27	$40-$50		$65-$90	$75-$100	$100-$125	$60-$90 up	
Wright, William Harry Active 1869-93. Deceased 1895	$95-$110	$175-$200			$225-$250	$400-$600	$225-$350 up	
1954 INDUCTION								
Dickey, William Malcolm "Bill" Active 1928-46	$1-$2	$3-$5		$15-$20	$5-$10	$15-$25	$5-$20 up	Yellow Plaque: $5-$10 Perez-Steele Card: $10-$15
Maranville, Walter James "Rabbit" Active 1912-35. Deceased 1954	$25-$50	$45-$55		$75-$100	$65-$90	$90-$115	$75-$100 up	
Terry, William Harold "Bill" Active 1923-41.	$1-$2	$2-$3		$15-$20	$4-$8	$15-$25	$5-$15 up	Yellow Plaque: $4-$8 Perez-Steele Card: $10-$15
1955 INDUCTION								
Baker, John Franklin "Homerun" Active 1908-22. Deceased 1963	$20-$25	$30-$35		$35-$50	$35-$50	$40-$50	$25-$50 up	Centennial Baseball Stamp: $60 (recent)
DiMaggio, Joseph Paul Active 1936-51	$2-$4	$4-$6		$20-$30	$5-$12	$25-$35	$15-$25 up	Yellow Plaque: $5-$9 Perez-Steele Card: $12-$17.
Hartnett, Charles Leo "Gabby" Active 1922-41. Deceased 1972	$4-$6	$6-$10		$17-$25	$8-$15	$20-$30	$7-$20 up	A.L.S.: $20 (recent) Yellow Plaque: $10-$20 Centennial Baseball Stamp: $20 (recent)

92 Collecting Autographs For Fun and Profit

Hall of Fame Members: Values 93

MEMBER OF BASE-BALL'S HALL OF FAME (Their Values)	CUT SIGNA-TURE	3x5 CARD	ALBER-TYPE PLACQUE	ARTVUE PLACQUE	PHOTO-GRAPH	BASEBALL	BASEBALL CARD	OTHER (Their Values)
Lyons, Theodore Amar "Ted" Active 1923-46	$1.50-$3	$3.50-$5		$15-$20	$6-$10	$15-$20	$6-$15 up	Yellow Plaque: $6-$10 Perez-Steele Card: $10-$15 A.L.S.: $25 (recent)
Schalk, Raymond William "Ray" Active 1912-29. Deceased 1970	$3-$5	$6-$10		$20-$25	$10-$15	$20-$30	$7-$15 up	Yellow Plaque: $10-$15
Vance, Clarence Arthur "Dazzy" Active 1915-35. Deceased 1961	$20-$25	$30-$35		$50-$75	$35-$50	$65-$100	$35-$75 up	

1956 INDUCTION

Cronin, Joseph Edward "Joe" Active 1926-47	$1-$2	$2-$4		$8-$15	$5-$10	$15-$25	$3-$10 up	Yellow Plaque: $4-$7 Perez-Steele Card: $10-$15 A.L.S.: $30 (recent)
Greenberg, Henry Benjamin "Hank" Active 1930-47	$1-$2	$2-$4		$15-$20	$4-$8	$17-$25	$6-$20 up	Yellow Plaque: $8-$12 Perez-Steele Card: $10-$15

1957 INDUCTION

Crawford, Samuel Earl "Wahoo Sam" Active 1899-1917. Deceased 1968	$10-$15	$20-$25		$30-$40	$25-$30	$40-$50	$20-$50 up	Yellow Plaque: $20-$25
McCarthy, Joseph Vincent "Joe" Active 1929-50. Deceased 1978	$1.50-$3	$3-$5		$18-$25	$7-$10	$20-$25	$6-$15 up	Yellow Plaque: $7-$12

1958 INDUCTION

No one was inducted into the Hall of Fame this year.

1959 INDUCTION

Wheat, Zachariah Davis "Zack" Active 1909-27. Deceased 1972	$3-$5	$6-$11		$20-$25	$10-$17	$20-$25	$8-$15 up	Yellow Plaque: $10-$15

MEMBER OF BASE-BALL'S HALL OF FAME (Their Values)	CUT SIGNA-TURE	3x5 CARD	ALBER-TYPE PLACQUE	ARTVUE PLACQUE	PHOTO-GRAPH	BASEBALL	BASEBALL CARD	OTHER (Their Values)
1960 INDUCTION No one was inducted into the Hall of Fame this year.								
1961 INDUCTION Carey, Max George Active 1910-33. Deceased 1976	$1.50-$2.50	$3-$5		$15-$20	$7-$12	$15-$20	$5-$10 up	Yellow Plaque: $7-$10 A.L.S.: $35 (recent)
Hamilton, William Robert "Billy" Active 1888-1901. Deceased 1940	$125-$150	$225-$250			$175-$225	$350-$500	$175-$250 up	
1962 INDUCTION Feller, Robert William Andrew "Bob" Active 1936-56	$1-$2	$2-$3		$17-$25	$6-$10	$15-$20	$5-$10 up	Yellow Plaque: $5-$10 Perez-Steele Card: $10-$15 A.L.S.: $25 (recent)
McKechnie, William Boyd "Bill" Active 1907-46. Deceased 1965	$14-$19	$25-$30		$40-$50	$25-$30	$35-$45	$25-$50 up	Yellow Plaque: $30-$35 A.L.S.: $45 (recent)
Robinson, Jack Roosevelt "Jackie" Active 1947-56. Deceased 1972	$10-$15	$20-$25		$40-$50	$25-$35	$65-$100	$30-$50 up	Yellow Plaque: $20-$25 A.N.S.: $40 (recent) L.S.: $20 (recent)
Rousch, Edd J. Active 1913-31	$1-$2	$2.50-$4		$20-$25	$4-$10	$12-$17	$3-$10 up	Yellow Plaque: $4-$8 Perez-Steele Card: $10-$15 A.L.S.: $12.50 (recent)
1963 INDUCTION Clarkson, John Gibson Active 1882-94. Deceased 1909	$175-$200	$275-$325			$275-$325	$600-$800	$225-$500 up	A.L.S.: $375 (recent)
Flick, Elmer Harrison Active 1898-1910. Deceased 1971	$4-$6	$7-$12		$30-$45	$10-$15	$20-$30	$10-$15	Yellow Plaque: $10-$15

Hall of Fame Members: Values 95

MEMBER OF BASE-BALL'S HALL OF FAME (Their Values)	CUT SIGNA-TURE	3x5 CARD	ALBER-TYPE PLACQUE	ARTVUE PLACQUE	PHOTO-GRAPH	BASEBALL	BASEBALL CARD	OTHER (Their Values)
Rice, Edgar Charles "Sam" Active 1915-34. Deceased 1974	$2-$4	$4-$8		$20-$25	$6-$15	$20-$25	$8-$15	Yellow Plaque: $8-$13
Rixey, Eppa Active 1912-33. Deceased 1963	$15-$20	$30-$35		$45-$50	$30-$35	$40-$50	$30-$50 up	Check: $25 (recent)
1964 INDUCTION								
Appling, Lucius Benjamin "Luke" Active 1930-50	$1-$2	$2.50-$3.50			$2-$5	$10-$15	$2-$10 up	Yellow Plaque: $3-$5 Perez-Steele Card: $10-$15
Faber, Urban Charles "Red" Active 1914-33. Deceased 1976	$1.50-$3	$4-$7			$5-$10	$14-$20	$6-$15 up	Yellow Plaque: $8-$15
Grimes, Burleigh Arland Active 1916-38	$1-$2	$2.50-$4			$4-$8	$15-$20	$4-$15 up	Perez-Steele Card: $10-$15 Yellow Plaque: $6-$10
Huggins, Miller James Active 1904-29. Deceased 1929	$150-$200	$225-$275			$200-$250	$350-$500	$200-$250 up	A.L.S.: $300 (recent)
Keefe, Timothy J. Active 1880-93. Deceased 1933	$150-$200	$275-$325			$225-$300	$600-$1,000	$250-$350 up	A.N.S.: $350 (recent)
Manush, Henry Emmett "Heinie" Active 1923-39. Deceased 1971	$3-$5	$7-$12			$7-$15	$20-$25	$8-$15 up	Yellow Plaque: $10-$15
Ward, John Montomery Active 1878-94. Deceased 1925	$150-$200	$275-$325			$275-$350	$600-$900		$225-$500 up
1965 INDUCTION								
Galvin, James F. "Pud" Active 1879-92. Deceased 1902	$275-$350	$375-$450			$325-$400	$800-$1,000 up	$325-$500 up	A.L.S.: $550 (recent)
1966 INDUCTION								
Stengel, Charles Dillon "Casey" Active 1912-65. Deceased 1975	$3-$5	$5-$10			$12-$17	$25-$35	$12-$17 up	Yellow Plaque: $12-$17
Williams, Theodore Samuel "Ted" Active 1939-72	$5-$8	$10-$15			$15-$20	$30-$35	$13-$20 up	Yellow Plaque: $12-$17 Perez-Steele Card: $15-$20

MEMBER OF BASE-BALL'S HALL OF FAME (Their Values)	CUT SIGNA-TURE	3x5 CARD	ALBER-TYPE PLACQUE	ARTVUE PLACQUE	PHOTO-GRAPH	BASEBALL	BASEBALL CARD	OTHER (Their Values)
1967 INDUCTION								
Rickey, Wesley Branch Active 1905-64. Deceased 1965	$20-$25	$30-$35			$35-$40	$40-$45	$30-$50 up	L.S.: $65 (recent)
Ruffing, Charles Herbert "Red" Active 1924-47	$2-$3	$3.50-$5			$4-$8	$12-$20	$5-$10 up	Yellow Plaque: $6-$10 Perez-Steele Card: $10-$15
Waner, Lloyd James "Little Poison" Active 1927-45. Deceased 1982	$1-$2	$2.50-$3.50			$5-$10	$15-$20	$4-$10 up	Yellow Plaque: $4-$10 A.L.S.: $35 (recent) A.N.S.: $27.50 (recent)
1968 INDUCTION								
Cuyler, Hazen Shirley "Kiki" Active 1921-38. Deceased 1950	$30-$35	$55-$75			$50-$75	$85-$100	$50-$90 up	A.N.S.: $85 recent
Goslin, Leon Allen "Goose" Active 1921-38. Deceased 1971	$5-$7.50	$9-$14			$10-$15	$20-$25	$8-$15 up	Yellow Plaque: $12-$17
Medwick, Joseph Michael "Ducky" Active 1932-48. Deceased 1975	$2-$4	$5-$8			$8-$12	$12-$16	$5-$10 up	Yellow Plaque: $10-$15 A.L.S.: $25 (recent)
1969 INDUCTION								
Campanella, Roy Active 1948-57 *All of Campanella's new signatures are stamped rather than personally signed since his accident.	$35-$40	$50-$65			$50-$75	$90-$115	$55-$75 up	Perez-Steele Card: $5-$7.50* A.N.S.: $70 (recent) A.L.S.: $95 (recent)
Coveleski, Stanley Anthony "Stan" Active 1912-28	$1-$2	$2-$3			$3-$8	$15-$20	$3-$10 up	Yellow Plaque: $4-$10 Perez-Steele Card: $10-$15 A.L.S.: $25 (recent)

Hall of Fame Members: Values 97

MEMBER OF BASE-BALL'S HALL OF FAME (Their Values)	CUT SIGNA-TURE	3x5 CARD	ALBER-TYPE PLACQUE	ARTVUE PLACQUE	PHOTO-GRAPH	BASEBALL	BASEBALL CARD	OTHER (Their Values)
Hoyt, Waite Charles Active 1918-38	$1-$2	$1.50-$2.50			$3-$5	$6-$10	$2.50-$7.50	Yellow Plaque: $2.50-$3.50 Perez-Steele Card: $10-$15 A.L.S.: $25 (recent) A.N.S.: $20 (recent)
Musial, Stanley Frank "Stan the Man" Active 1941-63	$1-$2	$2.50-$4			$6-$10	$14-$19	$5-$10 up	Yellow Plaque: $6-$10 Perez-Steele Card: $12-$17
1970 INDUCTION								
Boudreau, Louis "Lou" Active 1938-60	$1-$2	$2-$3			$4-$10	$12-$17	$3-$10 up	Yellow Plaque: $4-$8 Perez-Steele Card: $10-$15
Coombs, Earl Bryan "Colonel" Active 1924-35. Deceased 1976	$2-$3	$4-$8			$6-$10	$15-$20	$5-$15 up	Yellow Plaque: $8-$15 A.L.S.: $25 (recent) Check: $10 (recent)
Frick, Ford Christopher Active 1934-51. Deceased 1978	$2-$3	$4-$9			$7-$15	$15-$22	$7-$12 up	Yellow Plaque: $8-$12 A.L.S.: $37.50 (recent)
Haines, Jesse Joseph "Pop" Active 1918-37. Deceased 1978	$2-$5	$4-$8			$6-$10	$15-$20	$9-$15 up	Yellow Plaque: $10-$15 A.L.S.: $35 (recent)
1971 INDUCTION								
Bancroft, David James Active 1915-30. Deceased 1972	$2-$5	$4-$8			$9-$14	$20-$25	$9-$15 up	Yellow Plaque: $14-$19. A.L.S.: $25 (recent)
Beckley, Jacob Peter Active 1888-1907. Deceased 1918	$225-$275	$350-$400			$450-$500	$550-$750	$350-$500 up	

98 Collecting Autographs For Fun and Profit

Hall of Fame Members: Values 99

MEMBER OF BASE-BALL'S HALL OF FAME (Their Values)	CUT SIGNA-TURE	3x5CARD	ALBER-TYPE PLACQUE	ARTVUE PLACQUE	PHOTO-GRAPH	BASEBALL	BASEBALL CARD	OTHER (Their Values)
Hafey, Charles James "Chick" Active 1924-37. Deceased 1973	$3-$4	$6-$10			$10-$15	$20-$25	$10-$15 up	Yellow Plaque: $10-$15 L.S.: $25 (recent) A.L.S.: $30 (recent)
Hooper, Harry Bartholomew Active 1909-25. Deceased 1974	$2-$3	$4-$6			$6-$10	$14-$20	$5-$10 up	Yellow Plaque: $8-$12 A.L.S.: $35 (recent) Check: $30 (recent)
Kelley, Joseph James Active 1891-1908. Deceased 1943	$125-$150	$200-$250			$175-$250	$350-$500	$200-$500 up	
Marquard, Richard William "Rube" Active 1908-25. Deceased 1980	$1.50-$2.50	$3-$4			$5-$10	$15-$20	$4-$10 up	Yellow Plaque: $5-$10 A.L.S.: $17.50 (recent)
Paige, Leroy Robert "Satchel" Active 1926-53 and 1965. Deceased 1982	$2-$3	$3-$5			$8-$12	$17-$25	$5-$10 up	Yellow Plaque: $10-$15
Weiss, George Martin Active 1949-60. Deceased 1972	$12-$15	$20-$25			$20-$25	$30-$40		Yellow Plaque: $35-$50*

*Extremely rare finds.

1972 INDUCTION

Berra, Lawrence Peter "Yogi" Active 1946 to Present	$1-$2	$2-$3			$5-$10	$15-$20	$5-$10 up	Yellow Plaque: $5-$9 Perez-Steele Card: $10-$15 A.N.S.: $12-$17
Gibson, Joshua "Josh" Active 1930-46. Deceased 1947	$125-$150	$225-$275			$250-$300	$350-$500		
Gomez, Vernon Louis "Lefty" Active 1930-43.	$2-$3	$3-$4			$6-$10	$15-$20	$6-$10 up	Yellow Plaque: $6-$10 Perez-Steele Card: $14-$20
Harridge, William "Will" Active 1931-59. Deceased 1971	$10-$15	$20-$25			$25-$35	$35-$50	$25-$35 up	

MEMBER OF BASE-BALL'S HALL OF FAME (Their Values)	CUT SIGNA-TURE	3x5 CARD	ALBER-TYPE PLACQUE	ARTVUE PLACQUE	PHOTO-GRAPH	BASEBALL	BASEBALL CARD	OTHER (Their Values)
Koufax, Sanford "Sandy" Active 1955-66	$1-$2	$2-$3			$5-$10	$15-$20	$5-$15 up	Yellow Plaque: $5-$10 Perez-Steele Card: $10-$15
Leonard, Walter Fenner "Buck" Active 1933-50	$1-$2	$2-$3			$3-$10	$10-$15	$3-$10 up	Yellow Plaque: $4-$8 Perez-Steele Card: $10-$15
Wynn, Early Active 1939-63. *Early never signs baseball cards now that he's retired. He says they are "unauthorized" and refuses collectors.	$1-$2	$2-$3			$6-$10	$15-$20	$6-$15 up*	Yellow Plaque: $10-$15 Perez-Steele Card: $10-$15
Youngs, Ross Middlebrook Active 1917-26. Deceased 1927	$175-$200	$250-$300			$275-$325	$550-$800	$225-$300 up	A.L.S.: $675 (recent) A.N.S.: $37.50 (recent)
1973 INDUCTION								
Clemente, Roberto Walker Active 1955-72. Deceased 1972	$20-$25	$26-$35			$35-$50	$75-$125	$50-$100 up	Scorebook: $45 (recent)
Evans, William George Active 1906-27. Deceased 1965	$30-$35	$55-$65			$60-$85	$125-$200		
Irvin, Monford "Monte" Active 1938-56	$1-$1.50	$1.50-$2.50			$4-$8	$10-$15	$3.50-$5 up	Yellow Plaque: $4-$6 Perez-Steele Card: $10-$15
Kelly, George Lange Active 1915-32	$1-$2	$2.50-$4			$3-$7	$10-$15	$4-$10 up	Yellow Plaque: $4-$8 Perez-Steele Card: $10-$15
Spahn, Warren Edward Active 1942-65	$1-$2	$2-$3			$4-$10	$15-$20	$4-$10 up	Yellow Plaque: $4-$8 Perez-Steele Card: $10-$15

MEMBER OF BASE-BALL'S HALL OF FAME (Their Values)	CUT SIGNA-TURE	3x5 CARD	ALBER-TYPE PLACQUE	ARTVUE PLACQUE	PHOTO-GRAPH	BASEBALL	BASEBALL CARD	OTHER (Their Values)
Welch, Michael Francis Active 1880-92. Deceased 1941	$175-$200	$275-$350			$300-$350	$550-$800	$250-$500 up	
1974 INDUCTION								
Bell, James Thomas "Cool Papa" Active 1922-46 *As of June 1983 "Cool Papa" could no longer sign autographs due to his failing eyesight.	$2-$3	$4-$5			$8-$15	$15-$20	$4-$10 up	Yellow Plaque: $6-$10 Perez-Steele Card: $20-$25*
Bottomley, James Leory Active 1922-37. Deceased 1959	$30-$35	$45-$50			$75-$100	$100-$125	$40-$80 up	
Conlon, John Bertrand "Jocko" Active 1941-65	$1.50-$3	$3-$4			$5-$10	$13-$20	$4-$10 up	Yellow Plaque: $6-$10 Perez-Steele Card: $10-$15
Ford, Edward Charles "Whitey" Active 1950-67	$1.50-$2.50	$3-$4			$5-$10	$15-$20	$4-$10 up	Yellow Plaque: $7-$12 Perez-Steele Card: $10-$15
Mantle, Mickey Charles Active 1951-68	$8-$12	$14-$18			$18-$40	$50-$65	$15-$25 up	Yellow Plaque: $15-$20 Perez-Steele Card: $20-$25 Book: $35 (recent)
Thompson, Samuel L. Active 1885-1906. Deceased 1922	$2.25-$2.75	$3.75-$4.25			$300-$350	$550-$800	$250-$300 up	
1975 INDUCTION								
Averill, Howard Earl Active 1929-41. Deceased 1983	$1-$2	$2.50-$3.50			$5-$10	$10-$15	$3-$6 up	Yellow Plaque: $4-$8 Perez-Steele Card: $20-$25
Harris, Stanley Raymond "Bucky" Active 1919-56. Deceased 1977	$1.50-$2.50	$3-$4			$5-$10	$15-$20	$5-$10 up	Yellow Plaque: $8-$12
Herman, William Jennings "Billy" Active 1931-66	$1-$2	$2-$3			$4-$8	$10-$15	$4-$10 up	Yellow Plaque: $5-$10 Perez-Steele Card: $10-$15

102 Collecting Autographs For Fun and Profit

MEMBER OF BASE-BALL'S HALL OF FAME (Their Values)	CUT SIGNA-TURE	3x5 CARD	ALBER-TYPE PLACQUE	ARTVUE PLACQUE	PHOTO-GRAPH	BASEBALL	BASEBALL CARD	OTHER (Their Values)
Johnson, William Julius "Judy" Active 1921-38	$1-$2	$2.50-$3.50			$5-$10	$12-$20		Yellow Plaque: $6-$10 Perez-Steele Card: $10-$15 A.L.S.: $25 (recent)
Kiner, Ralph McPherran Active 1946-55	$1-$2	$2-$3			$5-$10	$10-$15	$4-$10 up	Yellow Plaque: $4-$8 Perez-Steele Card: $10-$15
1976 INDUCTION								
Charleston, Oscar McKinley Active 1915-30. Deceased 1931	$100-$150	$175-$225			$200-$250	$250-$300	$200-$400 up	
Connor, Roger Active 1880-97. Deceased 1931	$175-$225	$225-$300			$275-$325	$550-$800	$225-$500 up	
Hubbard, Robert Cal Active 1936-51. Deceased 1977	$4-$6	$10-$14			$10-$15	$25-$35	$10-$20 up	Yellow Plaque: $15-$20 A.L.S.: $27.50 (recent)
Lemon, Robert Granville "Bob" Active 1941 to present)	$1-$2	$2.50-$3.50			$5-$10	$12-$20	$3-$10 up	Yellow Plaque: $5-$8 Perez-Steele Card: $10-$15
Lindstrom, Frederick Charles Active 1924-36. Deceased 1981	$1.50-$2.50	$2.50-$3.50			$5-$10	$15-$20	$4-$10	Yellow Plaque: $6-$10 A.L.S.: $17.50 (recent) A.N.S.: $12 (recent)
Roberts, Robin Evan Active 1948-66	$1-$2	$2.50-$3.50			$5-$10	$15-$20	$4-$10 up	Yellow Plaque: $5-$8 Perez-Steele Card: $10-$15
1977 INDUCTION								
Banks, Ernest Active 1953-71	$1.50-$2.50	$3-$5			$8-$15	$15-$20	$6-$15 up	Yellow Plaque: $6-$10 Perez-Steele Card: $15-$20

MEMBER OF BASE-BALL'S HALL OF FAME (Their Values)	CUT SIGNA-TURE	3x5 CARD	ALBER-TYPE PLACQUE	ARTVUE PLACQUE	PHOTO-GRAPH	BASEBALL	BASEBALL CARD	OTHER (Their Values)
Dihigo, Martin Active 1923-45. Deceased 1971	$100-$125	$175-$225			$175-$225	$350-$500		
Lloyd, John Henry Active 1905-31. Deceased 1964	$90-$110	$175-$200			$175-$200	$275-$400		
Lopez, Alfonso Ramon Active 1928-69	$1-$2	$2.50-$3.50			$4-$8	$10-$15	$3-$5 up	Yellow Plaque: $5-$10 Perez-Steele Card: $10-$15 up
Rusie, Amos Wilson Active 1889-1901. Deceased 1942	$225-$250	$350-$400			$300-$350	$700-$1,000	$350-$500 up	
Sewell, Joseph Wheeler "Joe" Active 1920-33	$1-$2	$2.50-$3.50			$3-$7	$15-$20	$4-$10 up	Yellow Plaque: $3-$8 Perez-Steele Card: $10-$15 A.L.S.: $40 (recent)
1978 INDUCTION								
Joss, Adrian "Addie" Active 1902-10. Deceased 1911	$225-$250	$350-$400			$350-$400	$550-$800	$350-$400 up	
MacPhail, Leland Stanford "Larry" Active 1933-47. Deceased 1975	$15-$20	$25-$30			$30-$35	$35-$40		
Mathews, Edwin Lee "Eddie" Active 1952-74	$1-$2	$2.50-$3.50			$4-$8	$15-$20	$3.50-$10 up	Yellow Plaque: $5-$10 Perez-Steele Card: $10-$15
1979 INDUCTION								
Giles, Warren Christopher Active 1937-69. Deceased 1979	$2-$3	$5-$8			$8-$15	$17-$25	$9-$15 up	Yellow Plaque: $10-$15 A.L.S.: $35 (recent)
Mays, Willie Howard Active 1951-73	$2-$3	$5-$10			$10-$15	$20-$25	$10-$15 up	Yellow Plaque: $10-$15 Perez-Steele Card: $20-$25
Wilson, Lewis Robert "Hack" Active 1923-34. Deceased 1948	$50-$60	$85-$100			$125-$175	$175-$250	$100-$125 up	

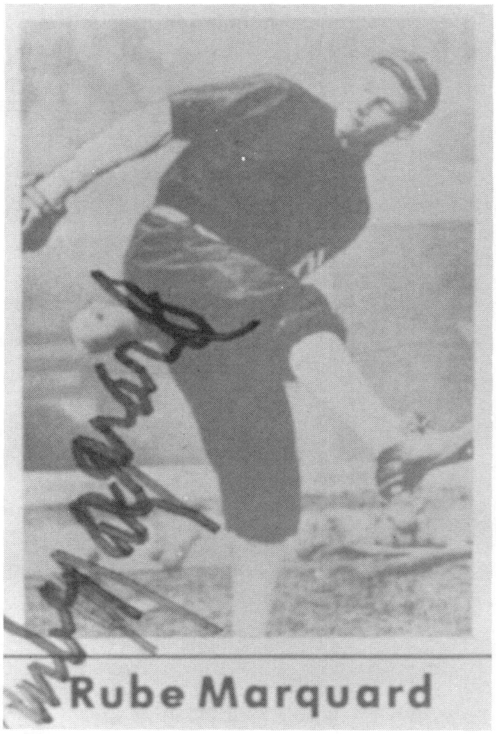
Rube Marquard

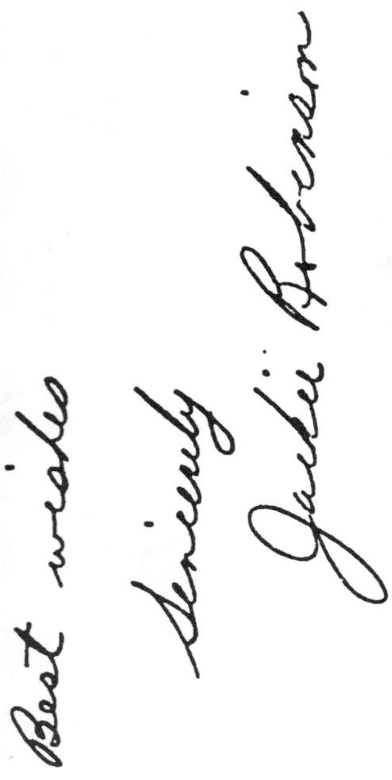

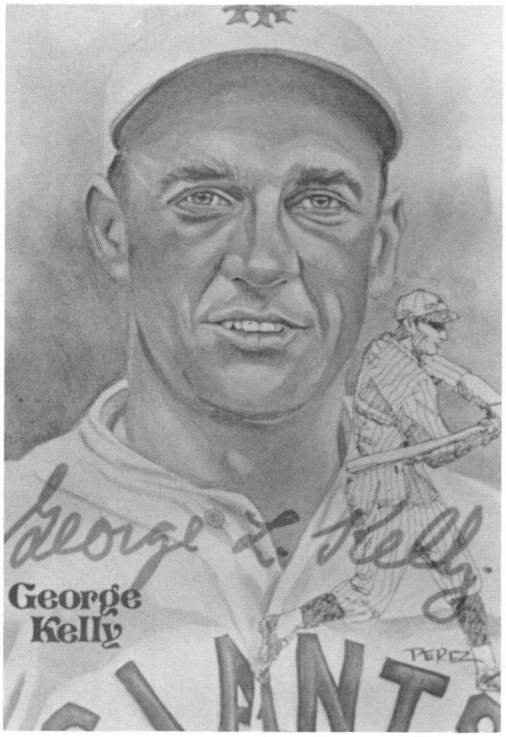
George
Kelly
PEREZ

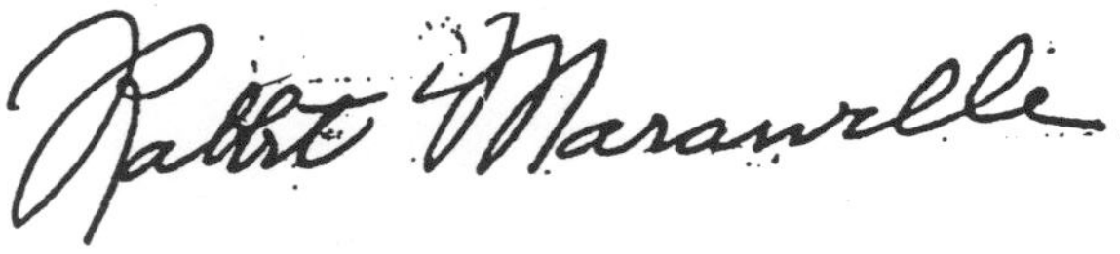

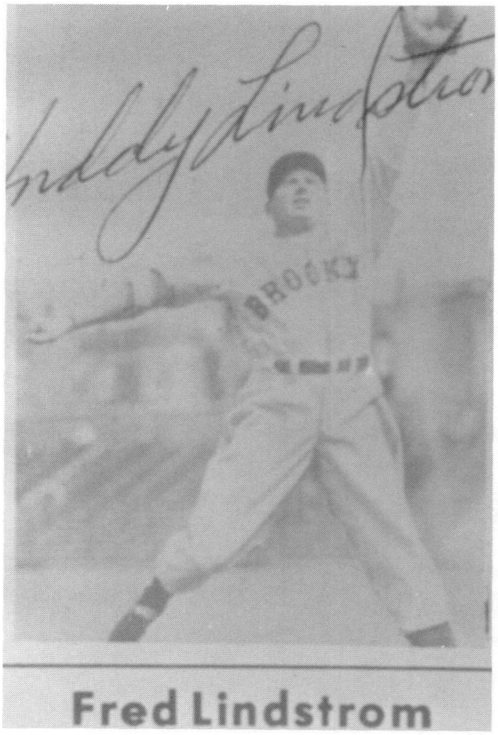
Fred Lindstrom

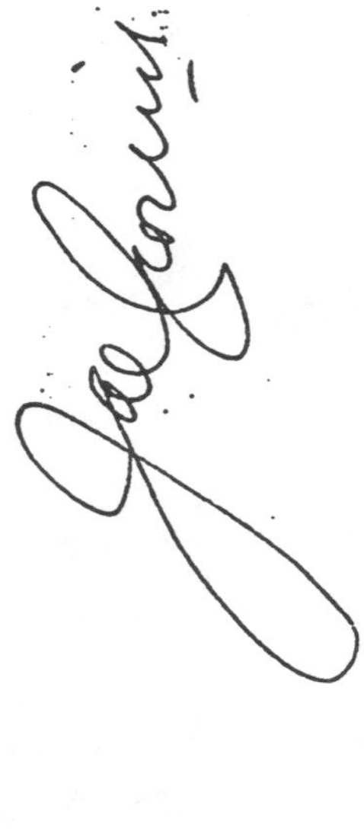

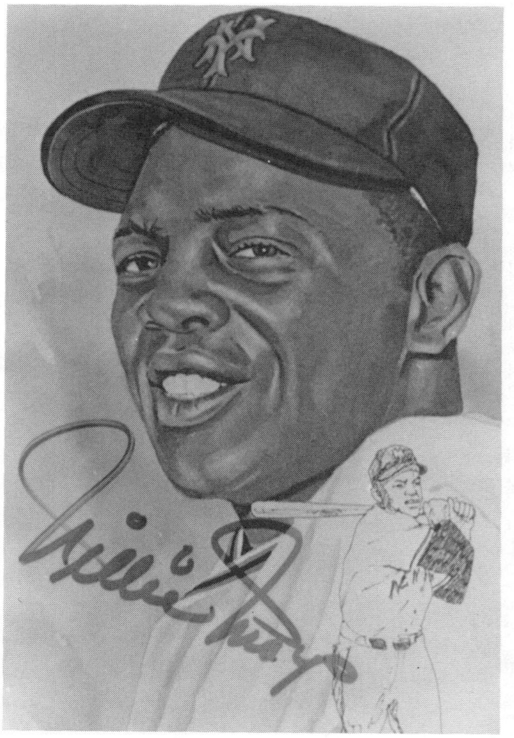

Hall of Fame Members: Values 105

MEMBER OF BASE-BALL'S HALL OF FAME (Their Values)	CUT SIGNA-TURE	3x5CARD	ALBER-TYPE PLACQUE	ARTVUE PLACQUE	PHOTO-GRAPH	BASEBALL	BASEBALL CARD	OTHER (Their Values)
1980 INDUCTION								
Kaline, Albert William "Al" Active 1953-74	$1-$2	$2.50-$3.50			$6-$10	$15-$20	$5-$10 up	Yellow Plaque: $5-$10 Perez-Steele Card: $10-$15
Klein, Charles Herbert "Chuck" Active 1928-44. Deceased 1958	$30-$35	$55-$75			$40-$60	$95-$125	$40-$50 up	
Snider, Edwin Donald "Duke" Active 1947-64	$1-$2	$2.50-$3.50			$6-$10	$15-$20	$5-$10 up	Yellow Plaque: $5-$10 Perez-Steele Card: $10-$15
Yawkey, Thomas Austin "Tom" Active 1933-76. Deceased 1976	$14-$18	$25-$30			$30-$35	$35-$50		
1981 INDUCTION								
Foster, Andrew "Rube" Active 1902-26. Deceased 1930	$20-$25	$30-$35			$50-$75	$100-$150		
Gibson, Robert "Bob" Active 1959-75	$2-$3	$4-$6			$8-$15	$15-$20	$10-$15 up	Yellow Plaque: $10-$15 Perez-Steele Card: $10-$15
Mize, John Robert "Johnny" Active 1936-53	$1-$2	$2.50-$3.50			$5-$10	$15-$20	$3-$6	Yellow Plaque: $3-$6 Perez-Steele Card: $10-$15
1982 INDUCTION								
Aaron, Henry Louis "Hank" Active 1954-76	$3-$5	$8-$12			$10-$15	$20-$25	$15-$20 up	Yellow Plaque: $10-$15 Perez-Steele Card: $15-$20 Check: $18.50 (recent)
Chandler, Albert Benjamin "Happy" Active 1945-51	$1-$2	$2.50-$3.50			$5-$10	$15-$25	$4-$6 up	Yellow Plaque: $4-$8 Perez-Steele Card: $10-$15

MEMBER OF BASE-BALL'S HALL OF FAME (Their Values)	CUT SIGNA-TURE	3x5 CARD	ALBER-TYPE PLACQUE	ARTVUE PLACQUE	PHOTO-GRAPH	BASEBALL	BASEBALL CARD	OTHER (Their Values)
Jackson, Travis Clavin "Stonewall" Active 1922-36	$1-$2	$2.50-$3.50			$5-$10	$15-$20	$4-$10 up	Yellow Plaque: $4-$8 Perez-Steele Card: $10-$15
Robinson, Frank Active 1956-76	$1.50-$2.50	$3-$5			$5-$10	$15-$20	$5-$10 up	Yellow Plaque: $5-$10 Perez-Steele Card: $10-$15
1983 INDUCTION								
Alston, Walter Emmons "Walt" Active 1954-76	$.50-$.75	$1-$2			$5-$10	$10-$15	$1-$5 up	Perez-Steele Card: $10-$15
Kell, George Clyde Active 1943-57	$.50-$.75	$1-$2			$5-$10	$15-$20	$1-$5 up	Perez-Steele Card: $10-$15
Marichal, Juan Antonio Active 1960-75	$.50-$.75	$1-$2			$7-$12	$15-$20	$1-$5 up	Perez-Steele Card: $10-$15
Robinson, Brooks Calbert Active 1955-77	$.50-$.75	$1-$2		$5-$10	$10-$15	$1-$5 up	Perez-Steele Card: $10-$15	
1984 INDUCTION								
Aparicio, Luis Ernest Active 1956-73	$.50-$.75	$1-$2			$4-$8	$7-$10	$1-$3 up	
Drysdale, Donald Scott "Don" Active 1956-69	$.50-$.75	$1-$2			$5-$10	$10-$15	$1-$3 up	
Ferrell, Richard Benjamin "Rick" Active 1929-47	$1-$1.50	$1.50-$3			$5-$10	$12-$17	$3-$5 up	
Killebrew, Harmon Clayton Active 1954-75	$.50-$.75	$1-$2			$4-$8	$10-$15	$2-$6 up	
Reese, Harold Henry "Pee Wee" Active 1940-58	$.50-$75	$1-$2			$3-$8	$10-$15	$2-$5 up	

8.
Some Living Hall of Famers: Addresses

A marvelous autograph collection of baseball greats can be built around those players who have been voted into the Hall of Fame. A great number of these men are still living, and most of them are extremely generous in responding to the requests of fans and collectors.

Complete collections of limited edition Hall of Fame art postal cards are available in color from Perez-Steele Galleries. A series of official Hall of Fame plaque cards can be ordered from the National Baseball Hall of Fame. Other excellent card sets, including "All Time Greats" and "Baseball Immortals," as well as numerous 8x10 photographs in color and black and white, are available from Den's Collectors Den. See Chapter 16 for addresses and phone numbers.

Any or all of the above items are ideal for sending out to the famous players of your choice for autographs. Never send more than two cards or photographs for signing at any one time. Don't forget to include a sincere letter of request with a self-addressed, stamped envelope for their return.

Quite a few Hall of Famers willingly include extra or bonus autographic material with each answer to a collector's request. For example, when "Happy" Chandler responds, not only does he sign both pictures, but he tosses in a couple of signed sheets of note paper. Mickey Mantle sometimes includes a bonus signed black and white photo, as does the well known Ted Lyons.

The unforgettable Willie Mays always responds to autograph requests rather quickly. He

Enos Slaughter's major league statistics far surpass those held by many current members of baseball's Hall of Fame. Why it took so long for this fabulous star to be voted into this select group is a continuing major controversy in support circles. Such a slight to one of baseball's greatest stars is an unpardonable insult to both the man and his fans.

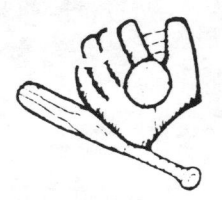

WILLIE MAYS "Say Hey" FOUNDATION, INC.

Directors:

Willie Mays
Mae Mays
Carl Kiesler
Tommy Lasorda
Don Zimmer
Willie Stargel
Don Newcombe
Bob Watson

May 11, 1983

Mr. Wayne Roberts
Box 290081
San Antonoio, TX 78280-1481

Dear Wayne,

Thank you for your letter. I'm sorry it has taken me so long to reply, but my schedule requires extensive travel. Although I am very busy, I enjoy answering letters and requests for autographs. I appreciate that the fans remember my contribution to baseball.

For twenty years I was able to participate in baseball and I truly loved the game. Now I have other goals. I am dedicated to helping youth develop direction in their lives through educational scholarships and athletic programs. The vehicle for accomplishing my goals is the **Willie Mays "Say Hey" Foundation.** I would like the assistance and support of you, my fans and friends. Any contribution to the Foundation will assist us in reaching our goals. I would greatly appreciate your assistance, or the aid of your parents in helping other youth. Contributions to the Foundation can be mailed to:

Willie Mays "Say Hey" Foundation
652 Bair Island Road
Redwood City, CA 94063

Thank you for your support.

Best wishes,

Willie Mays
Willie Mays

652 Bair Island Road • Suite 110 • Redwood City, California 94063 • (415) 369-MAYS

Some Living Hall of Famers: Addresses 109

This is "Cool Papa's" autograph when he could see well enough to write.

Up until June of 1983, "Cool Papa" Bell was very generous about signing any and all items sent to him. He would also write his name and address on the collector's return envelope. After this period, all photos were returned unsigned, but included was a strip of paper with his signature and a short note from a family member or a friend.

will sign and return his photographs, accompanied by a bonus signed letter telling about his work with young people. See illustration.

Travis Jackson gives his fans a couple of 3x5 signed cards and/or two signed plaque cards as extras. And he sometimes includes a signed black and white photo taken during his playing days. Jackson, Jud Johnson and Ted Lyons will inscribe either their name and address, or their address alone on a return envelope—thus providing more terrific autograph specimens!

Up until June of 1983, "Cool Papa" Bell was very generous about signing any and all items sent to him. He would also write his name and address on the collector's return envelope. After this period, all photos were returned unsigned, but included was a strip of paper with his signature and a short note from a family member or a friend. Lou Boudreau usually sends at least two signed plaque Hall of Fame cards as a bonus.

Jocko Conlon always honors autograph requests promptly. He signs your photographs and returns your request letter signed, "jocko", or "Jocko Conlon", following a note such as, "Bless you all", or "A blessed Xmas to your family".

Joe Sewell will autograph photos and cards and then write his name and address on the return envelope provided with the request. Joe also writes a note on the letter sent to him which usually goes like this: "Dear Robert: Glad to autograph the cards for you. Thanks for remembering me. Sincerely, Joe Sewell."

Roy Campenella hasn't been able to autograph anything since his unfortunate accident years ago. Yet, this man does honor all autograph requests by utilizing a rubber stamp for his signature. And he, as well as Sandy Koufax, use the Dodger's Stadium in Los Angeles as their mailing address.

Early Wynn is quite good about signing specific kinds of materials. He will autograph *only* 8x10 photographs, Perez-Steele limited edition Hall of Fame Cards and the official plaque cards issued by the baseball Hall of Fame in Cooperstown. All other requests are refused but returned with a form letter saying that the material is "unauthorized", and therefore not acceptable for signing. If Early is away for an extended period of time, his daughter returns your photographs or cards with a note—a nice gesture which keeps the collector from waiting and wondering about the request. See the illustration.

One of the toughest autographs to obtain is that of the busy Ernie Banks. A collector may have to send out requests a half-dozen times in order to achieve decent results. Equally difficult specimens to get include those of Bob Gibson, Frank Robinson, Juan Marichial and Lefty Gomez. Lastly, Luis Aparicio is rather elusive since he is the only Hall of Famer to reside in a foreign country—Venezuela. All the others respond fairly promptly—some within a two week period. Others in a month or more.

110 Collecting Autographs For Fun and Profit

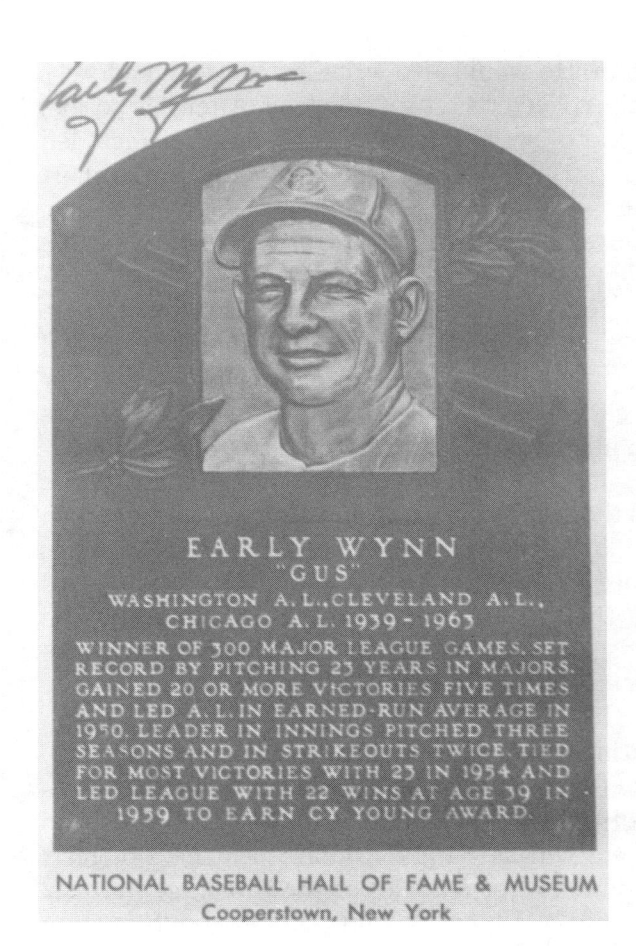

Mr. Wynn is working in Chicago for the summer and will not return home until Nov. 1st.

Loraine F. Wynn

Ted Williams is always willing to sign material for collectors, but a record of sorts is kept of who is sent autographs. To stop the unscrupulous dealer or collector who tries to obtain numerous autographs for resale, the above letter is sent out as a response—and the photos are returned promptly and unsigned.

```
                    P. O. BOX 481
                 ISLAMORADA, FLORIDA KEYS
                         33036


Thank you for your recent letter to Ted Williams.

Due to his heavy business schedule and his duties as
consultant for the Boston Red Sox, Ted spends very little
time here in Islamorada.  As a result, it is impossible
for him to comply with all his autograph requests unless
he limits the number of times he answers each person.

It is with regret, therefore, that I am returning
herewith the latest material you sent for his signature.

Ted really appreciates your interest and is glad to know
that you share his enthusiasm for the great game of
baseball.

                              Sincerely,


                              Stacia H. Gerow for
                              Ted Williams
```

Addresses of Some Living Hall of Famers

Henry Louis "Hank" Aaron: 1611 Adams Drive, S.W., Atlanta, GA 30311.

Luis Ernest Aparicio: Calle 73, No. 14-53, Maracaibo, Venezuela.

Lucius Benjamin "Luke" Appling: RR#7, Bragg Road, Cummings, GA 30130.

Ernest "Ernie" Banks: 1440 North State Parkway, No. 3-D, Chicago, IL 60610.

James "Cool Papa" Bell: 3034 Dickson Street, St. Louis, MO 63106.

Lawrence Peter "Yogi" Berra: 19 Highland Avenue, Montclair, NJ 07042.

Louis "Lou" Boudreau: 15600 Ellis Avenue, Dolton, IL 60419.

Lewis Clark "Lou" Brock: 12595 Durbin Drive, St. Louis, MO 63141.

Roy Campenella: 1000 Elysian Park Avenue, Los Angeles, CA 90012.

Albert Benjamin "Happy" Chandler: RR, Versailles, KY 40383.

John Bertrand "Jocko" Conlan: 5937 Cheney Road, Scottsdale, AZ 85251.

William Malcolm "Bill" Dickey: 114 East 5th Street, Little Rock, AR 72203.

Joseph Paul "Joe" DiMaggio: 2150 Beach Street, San Francisco, CA 94123.

Donald Scott "Don" Drysdale: 78 Colgate Street, Rancho Mirage, CA 92270.

Robert William Andrew "Bob" Feller: P.O. Box 157, Gates Mills, OH 44040.

Richard Benjamin "Rick" Ferrell: 2199 Golfview, #203, Troy, MI 48084.

Edward Charles "Whitey" Ford: 38 Schoolhouse Lane, Lake Success, NY 11020.

Charles Leonard "Charlie" Gehringer: 32301 Lahser Road, Birmingham, MI 48010.

Robert "Bob" Gibson: 215 Belleview Blvd South, Belleview, NE 68005.

Vernon Louis "Lefty" Gomez: 26 San Benito Way, Novato, CA 94947.

Henry Benjamin "Hank" Greenberg: 1129 Miradero Road, Beverly Hills, CA 90210.

Burleigh Arland Grimes: Rt. #3, Box 89, Holcombe, WI 54745.

William Jennings "Billy" Herman: 3111 Garden East, Apt. 33, Palm Beach Gardens, FL 33410.

Carl Owen Hubbell: Suncrest Apt. No. 8, 130 North Leseur, No. 1, Mesa, AZ 83205.

Monford "Monte" Irvin: 243 South Harrison Street, East Orange, NJ 07018.

Travis Calvin Jackson: Waldo, AZ 71770.

William Julius "Judi" Johnson: 3701 Kiamensi Street, Marshalltown, DE 19808.

Albert William "Al" Kaline: 945 Timberlake Drive, Bloomfield Hills, MI 48013.

George Clyde Kell: P.O. Box 158, Swifton, AK 72471.

Harmon Clayton Killebrew: P.O. Box 626, Ontario, OR 97914.

Ralph McPherran Kiner: Bote Road, Greenwich, CT 06830.

Sanford "Sandy" Koufax: 1000 Elysian Avenue, Los Angeles, CA 90012.

Robert Granville "Bob" Lemon: 1141 Clairborne Drive, Long Beach, CA 90807.

Walter Fenner "Buck" Leonard: 605 Atlantic Avenue, Rocky Mount, NC 27801.

Alfonso Ramon "Al" Lopez: 3601 Beach Drive, Tampa, FL 33609.

Theodore Amar "Ted" Lyons: 1401 Loree Street, Vinton, LA 70668.

Mickey Charles Mantle: 5730 Watson Circle, Dallas, TX 75225.

Juan Antonio Marichal: 170 Joost Avenue, San Francisco, CA 94134.

112   Collecting Autographs For Fun and Profit

To Bob
Best Wishes
PeeWee Reese

WILLIAM MALCOLM DICKEY
NEW YORK A.L. 1928-1946
SET RECORD BY CATCHING 100 OR MORE GAMES 13 SUCCESSIVE SEASONS. PLAYED WITH YANKEES, CHAMPIONS OF 1932-36-37-38-39-41-42-43, WHEN CLUB WON 7 WORLD SERIES TITLES. HOLDS NUMEROUS WORLD SERIES RECORDS FOR CATCHERS, INCLUDING MOST GAMES, 38. PLAYED ON 8 ALL-STAR TEAMS FROM 1932 TO 1946. LIFETIME BATTING AVERAGE OF .313 IN 1789 GAMES.
NATIONAL BASEBALL HALL OF FAME AND MUSEUM
COOPERSTOWN, NEW YORK

Bill Dickey

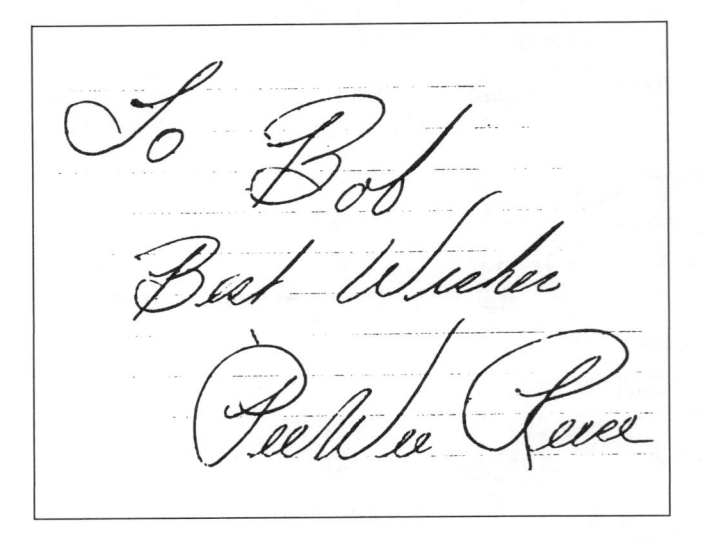

HENRY "HANK" L. AARON
MILWAUKEE N.L., ATLANTA N.L., MILWAUKEE A.L., 1954-1976
HIT 755 HOME RUNS IN 23-YEAR CAREER TO BECOME MAJORS' ALL-TIME HOMER KING. HAD 20 OR MORE FOR 20 CONSECUTIVE YEARS, AT LEAST 30 IN 15 SEASONS AND 40 OR BETTER EIGHT TIMES. ALSO SET RECORDS FOR GAMES PLAYED (3,298), AT-BATS (12,364), LONG HITS (1,477), TOTAL BASES (6,856), RUNS BATTED IN (2,297). PACED N.L. IN BATTING TWICE AND HOMERS, RUNS BATTED IN AND SLUGGING PCT. FOUR TIMES EACH. WON MOST VALUABLE PLAYER AWARD IN N.L. IN 1957.
Hank Aaron
NATIONAL BASEBALL HALL OF FAME & MUSEUM
Cooperstown, New York

Hank Aaron, one of the most popular of the more recent Hall of Fame inductees. This man was voted into this select group in 1982 after finishing a remarkable career spanning 22 years in the major leagues. He hit a total of 755 homers and broke Babe Ruth's record.

4/15/50

Bobby,
I like your sincerity that's why I really mean this autograph

Yogi Berra

Some Living Hall of Famers: Addresses

Edwin Lee "Eddie" Mathews: 13744 Recuerdo Drive, Del Mar, CA 92014.

Willie Howard Mays: 51 Mt. Vernon Lane, Atherton, CA 94025.

John Robert "Johnny" Mize: P.O. Box 112, Demorest, GA 30536.

Stanley Frank "Stan" Musial: 85 Trent Drive, Ladue, MO 63124.

Harold Henry "Pee Wee" Reese: 3211 Beals Branch Road, Louisville, KY 40206.

Robin Evan Roberts: 504 Terrace Hill Road, Temple Terrace, 33617.

Brooks Calbert Robinson: 1506 Sherbrook Road, Lutherville, MD 21093.

Frank Robinson: 15557 Aqua Verde Drive, Bel Air, CA 90024.

Edd J. Roush: 122 South Main Street, Oakland City, IN 47560.

Charles Herbert "Red" Ruffing: 25382 Concord Drive, Cleveland, OH 44122.

Joseph Wheeler "Joe" Sewell: 1618 Dearing Place, Tuscaloosa, AL 35401.

Enos Bradsher "Country" Slaughter: RR #2, Roxboro, NC 27573.

Edwin Donald "Duke" Snider: 3037 Lakemont Drive, Fallbrook, CA 92028.

Warren Edward Spahn: RR #2, Hartshorne, OK 74547.

William Harold "Bill" Terry: P.O. Box 2177, Jacksonville, FL 32203.

Theodore Samuel "Ted" Williams: P.O. Box 481, Islamorada, FL 33036.

James Hoyt Wilhelm: P.O. Box 2217, Sarasota, FL 33578.

Early Wynn: 525 Bayview Parkway, Nokomis, FL 33555.

Bill Terry is one of the few major league ball players to hit over .400 in a season. He was an outstanding hitter with a lifetime batting average of an astounding .341. Bill was brought into baseball's Hall of Fame in 1954.

114   Collecting Autographs For Fun and Profit

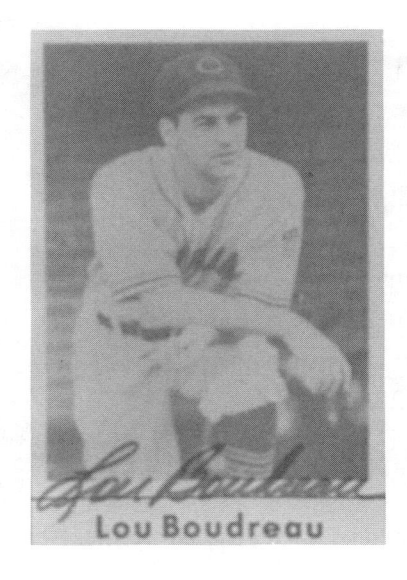

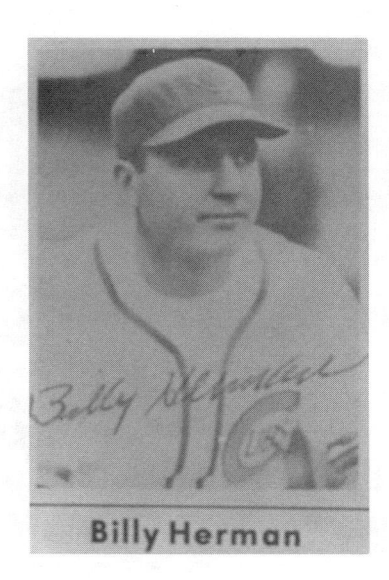

Lou Boudreau

Rick Ferrell

Billy Herman

Bob Lemon

Joe Sewell

Travis Jackson was best known as a premier fielding shortstop who also hit well during his 14 years in the major leagues. He batted over .300 in six of his playing years. His election to baseball's Hall of Fame came in 1982.

9. Directory of Major League Baseball Parks

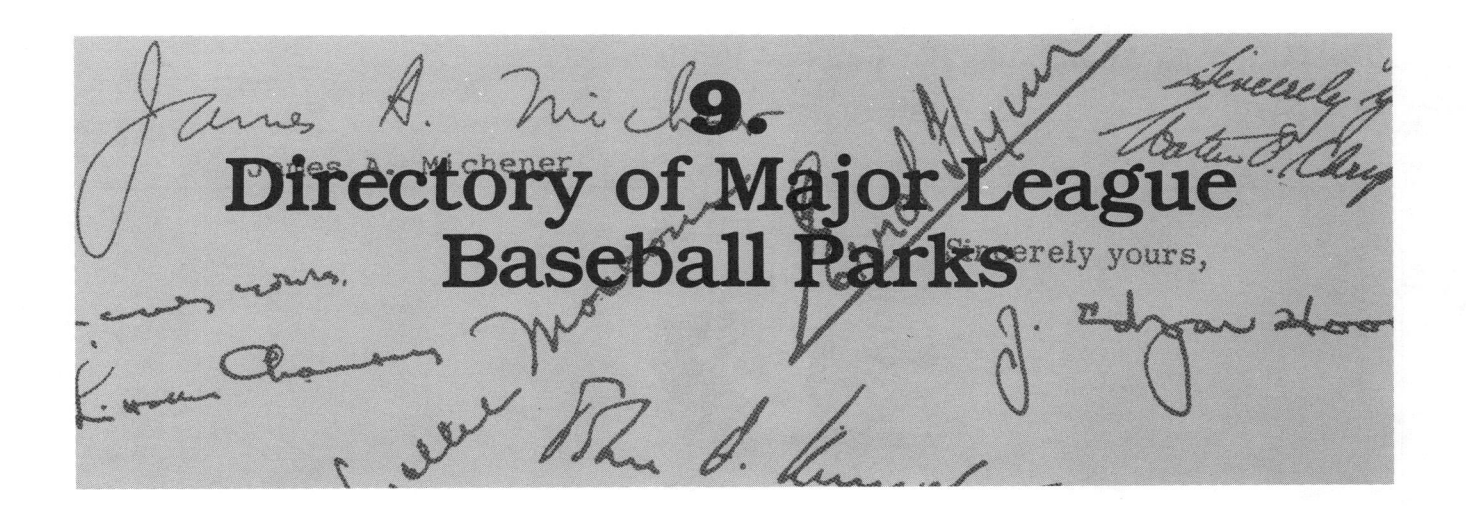

A collector always takes somewhat of a risk when writing away for an autograph. He or she is actually betting the price of postage and the time it takes to write a letter against the possibility of obtaining, a highly valued prize—a signature, a photograph, a letter or a signed baseball. In most cases, the chances of getting the desired autograph are excellent. Baseball players, as well as those in all other professional sports, are usually pleased to honor sincere requests from fans and collectors.

Team requests are often quite different! The collector is brashly asking a stranger to go to a lot of time and trouble to acquire the signatures of an entire baseball team on a ball, in an official yearbook, on a group photograph, or in a program. A whole team can only be acquired during the regular season, or while in Spring training, when all the players are present.

Should a request be rejected, try again and again. Surprising results are sometimes in the making! Your intrepid author wrote to all 14 teams in the American and all 12 teams in the National League during the 1983 season. The results were most astounding: 10 signed baseballs from the American League teams; 9 signed baseballs from the National League teams! The others never even bothered answering the requests. Here are some of the responses:

> Enclosed is the Oakland A's autographed baseball you have requested for your son. We hope he will enjoy the ball for years to come. Thank you for your interest in the Oakland A's.
>
> Sincerely
> Emil Roy Eisenhardt
> Chairman, President

On behalf of the Chicago White Sox, I would like to take this opportunity to thank you for your letter of June 7th. I apologize for the delay in responding, however, my schedule has kept me out of the office quite a lot lately on baseball business. Enclosed please find one autographed baseball for your son. I do hope that your son is enjoying the race for the pennant! If you are ever in the Chicago area join us out at Comisky Park to cheer the White Sox on to victory!

Sincerely
Eddie Einhorn
President

Thank you for your recent note and request for an autographed baseball for your son. Per your request, I am delighted to enclose the baseball autographed by our team members. I hope you enjoy this special souvenir, and that you may continue to enjoy the game of baseball together for a long time to come. Again, many thanks for your letter and for your loyal, long-distance support for the Giants. On behalf of the entire team, warmest wishes to you.

Sincerely
Robert A. Lurie
President

We have heard that you are a great fan of the Pirates, and we wanted to take this opportunity to thank you for being such a loyal friend of the team. The Bucs have had problems this year and we just don't seem to be getting the hits when we need them or good pitching. It's a good thing the season is early enough for us to still have a crack at the pennant. Hopefully the Pirates will put it together before too long and get started on a long winning streak. Our fans are important to us, especially those, like you, who stick by the team whether

June 3, 1983

Mr. Robert W. Pelton
119 Bluehill Road
San Antonio, Texas 78229

Dear Mr. Pelton:

Thank you for your letter of May 27th. We will be happy to arrange something for your son. Let me know when you are coming and we will work with you.

I am enclosing a schedule of our games and an autographed baseball for your son.

Sincerely,

Larry Schmittou
Vice President

LS:js
encl.

Texas Rangers Baseball Club   P.O. Box 1111 Arlington, Texas 76010   Executive Offices: 817 273 5222   Ticket Office: (Metro) 273 5100

they win or lose. So we are happy to send you under separate cover a Pirate cap, Yearbook, and autographed baseball, which we hope you will enjoy. All of us in the Pirate family join in sending you our best wishes and hope you'll keep rooting for the Bucs to win.

Chuck Tanner Kindest regards,
Manager Harding Peterson
  Executive Vice President

Some years ago, the only baseball players who continually ignored my requests for autographs were those playing with the fabled Brooklyn Dodgers. Why this was the case I could never understand, particularly in view of the fact that every other major league team so conscientiously labored to present a good public image. Many members of other teams simply wrote their signatures on a plain postcard, answering all their requests in this manner. Still others, such as those who played with the Cleveland Indians, Pittsburg Pirates and the St. Louis Cardinals, were supplied with an unlimited number of picture postcards of themselves, courtesy of the management. Each man took the time to sign these pictures personally, on request. The club then paid the postage out of a general expense fund so that the sometimes staggering cost of this operation wouldn't have to be borne by their players. The same teams also provided a secretary to write the return addresses on the cards in order to relieve the players from this time consuming task.

I became a rather desperate young collector regarding the Brooklyn club. The Dodgers appeared to be well on the way to a National League championship. Finally, I decided to go all out in my effort and write a polite letter to the top man, Mr. Branch Rickey, who owned the organization! You may recall that Rickey was the courageous man who brought the first Negro, Jackie Robinson, into the major leagues. In my letter, I pointed out my lack of success in obtaining autographs from members of the team, and I explained that players on each of the other fifteen major league clubs had willingly sent me photographs as well as other autographs. A short time later, the mailman brought a letter from the Dodger publicity director. It went as follows:

This is to acknowledge receipt of your letter of August 5th addressed to Mr. Branch Rickey and referred to me for reply. In this connection, I am appending hereto a sheet bearing the autographs of our players. However, I think you should know that this is a deviation from our policy. Annually, we receive thousands of requests very similar to yours and, while our players would like to honor each request, they find it physically impossible to do so. We had hoped that you would appreciate their problem in this matter.

At last, the autographs I had tried so long and hard to obtain were in my hands. Today, this sheet of signatures is invaluable. It contains four present members of baseball's Hall of Fame: Jackie Robinson, Roy Campanella, Duke Snider, and Pee Wee Reese.

The Brooklyn Dodgers—1949 World Champions of Baseball. This is an example of a complete set of autographs obtained from a baseball team simply by corresponding with the right person. This sheet of signatures was received from Branch Rickey, the man who owned the team at that time. The astericks denote those players who are presently members of the Baseball Hall of Fame in Cooperstown, New York.

WHERE TO WRITE MAJOR LEAGUE TEAMS

American League Teams:

1. Baltimore Orioles, Memorial Stadium, Baltimore, MD 21218.
2. Boston Red Sox, Fenway Park, 24 Yawkey Way, Boston, MA 02215.
3. California Angels, Anaheim Stadium, P.O. Box 2000, 2000 State College Blvd., Anaheim, CA 92806.
4. Chicago White Sox, Comiskey Park, 324 West 35th Street, Chicago, IL 60616.
5. Cleveland Indians, Municipal Stadium, Boudreau Blvd, Cleveland, OH 44114.
6. Detroit Tigers, Tiger Stadium, Detroit, MI 48216.*
7. Kansas City Royals, Royals Stadium, P.O. Box 1969, Kansas City, MO 64141.*
8. Milwaukee Brewers, County Stadium, 201 South 46th Street, Milwaukee, WI 53214.
9. Minnesota Twins, Hubert H. Humphrey Metrodome, 501 Chicago Avenue South, Minneapolis, MN 55415.*Avenue, Atlanta, GA 30302.*

11. Oakland A's, Oakland Stadium, Oakland, CA 94621.
12. Seattle Mariners, The Kingdome, P.O. Box 4100, 419 Second Avenue, Seattle, WA 98104.
13. Texas Rangers, Arlington Stadium, P.O. Box 1111, Arlington, TX 76010.
14. Toronto Blue Jays, Exhibition Stadium, P.O. Box 7777, Adelaide Street Post Office, Toronto, Ontario, Canada M5C 2K7.*

National League Teams:

1. Atlanta Braves, Atlanta Stadium, P.O. Box 4064, 521 Capitol Avenue, Atlanta, GA 30302.*
2. Chicago Cubs, Wrigley Field, 1060 West Addison Street, Chicago, IL 60613.
3. Cincinnati Reds, 100 Riverfront Stadium, Cincinnati, OH 45202.
4. Houston Astros, The Astrodome, P.O. Box 288, 8701 Kirby Street, Houston, TX 77001.
5. Los Angeles Dodgers, Dodger Stadium, 1000 Elysian Park Avenue, Los Angeles, CA 90012.
6. Montreal Expos, Olympic Stadium, P.O. Box 500, Station M, 4545 Pierre de Coubertin, Montreal, Quebec, Canada HIV 3P2.
7. New York Mets, Shea Stadium, 126th Street and Roosevelt Avenue, Flushing, NY 11368.
8. Philadelphia Phillies, Veterans Stadium, P.O. Box 7575, Broad Street and Pattison Avenue, Philadelphia, PA 19148.*
9. Pittsburg Pirates, Three Rivers Stadium, 600 Stadium Circle, Pittsburg, PA 15212.
10. St. Louis Cardinals, Busch Memorial Stadium, 250 Stadium Plaza, St. Louis, MO 63122.*
11. San Diego Padres, San Diego Stadium, P.O. Box 2000, 9449 Friars Road, San Diego, CA 92120.
12. San Francisco Giants, Candlestick Park, P.O. Box 24308, San Francisco, CA 94124.

*The only teams not honoring a request for a signed baseball.

The Brooklyn Dodgers—1949 World Champions of Baseball. This is an example of a complete set of autographs obtained from a baseball team simply by corresponding with the right person. This sheet of signatures was received from Branch Rickey, the man who owned the team at that time. The astericks denote those players who are presently members of the Baseball Hall of Fame in Cooperstown, New York.

10. Career Leaders and Record Holders: Addresses

Jim Bunning has the distinction of pitching no-hitters in both major leagues: against the Boston Red Sox when he played with the Detroit Tigers in the American League; and as a Philadelphia Phillies pitcher against the New York Mets in the National League.

Ball players such as Bunning, Johnny Bench, Rusty Staub, Lou Brock, Gaylord Perry, and others made quite a name for themselves in the baseball world. Autographs of these outstanding stars are relatively easy to obtain by simply writing to them, or through inexpensive purchases made at baseball card shows which are regularly held throughout the nation.

Each of these players was much celebrated during his career and has a special claim to fame. Many of these stars will eventually be nominated and voted on, for membership in baseball's most exclusive club—the Hall of Fame in Cooperstown, New York. Photographs of various sizes, as well as picture baseball cards suitable for autographing, are readily available from the sources given in Chapter 16.

SOME MAJOR LEAGUE CAREER LEADERS

Over 2200 Hits:

Dagoberto Campaneris, P.O. Box 16901, Raytown, MO 64133.

Over 450 Doubles:

Daniel Joseph "Rusty" Staub, 1271—3rd Avenue, New York, NY 10021.

Over 300 Homeruns:

Bobby Lee Bonds, 175 Lyndhurst, San Carlos, CA 94076.

Over 10 Grand Slams:

David Arthur Kingman, 818 West Busse Avenue, Mount Prospect, IL 60056.

Joseph Owen Rudi, P.O. Box 98, Laguna Beach, CA 92652.

Over 400 Stolen Bases:
Louis Clark Brock, 12595 Durbin Drive, St. Louis, MO 63141.

Cesar Eugenito Cedeno, 9919 Sage Doune, Houston, TX 77034.

Ronald LeFlore, 10448 Somerset Street, Detroit, MI 48224.

Over 1250 Runs Batted In:
John Lee Bench, 661 Reisling Knoll, Cincinnati, OH 45226.

Pitchers with Over 2100 Strikeouts:
James Paul David Bunning, 30 Winston Hill Road, Fort Thomas, KY 41075.

Jerry Martin Koosman, RR #2, Box 67E, Chaska, MN 55318.

Michael Stephen Lolich, 6252 Robinhill, Washington, MI 48094.

Pitchers with Over 40 Shutouts:
Rikalbert Bert Blyleven, 18992 Canyon Drive, Villa Park, CA 92667.

Donald Howard Sutton, 4367 North Park Vincente, Calabasas Park, CA 91302.

Luis Clemente Tiant, P.O. Box 298, Sudbury, MA 01776.

Pitchers with Over 200 Wins:
Thomas Edward John, 845 Shadow Ridge Road, Franklin Lakes, NJ 07417.

George Thomas Seaver, Larkspur Lane, Greenwich, CT 06830.

Pitchers with Over 4400 Innings Pitched:
James Lee Kaat, Sweetwater Farm, Glen Mills, PA 19342.

Gaylord Jackson Perry, RR#3, Box 565, Williamston, NC 27892.

Pitchers with Over 600 Games Pitched:
Thomas Henry Burgmeier, 12104 West 100th Street, Lenexa, KS 66215.

Elroy Leon Face, 3917 Main Street, McKeesport, PA 15132.

Lyndall Dale McDaniel, 5024 South Osage Street, Kansas City, MO 64133.

Frank Edwin "Tug" McGraw, Coleshill Rose Valley Road, Media, PA 19063.

Donald John McMahon, 11131 Fraley Street, Garden Grove, CA 92641.

Ronald Peter Perranoski, 1000 Elysian Park Avenue, Los Angeles, CA 90012.

James Hoyt Wilhelm, P.O. Box 2217, Sarasota, FL 33578.

Pitchers with Over 100 Saves:
David John Giusti, 524 Clair Drive, Pittsburg, PA 15241.

Darold Duane Knowles, 1004 Rainbow Lane, Blue Springs, MO 64015.

David Eugene LaRoche, 36 Harbor Sight Drive, Rolling Hills Estates, CA 90274.

Albert Walter Lyle, 107 Pine Terrace Drive, DeMarest, NJ 07627.

Kenton Charles Tekulve, 1531 Sequoia Street, Pittsburg, PA 15241.

Manager with Over 14 Years Managing:
Earl Sidney Weaver, 19016 West Lake Drive, Hialeah, FL 33015.

SOME MAJOR LEAGUE SEASON RECORDS

Most Singles in One Season:
Don Richard Ashburn, Gladwynne, PA 19035. (181 in 1951).

Ralph Allan Garr, 7819 Chaseway Drive, Missouri City, TX 77459. (180 in 1971).

Peter Edward Rose, 5946 Country Hills, Cincinnati, OH 45238. (181 in 1973).

Most Triples in One Season:
Loren Dale Mitchell, 3434 East 75th Place South, Tulsa, OK 74136. (23 in 1949).

Most Homeruns in One Season:
George Arthur Foster, 14400 Cerose Street, Hawthorne, CA 90250. (52 in 1977).

Adolph Louis "Dolph" Camilli, 2831 Hacienda Street, San Mateo, CA 94403. (34 in 1941).

Theodore Bernard "Ted" Kluszewski, 8353 Island Lane, Maineville, OH 45039. (49 in 1954).

Nicholas Raymond Tom "Nick" Etten, 21 Spinning Wheel Road, Hinsdale, IL 60521. (22 in 1944).

Gus Edward Zernial, Box 2373 Rural Bridge, Coarse Gold, CA 93614. (33 in 1951).

Roy Edward Sievers, 11505 Bellefontaine Road, Spanish Lake, MO 63138. (42 in 1957).

Most Stolen Bases in One Season:
Rickey Henley Henderson, 7237 Skyline Drive, Oakland, CA 94611. (100 in 1980).

David Earl Lopes, 16984 Avenue de Santa Ynez, Pacific Palisades, CA 90272. (77 in 1975).

William Alex North, 3303 East Madison, Seattle, WA 98102. (75 in 1976).

Maurice Morning Wills, 245 Fowling Street, Playa del Rey, CA 90291. (104 in 1962).

Most Strikeouts in One Season:
Steve Norman Carlton, 16240 Holts Lake Drive, Chesterfield, MO 63017. (310 in 1972).

Samuel Edward McDowell, 201 Penn Center Blvd, Pittsburg, PA 15235. (325 in 1965).

James Rodney Richard, 10235 Sageville Street, Houston, TX 77089. (313 in 1979).

Lynn Nolan Ryan, P.O. Box 409, Alvin, TX 77511. (383 in 1973).

Best Winning Percentage for One Season:
John Robert Candelaria, 312—32nd Avenue East, Bradenton, FL 33505. (.800 in 1977).

Ronald Ames Guidry, 109 Conway Street, Lafayette, LA 70507. (.893 in 1978).

David Arthur McNally, 3305 Ramada Drive, Billings, MT 59102. (.808 in 1971).

Elwin Charles "Preacher" Roe, 936 Nicholas Drive, West Plains, MO 65775. (.880 in 1951).

Most Shutouts in One Season:
Wilmer Dean Chance, 1413 Tr. 13, Road 2, Jeromesville, OH 44840. (11 in 1964).

James Alvin Palmer, P.O. Box 145, Brooklandville, MD 21022. (10 in 1975).

Most Games Saved in One Season:
Jack Delane Akers, 329 Reno Drive, Lynchburg, VA 24502. (32 in 1966).

Clay Palmer Carroll, 4515-26th Avenue, Bradenton, FL 33503. (37 in 1972).

Richard Allen "Goose" Gossage, 32 North Foote, Colorado Springs, CO 80909. (33 in 1980).

Wayne Allen Granger, P.O. Box 134, Aldrich Avenue, Huntington, MA 01050. (35 in 1970).

John Frederick Hiller, 102 West Arrowhead Road, Duluth, MN 55803. (38 in 1973).

Daniel Raymond Quisenberry, 811 Arno Road, Kansas City, MO 64113. (33 in 1980).

Howard Bruce Sutter, 12009 Tindall Drive, Town and Country, MO 63131. (37 in 1979).

11. MVP's: Addresses

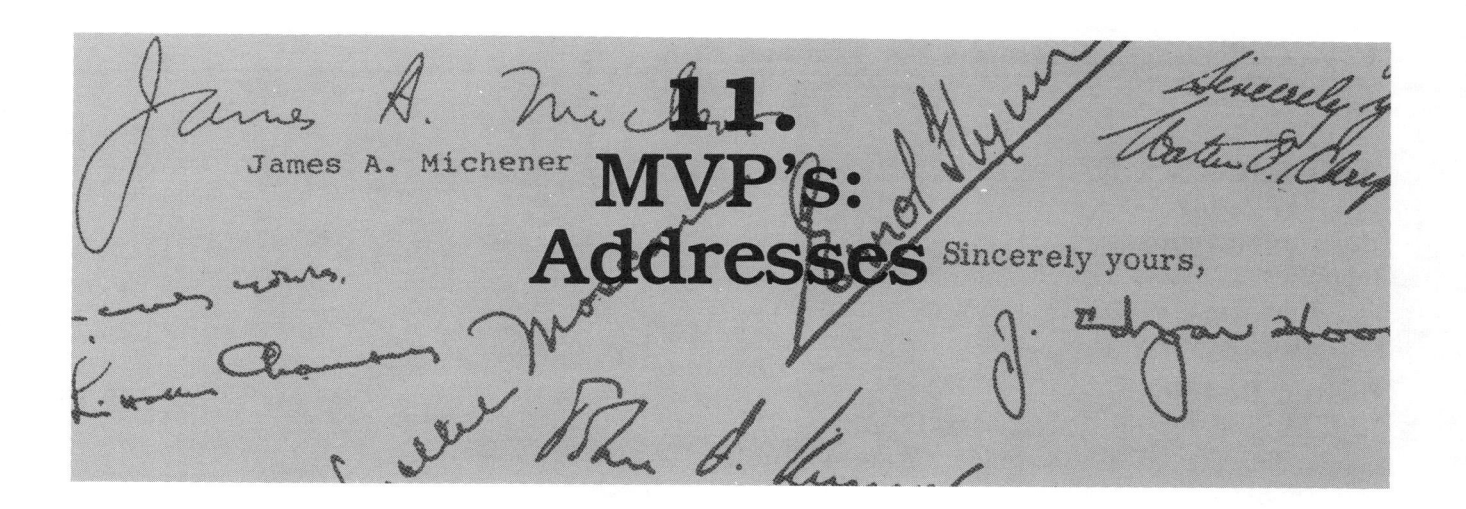

Each year, the members of the Baseball Writers' Association of America consider a number of outstanding major leaguers for the coveted Most Valuable Player Award. A secret ballot is held and the winner is given this prestigious honor—in much the same way as actors and actresses win Academy Awards for films, and Emmys for superb television performances.

Hal Newhouser of the Detroit Tigers was the only major league pitcher ever to win the Most Valuable Player Award for two years in succession (1944 and 1945). Don Newcombe of the Brooklyn Dodgers shares the National league record for the number of homeruns hit by a pitcher in one season. He belted seven big ones out of the park! Big Don won the MVP in 1956.

Marty Marion, the slick fielding St. Louis Cardinals shortstop, led his club with a .357 batting average during the 1943 World Series. He was voted the league's Most Valuable Player in 1944.

And lastly, Al Rosen of the Cleveland Indians set the Amerian League record for third basemen by hitting 43 homers in a single season! He won the award for his outstanding performance during the 1953 season. Today this same man is President of the Houston Astros!

Collectors can obtain photographs or picture cards of these famous players from the sources given in Chapter 16. Each man will graciously honor sincere requests for autographs.

AMERICAN LEAGUE

Baltimore Orioles:
John Wesley "Boog" Powell, U.S. Anglers Marina, Key West, FL 33040. (First baseman. Won MVP in 1970).

Boston Red Sox:
Jack Eugene Jensen, RR#2, Box 170A2, Scottsville, VA 24590. (Outfielder. Won MVP in 1958).

Carl Michael Yastrzemski, Highland Beach, FL 33444. (Outfielder. Won MVP in 1967).

Frederic Michael Lynn, 6961 East Via El Estribo, Anaheim Hills, CA 92807. (Outfielder. Won MVP in 1975).

James Edward Rice, RR#8, Box 686, Anderson, SC 29621. (Outfielder. Won MVP in 1978).

Calfornia Angels:
Donald Eugene Baylor, 260 Cagney Lane, No. 109, Newport Beach, CA 92663. (Outfielder. Won MVP in 1979).

Cleveland Indians:
Albert Leonard Rosen, P.O. Box 288, Houston, TX 77001. (Third baseman. Won MVP in 1953).

Detroit Tigers:
Harold "Hal" Newhouser, 2584 Marcy Street, Bloomfield Hills, MI 48013. (Pitcher. Won MVP in 1944 and 1945).

Kansas City Royals:
George Howard Brett, Lot E, Kaw Lane, Lake Quivira, Kansas City, KS 66106. (Third baseman. Won MVP in 1980).

Milwaukee Brewers:
Roland Glen "Rollie" Fingers, 1437 De La Warr Circle, Mequon, WI 53902. (Pitcher. Won MVP in 1981).

Minnesota Twins:
Rodney Cline Carew, 5144 Crescent Drive, Anaheim, CA 92807. (First baseman. Won MVP in 1977).

New York Yankees:
Spurgeon Ferdinand "Spud" Chandler, 1591—77th Street North, St. Petersburg, FL 33710. (Pitcher. Won MVP in 1943).

1936 - 1939 Yankee Dynasty

Philip Francis Rizzuto, 912 Westminister Avenue, Hillside, NJ 07025. (Shortstop. Won MVP in 1950).

Oakland A's:
Vida Rochelle Blue, 10285 Royal Oak Drive, Oakland, CA 94605. (Pitcher. Won MVP in 1971).

Reginald Martinez Jackson, 22 Yankee Hill, Oakland, CA 94616. (Outfielder. Won MVP in 1973).

Philadelphia Athletics:
Robert Clayton "Bobby" Shantz, 152 Mount Pleasant Avenue, Ambler, PA 19002. (Pitcher. Won MVP in 1952).

Texas Rangers:
Jeffrey Alan Burroughs, 6155 Laguna Court, Long Beach, CA 90803. (Outfielder. Won MVP in 1974).

MVP's: Addresses

George Arthur Foster, 14400 Cerose Street, Hawthorne, CA 90250. (Outfielder. Won MVP in 1977).

Los Angeles Dodgers:

Steven Patrick Garvey, 4393 Park Vicente, Calabasa, CA 91302. (First baseman. Won MVP in 1974).

Philadelphia Phillies:

Michael Jack "Mike" Schmidt, 24 Lakewood Drive, Media, PA 19063. (Third baseman. Won MVP in 1980 and 1981).

Pittsburg Pirates:

Richard Morrow "Dick" Groat, 320 Beach Street, Pittsburg, PA 15218. (Shortstop. Won MVP in 1960).

David Gene "Dave" Parker, 4221 Middle Road, Allison Park, PA 15101. (Outfielder. Won MVP in 1978).

Wilver Dornel "Willie" Stargell, 126 Conover Road, Pittsburg, PA 15208. (First baseman. Won MVP in 1979*).

NATIONAL LEAGUE

Brooklyn Dodgers:

Adolph Louis "Dolph" Camilli, 2831 Hacienda Street, San Mateo, CA 94403. (First baseman. Won MVP in 1941).

Donald Newcombe, 20507 Peale Drive, Woodland Hills, CA 91364. (Pitcher. Won MVP in 1956).

Chicago Cubs:

Philip Joseph Cavaretta, 2206 Portside Passage, Palm Harbor, FL 33563. (First baseman. Won MVP in 1945).

Henry John "Hank" Sauer, 207 Vallejo Court, Millbrae, CA 94030. (Outfielder. Won MVP in 1952).

Cincinnati Reds:

William Henry "Bucky" Walters, 515 Fox Road, Glenside, PA 19038. (Pitcher. Won MVP in 1939).

Frank Andrew McCormick, 14 Vanderbilt Road, Manhasset, NY 11030. (First baseman. Won MVP in 1940).

San Francisco Giants:
Willie Lee McCovey, 220 Crest Road, Woodside, CA 94062. (First baseman. Won MVP in 1969).

St. Louis Cardinals:
Martin Whiteford "Marty" Marion, 201 South Broadway, St. Louis, MO 63102. (Shortstop. Won MVP in 1944).

Kenton Lloyd "Ken" Boyer, 1254 North Kirkwood Street, Saint Ann, MO 63074. (Third baseman. Won MVP in 1964).

Frank Joseph "Joe" Torre, 2300 Delmar Blvd, St. Louis, MO 63116. (Third baseman. Won MVP in 1971).

Keith Hernandez, P.O. Box 137, Chesterfield, MO 63017. (First baseman. Won MVP in 1979*).

*Stargell and Hernandez tied for MVP in 1979.

Bucky Walters

12. Old-Timers: Addresses

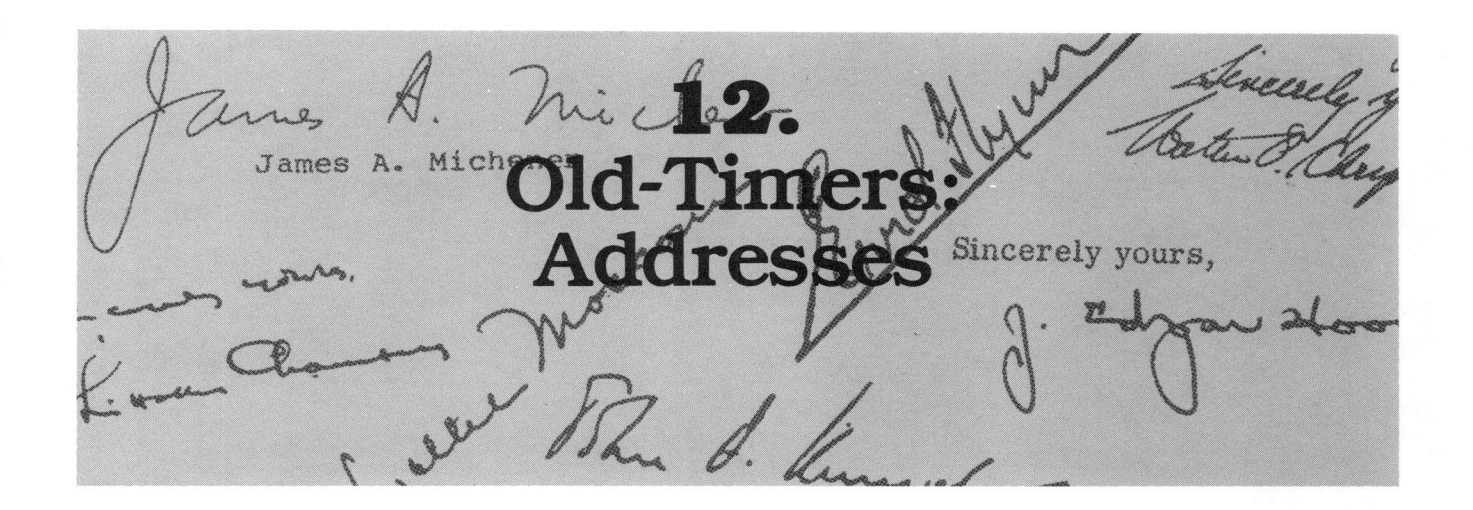

The autographs of many old-time baseball players are interesting to collect if only because they played many years ago. Others have some unique claim to fame or a career highlight often forgotten with the passage of time. Such autographic memorabilia will make a marvelous collection of unusual baseball nostalgia, and each player mentioned below will happily acknowledge courteous requests from collectors. Photographs of most of these old-timers can be purchased at reasonable prices and then sent through the mail for signing. One excellent picture source is Den's Collectors Den. (See Chapter 16 for address.) Ask for their current catalog.

"Bobo" Holloman of the St. Louis Browns pitched a no hitter in his first game as a rookie against the Philadelphia Athletics. He was then shipped back to the minors before the season ended. In 1921, George Torporcer became the first major league infielder to play while wearing glasses!

Johnny Cooney, known as baseball's worst homerun hitter, belted only *two* homers in 3,364 major league at-bats! Floyd Baker is another of baseballs all-time worst homerun hitters. He was able to hit only *one* homer in 2,280 at-bats during his major league career.

New York Yankee Allie Reynolds pitched the only no-hitter ever on the last day of a big league season. His great performance against the Boston Red Sox won the pennant for his club. In 1923, Pete Donohue was one of three twenty-game-winners with the Cincinnati Reds—and they still lost the pennant! Herb Score did the same thing in later years with the Cleveland Indians. Herb also holds the record for having 245 strikeouts in his rookie year. Bob Cain of the Detroit Tigers once pitched against and walked a 43-inch midget who played for the St. Louis Browns!

In 1920, Joe Oeschger, the Boston Braves' fast-ball pitcher, hurled the longest game in major league history—26 innings. The score was 1 to 1. It was finally called because of darkness. Ewell Blackwell was widely known as "The Whip" because of his unusual pitching motion. Lew Burdette was a good pitcher but a luckless fielder. This man once committed two errors which lost a World Series for his team. And Tommy Byrne was probably the best ever relief pitcher in the major leagues, when he played with the pennant winning New York Yankees.

Chicago White Sox Edgar Smith's claim to fame is certainly different! He was the pitcher off whom Joe DiMaggio singled on May 15, 1941, to begin his historic 56-consecutive game hitting streak. Jim Bagby, Jr., was the Cleveland Indian relief pitcher who stopped Joe's hitting streak in 1941 during a night game. And Kenny Keltner was the third baseman who robbed Joe of two certain hits during the same game.

Pete Gray was an exceptionally interesting ball player. He played in 77 games and batted .218 with the St. Louis Browns in 1945, despite having had only one arm! Monte Stratton gained fame when he lost his leg in a hunting accident. A movie, starring James Stewart, was made about his courageous life and career come-back.

Cleveland Indian catcher, Hank Helf, once caught a baseball tossed from 700 feet in the air! But the highest catch on record was made by another Indian, Joe Sprinz. This one was a ball

128 Collecting Autographs For Fun and Profit

Allie Reynolds

Monty Stratton

Johnny Vander Meer

dropped from 800 feet, and its force broke Joe's jaw! Hall of Famer Willie Mays is said to have made the greatest World Series catch ever accomplished by an outfielder. Who did Willie rob of an extra base hit? It was none other than Vic Wertz, hard hitting Cleveland Indian outfielder. But Vic went on to hit an astounding .500 in the 1954 World Series.

Harvey Haddix of the Pittsburg Pirates performed the greatest pitching feat of all time. He pitched a perfect game through 12 innings, but lost the game in the thirteenth by a 1 to 0 score. New York Yankee, Don Larsen, is the only man to ever pitch a perfect game in the World Series. He retired 27 batters in a row! And who was the unfortunate pitcher who went up against Larsen in this game? That was Sal Maglie of the Brooklyn Dodgers! Joe Nuxhall of the Cincinnati Reds was the youngest player to ever appear in a big league game. He was a mere 15 years old when he pitched against the St. Louis Cardinals.

Frenchy Bordagaray has the dubious distinction of being the only major leaguer to purposely spit in an umpire's eye during a disagreement. He was benched for 60 days and fined 500 big ones. But Frenchy was a topnotch outfielder-third baseman, with a career pinch-hitting average of .312—a figure no one laughed about.

Everyone has heard of Roger Maris, the man who finally topped Babe Ruth's 60 homerun record. But who is Jack Fisher? And who is Tracy Stallard?

Fisher, with the Baltimore Orioles, served up number 60 to Maris when he tied the long-standing record. Stallard, with the Boston Red Sox, threw a fastball in a later game's fourth inning. Maris promptly belted number 61 into the seats and made baseball history!

The great Johnny Vander Meer of the Cincinnati Reds once pitched two consecutive no hitters! His first was against Boston; the second, four days later was against Brooklyn. Virgil Trucks of the Detroit Tigers is one of only a few pitchers to have two no-hitters during the same season.

Bob Allison has the distinction of hitting a grand slam homerun in the same inning a teammate accomplished the identical feat. And Jim Gentile is the *only* major leaguer to ever hit back-to-back grand slam homers—in his first two appearances at the plate! Joe Adcock, Rocky Colavito and Pat Seery are three ball players who have had the distinction of hitting four home-runs in a single game.

Rex Barney had blinding speed and unlimited potential some years ago with the Brooklyn Dodgers, but control proved to be his ultimate downfall. Luckily, Hall of Famer Sandy Koufax, a pitcher with much the same problem, received help from a relatively obscure team mate. A catcher named Norm Sherry advised Sandy not to throw so hard in order to better develop his ability to find the plate. The rest is history.

Vic Raschi of the New York Yankees holds the American League record for retiring 32 batters in the ninth inning. Thus Bevins lost his no-hitter and the game. But he did win the dubious distinction of walking 10 batters—a new record!

Ray Fisher, who played for the Cincinnati Reds from 1910 to 1920, was one of the last legal spitball pitchers. He is only one of two alive today. The other Burleigh Grimes is in the baseball Hall of Fame. Carl Erskine became an overnight hero to the fans when he struck out 14 New York Yankees in a World Series game!

Eddie Yost had 1614 walks during his career in major league baseball. He is in the top 10 of the bases-on-balls leaders. And he played a record 576 consecutive games at third base for the hapless Washington Senators! Who is Eddie Miller? This man was one of the best fielding shortstops in major league history! Other impressive shortstops were Bobby Kerr, Billy Jurges, Alvin Dark, Eddie Joost, Bill Rogell and Dick Bartell, who led the 1936 New York Giants with an astounding .381 World Series batting average. Eddie Stanky, the great second baseman with the Brooklyn Dodgers, set the season record with 148 walks in 1945.

consecutively! He also has the honor of pitching to Hank Aaron when this man hit his first major league homerun! Who threw the homerun pitch to New York Giant Bobby Thompson in the championship playoff game? Yes—it was Ralph Branca of the Brooklyn Dodgers! Have you ever heard of Claude Passeau? He pitched for the Chicago Cubs and between 1941 and 1946 never committed a single error, while handling 273 consecutive fielding chances!

Mark Koenig was a teammate of Babe Ruth during the late twenties. He hit .500 in the 1927 World Series and was later traded. Koenig was voted only a half-share of the Chicago Cub's 1932 World Series bonus after hitting .353 when called up during mid-season. This infuriated his former Yankee pals and led to Ruth "calling" his famous World Series homerun against Chicago pitcher Charlie Root.

Floyd Bevins is best known for having *almost* pitched a World Series no-hitter against the Brooklyn Dodgers in 1947. Cookie Lavagetto gained a measure of fame by hitting a game winning double against this Yankee pitcher with two out

Lou Brissie once pitched for the Philadelphia Athletics although he had an artificial leg! Lou was an outstanding star in the major leagues despite his handicap.

130 Collecting Autographs For Fun and Profit

Mickey Owen was the unfortunate "goat" of the 1941 World Series between the Brooklyn Dodgers and the New York Yankees. He missed catching the final pitch, a spitball thrown by Hugh Casey, when Tommy Henrich struck out! Charlie Keller then followed with a double and the Yankees won the game by a 7 to 4 margin. Keller, by the way, led the Yankees with a .438 batting average in the 1939 World Series. Another Owen named Marv, third baseman for the Detroit Tigers, also experienced World Series futility! He couldn't get a hit in his last 12 at bats in the 1934 World Series against the St. Louis Cardinals. Then he was hitless in his first 19 at bats during the 1935 World Series against the Chicago Cubs. Marv Owen holds the record for a hitless streak during World Series play. He was 0 for 31!

What can be said that hasn't already been said about former Yankee star Frankie Crosetti? Hall of Famer Joe DiMaggio also had two brothers who made the big leagues—Dom and Vince. Dom set the American league record with 503 putouts in 1948 while an outfielder with the Boston Red Sox. And Leo Durocher! Well, who hasn't heard stories about this baseball great? Then we come to Joe Garagiola. Not well known as a player in his day, Joe gained fame later as a top notch game announcer.

Gene Bearden, forgotten by many fans, starred in the 1948 World Series. He pitched and won one complete game, saved a second game for his team, and held his opponents scoreless. Do you remember Riggs Stephenson? He was the Chicago Cubs leading batter during the 1932 World Series. Riggs belted out hits at a .444 clip! And Joe Moore hit .391 to lead the New York Giants in batting during the 1937 Series. Remember Frank McCormick? He was Cincinnati's leading hitter at .400, during the 1949 World Series! Lastly, Harry Walker led the St. Louis Cardinals with a .412 average in the 1946 Series.

Milt Gaston of the Chicago White Sox was one of two pitchers involved in four double plays in the same game. He did this during the 1932 season. Ferris Fain, first baseman for the Philadelphia Athletics, took part in a record 194 double plays during the 1949 season. Jimmie Reese was a 1930 New York Yankee infielder and close pal of the great Babe Ruth. He was born James Hymie Soloman but changed his name because he felt being Jewish would hinder his baseball career.

Does the name Freddie Shulte ring any bells? He was a Washington Senator star in 1933 when he hit .333 to lead his club in the World Series. Little remembered Bruce Campbell led the Detroit Tigers with a .360 batting average in the 1940 Series! Roger Cramer is yet another forgotten man. He hit .379 for Detroit in the 1945 Series. Larry Doby led the Cleveland Indians in the Series of 1948, with a .318 batting average. And Gene Woodling was the New York Yankee hero in two World Series. In 1950 this man walloped the ball at a .429 clip and in 1952 he sported a respectable .348 batting average.

Philadelphia "Whiz Kid" Andy Seminick is the only catcher to ever hit two homers in the same inning. Wes Westrum, former catcher with the New York Giants, once hit three sacrifice flies in one World Series game—a record. Gil McDougald was the New York Yankee star third baseman who hit a total of seven homers in various World Series games. Walt Dropo shares the first baseman major league record for getting hits in 12 consecutive times at bat. Tommy Holmes, outfielder for the old Boston Braves, once set a National League record when he hit safely in a total of 37 consecutive games. And Wally Berger shares a record of 38 homeruns as a rookie in 1930 when he first came up with the same ball club.

Johnny Marcum is noted for pitching two shutouts in a row for the Philadelphia Athletics when he began his major league career way back in 1933. Dave Ferriss did the same thing when he started with the Boston Red Sox in 1945. Don Grate, former outfielder with the Philadelphia Phillies, once tossed a baseball over 443 feet—the longest throw on record! And little known Forrest Jensen, 1936 Pittsburg Pirates player, holds the major league record with 696 times at bat during one season.

Red Schoendienst holds the National League record for top fielding at second base during one season and in a career. Hank Majeski set a fielding record for third basemen of .9883 while playing in 1947 for the Philadelphia Athletics. Jim Piersall, formerly with the Boston Red Sox, holds the best career fielding average (.9902) for an outfielder. Andy Pafko holds the World Series record for most chances handled by an outfielder while playing with the 1945 Chicago Cubs. And poor Dolph Camilli! He didn't fare so well in the realm of fielding. He committed three errors in one inning while playing first base for the Philadelphia Phillies during the 1935 season.

OLD TIMERS: CURRENT ADDRESSES

Adcock, Joseph Wilbur: P.O. Box 385, Coushatta, LA 71019.

Allison, William Robert: 6700 Galway Drive, Edina, MN 55424.

Bagby, James Charles Jacob, Jr.: 1910 South Cobb Drive, No. 48, Marietta, GA 30060.

Baker, Floyd Wilson: 33033 Idlewood Avenue, Youngstown, OH 44511.

Barney, Rex Edward: 4601 Hollins Ferry Road, Baltimore, MD 21227.

Bartell, Richard William: 1118 Island Drive, Alameda, CA 94501.

Bearden, Henry "Hank" Eugene: P.O. Box 176, Helena, AR 72342.

Berger, Walter "Wally" Antone: 124-21st Street, Manhattan Beach, CA 90266.

Bevins, Floyd Clifford: 5067-8th Avenue, N.E., Salem, OR 97303.

Blackwell, Ewell "The Whip": 84 Uloque Court, Brevard, NC 28712.

Bordagaray, Stanley "Frenchy" George: 395 Crestwood Avenue, Ventura, CA 93003.

Branca, Ralph Theodore Joseph: 791 North Street, White Plains, NY 10605.

Brissie, Leland "Lou" Victor: 653 Crestlyn Drive, North Augusta, SC 29841.

Burdette, Selva Lewis: 2837 Gulf of Mexico Drive, Longboat Key, FL 33548.

Byrne, Thomas Joseph: 442 Pineview Avenue, Wake Forest, NC 27587.

Cain, Robert Max: 161 East 226th Street, Euclid, OH 44123.

Camilli, Adolph "Dolph" Louis: 2831 Hacienda Street, San Mateo, CA 94403.

Campbell, Bruce Douglas: 4011 Bayside Road, Fort Meyers Beach, FL 33931.

Colavito, Rocco "Rocky" Domenico: 520 North Temple Blvd., Temple, PA 19560.

Cooney, John Walter: 818 Whitfield Avenue, Sarasota, FL 33580.

Cramer, Roger Maxwell: 5 Hilliard Drive, Manahawk, NJ 08050.

Crosetti, Frank Peter Joseph: 65 West Monterey Avenue, Stockton, CA 95204.

Dark, Alvin Ralph: 608 Neptune Avenue, Leucadia, CA 92024.

DiMaggio, Dominic Paul: 90 Beacon Street, Boston, MA 02108.

DiMaggio, Vincent Paul: 7528 Beck Avenue, North Hollywood, CA 91605.

Doby, Lawrence "Larry" Eugene: Nishuane Road 45, Montclair, NJ 07042.

Donohue, Peter Joseph: 8713 South Normandale Street, No. 261, Fort Worth, TX 76116.

Dropo, Walter: 7 Grant Road, Marblehead, MA 01945.

Durocher, Leo "The Lip" Ernest: 1400 East Palm Canyon, No. 210, Palm Springs, CA 92262.

Erskine, Carl Daniel: 6214 South Madison Avenue, Anderson, IN 46013.

Fain, Ferris Roy: Star Route No. 5, Georgetown, CA 95634.

Ferriss, David Meadow: 510 Robinson Drive, Cleveland, MS 38732.

Fisher, John Howard: 611 Hamilton Street, Easton, PA 18042.

Fisher, Raymond Lyle: 2112 Brockton Blvd., Ann Arbor, MI 48104.

Garagiola, Joseph Henry: 4514 Desert Park Place, Paradise Valley, AZ 85253.

Gaston, Nathaniel Milton: 5064 White Oak Court, Bradenton, FL 33507.

Gentile, James Edward: 1016 Neptune Street, Edmond, OK 73034.

Grate, Donald: 1245 N.W. 203rd Street, Miami, FL 33169.

Frank Crosetti

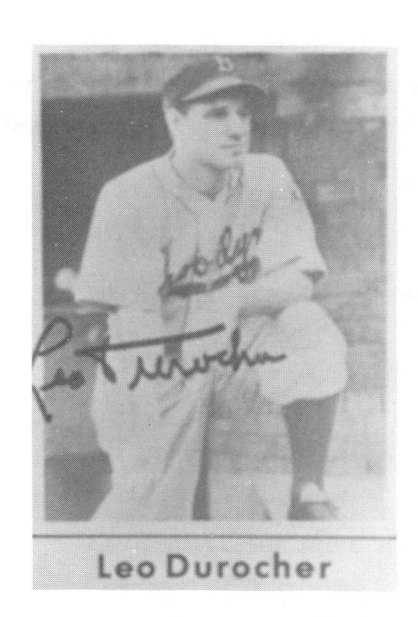

Joe Moore

Leo Durocher

Gray, Peter: 203 Phillips Street, Nanticoke, PA 18634.

Haddix, Harvey "Kitten": 4001 Vernon Ashbury Road, South Vienna, OH 45369.

Helf, Henry Hartz: 719 Postoak Street, Austin, TX 78704.

Henrich, Thomas David: 150 Cemetery West, Yellow Springs, OH 45387.

Holloman, Alva "Bobo" Lee: 650 Rivermont Road, Athens, GA 30601.

Holmes, Thomas Francis: 1 Pine Drive, Woodbury, N.Y. 11797.

Jensen, Forrest Docenus: 1311 North Parkwood Lane, Wichita, KS 67208.

Joost, Edwin David: P.O. Box 11515, Zephyr Cove, NV 89448.

Jurges, William Frederick: 2048 Bel Ombre Circle, Lake Wales, FL 33853.

Keller, Charles "King Kong" Ernest: 8238 Yellow Spring Road, Frederick, MD 21701.

Keltner, Kenneth Frederick: 3220 King Arthur's Court West, Greenfield, WI 53221.

Kerr, John "Buddy" Joseph: 341 Grove Street, Oradell, NJ 07649.

Koenig, Mark Anthony: 4295 Warm Springs Street, Glen Ellen, CA 95442.

Larsen, Donald James: 17090 Copper Hill Drive, Morgan Hill, CA 95037.

Lavegetto, Harry "Cookie" Arthur: 46 Tara Road, Orinda, CA 94563.

Maglie, Salvatore Anthony: 77 Morningside Drive, Grand Island, NY 14072.

Majeski, Henry: 12 Roosevelt Street, Staten Island, NY 10304.

Marcum, John Alfred: RR#2, Eminence, KY 40019.

McCormick, Frank Andrew: 14 Vanderbilt Road, Manhasset, NY 11030.

McDougald, Gilbert James: 10 Warren Avenue, Spring Lake, NJ 07762.

Miller, Edward Robert: 204 Cypress Drive, Lake Worth, FL 33460.

Moore, Joe Gregg: Gause, TX 77857.

Nuxhall, Joseph Henry: 5706 Lindenwood Lane, Fairfield, OH 45014.

Oeschger, Joseph Carl: Oeschger Lane, Ferndale, CA 95536.

Owen, Arnold Malcom: Greene County Sheriff, Springfield, MO 65802.

Owen, Marvin James: 42 Hawthorne Way, San Jose, CA 95110.

Passeau, Claude William: 113 London Street, Lucedale, MS 39452.

Piersall, James Anthony: WMAQ Radio, Chicago, IL 60601.

Raschi, Victor John Angelo: 1255 West Westlake Road, Conesus, NY 14435.

Reese, James Herman: 10797 Ashton Avenue, Los Angeles, CA 90024.

Reynolds, Allie Pierce: 2709 Cashion Place, Oklahoma City, OK 73112.

Rogell, William George: 17214 Glaston Bury Road, Detroit, MI 48219.

Rush, Robert Ransom: 1358 East 1st Place, Mesa, AZ 85201.

Schoendienst, Albert "Red" Fred: 331 Ladue Woods Court, Creve Coeur, MO 63141.

Schulte, Fred William: 336 West Boone Street, Belvidere, IL 61008.

Score, Herbert Jude: Radio Station WWWE, Cleveland, OH 44101.

Seerey, James Patrick: 9256 Leamont Street, St. Louis, MO 63136.

Seminick, Andrew Wasil: 1920 South Park Avenue, Melbourne, FL 32901.

Sherry, Norman Burt: 24181 Torena Circle, Mission Viejo, CA 92675.

Smith, Edgar: RR#130 Kinkover, Bordentown, NJ 08505.

Sprinz, Joseph Conrad: 1359-33rd Avenue, San Francisco, CA 94122.

Stallard, Evan Tracy: Herald, VA 24230.

Stanky, Edward Raymond: 2100 Spring Hill Road, Mobile, AL 36607.

Stephenson, Jackson Riggs: 917 Indian Hills Drive, Tuscaloosa, AL 35401.

Stratton, Monte Franklin Pierce: RR#2, Box 97, Greenville, TX 75401.

Thomson, Robert Brown: 122 Sunlit Drive, Watchung, NJ 07060.

Torporcer, George "Specs": 30 Teed Street, Huntington Station, NY 11747.

Trucks, Virgil Oliver: 2028 Buena Vista Drive, Birmingham, AL 35216.

Vander Meer, John Samuel: 4005 Leona Avenue, Tampa, FL 33606.

Walker, Harry "The Hat" William: RR#1, Box 145, Leeds, AL 35094.

Wertz, Victor Woodrow: P.O. Box 804, Mount Clemons, MI 48043.

Westrum, Wesley Noreen: P.O. Box 3001, Mesa, AZ 85205.

Woodling, Eugene Richard: 926 Remsen Road, Medina, OH 44256.

Yost, Edward Fred Joseph: 74 Eagle Lane, Hauppauge, NY 11788.

Dear Friend:

Thanks very much for your support. All the Cardinals and I appreciate it.

Sincerely,

Al Schoendienst

13. Exhibiting and Lecturing

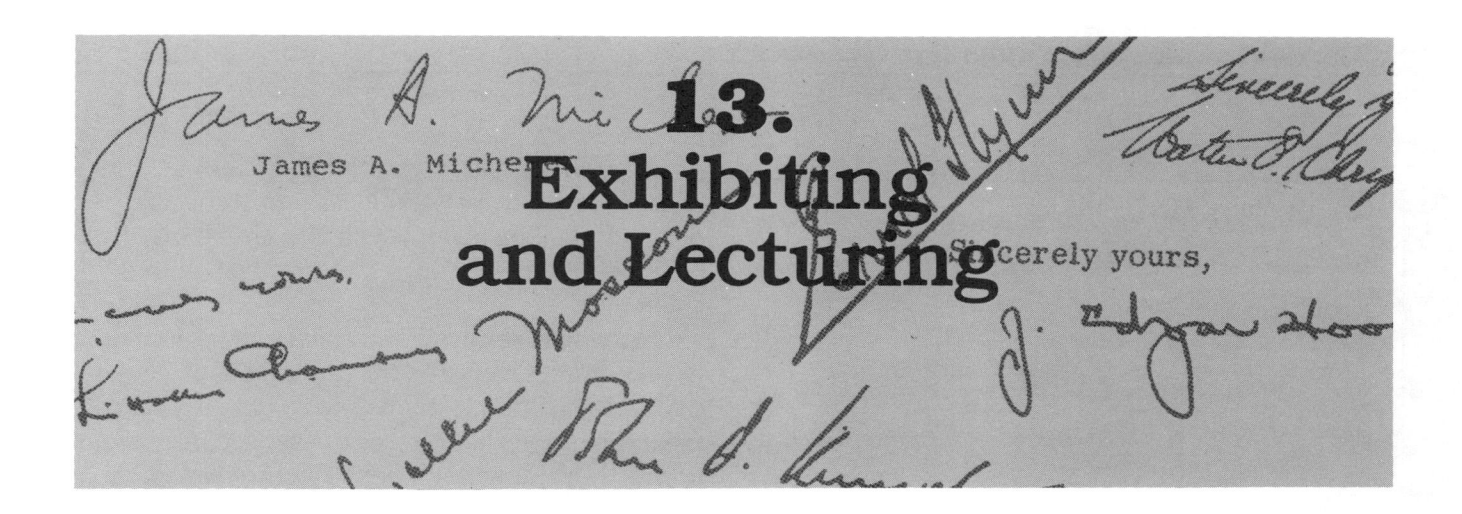

There's a continual demand for interesting exhibits of autographic materials, as well as openings for hobbyists who wish to take up lecturing as a sideline. This may serve only to attract new people to the hobby or merely to share the pleasure in their prizes with others. Hobbyists will find that libraries, schools, businesses and active civic organizations often need display items of general interest, and will welcome people with a unique avocation, who are capable of making a fascinating presentation of their specialty.

Start by setting up an appointment with a local librarian or high school principal. Offer to set up an exhibit of autographed photographs from your collection, selecting examples you feel might prove to be especially appealing. It's a good idea to take along a loose-leaf notebook or album of autographs when you keep the appointment. This will serve as a spring-board for discussing the theme of the display, and it will also help determine the categories of notables best suited for the particular exhibit.

A segment of my own collection was first put on display in Mobile, Alabama. I dropped by the library one day to browse around and while there met the head librarian. In the ensuing conversation, I brought up the subject of displays, and mentioned my collection. The librarian expressed an avid interest in the idea so I showed him a selection of my autographs, which were organized in a photograph album. Almost immediately he decided to add a two-week autograph exhibit to his activities calendar. The collection was subsequently lodged in securely locked glass display cases. The exhibit proved to be so popular that it was held over twice due to public demand. Later, the librarian, in a letter of thanks, said the display was "the most successful exhibit the library had ever sponsored".

Most libraries have small groups of locked glass display cases for valuable exhibits. Large libraries will have an abundance of such cases or cabinets and can schedule several exhibits to run concurrently. Each hobbyist or exhibitor is limited to the display area allocated for the particular collection. If locked display cases are not available, the collector must first stipulate that the exhibit be placed where it will be closely watched, preferably in a part of the library where an employee is on hand at all times. This is especially necessary if signed photographs or other valuable autographic materials must be placed on open display using a bulletin board, or if they're merely hung on a wall.

A few eye-catching signs, appropriately placed, will help attract the attention of potential viewers. Larger libraries usually have the necessary means of preparing such signs. A civic organization or a smaller library may require the collector to supply several hand-lettered announcements. A general display of the various categories included in your collection should be arranged in specific groupings. They should each be identified by signs. A few possibilities are: Military Leaders; The Space Age; Governors; Artists; The United Nations; The United States Senate; The Supreme Court; Stage and Screen; Literary Greats; Presidents; Baseball's Hall of Fame.

One other sign will be necessary for each glass exhibit case. It can be neatly hand-lettered by using a set of lettering guides available in any good

```
        FROM THE COLLECTION
               OF
          ROBERT W. PELTON

For information about lectures and exhibits,
phone 000-000 or write to: Street Address
                           Your Community
                           State, Zip Code
```

ing a set of lettering guides available in any good stationery store, or it can simply be typed. The message should be brief and to the point.

This kind of sign usually brings varying responses. Some calls or letters may lead to lecture invitations for the hobbyist capable of talking interestingly about his avocation. Opportunities to exhibit all or part of the collection elsewhere may be offered. And monetary offers may be made by viewers who wish to purchase an item shown in the display. Of course, some collectors do not desire to lecture, nor do they want to get involved in setting up other displays. Most aren't interested in purchase offers for any of their autographic treasures. In any of these cases, simply omit your phone number and address from the above sign. There is, in fact, no reason why a collector must even give his or her name if personal publicity is disliked. A collection or parts of it can be loaned for exhibit anonymously—as a public service.

The collector who would enjoy lecturing about autographs can register with any speakers' bureau located within his or her immediate area. In localities where there are no speakers' bureaus a would-be hobbyist lecturer should compile a list of possibilities. This can be accomplished in several ways. A local Chamber of Commerce usually maintains a current compilation of all professional organizations, civic groups and clubs in its area. This list will generally include the name of the group's president and/or the person who handles programming. Get in touch with the program chairperson for he or she is the one who arranges the entertainment at meetings. A Chamber of Commerce can also provide a church directory. Church groups and clubs have a continuing need for good program ideas and interesting speakers. A phone call or a note to various local ministers will produce information about which church groups would be most interested in a program on autograph collecting.

A would-be autograph collector-lecturer can't expect to receive a fee for talking about his hobby. Certainly, a collector has no right to expect payment if he or she has offered the service. Any group permitting a rank beginner to lecture before them is in effect doing the speaker a service—giving the person an opportunity to try their wings and gain much needed experience.

The situation is entirely different when a speakers' bureau or a club or organization initiates a lecture request. Then the collector is entitled to whatever fee is specified, either when registering with a bureau, or when negotiating with a group. Unless the beginning lecturer has some special claim to fame, making his appearance before an audience a matter of great public interest, he can't expect the same standard fee commanded by professionals for whom lecturing is a livelihood. Beginners can't expect to be invited immediately to lecture before the largest, most influential and most important organizations either. Small or nonpaying audiences, however, shouldn't be regarded as second-rate opportunities. They provide much free word-of-mouth publicity for the speaker who pleases them. Naturally, they will also spread the word about anyone who is boring, overly long-winded, or insufficiently knowledgeable about his or her specialty.

Many a successful lecture career has grown out of such modest beginnings. Most civic club meetings are reported in the local newspapers after the meeting is over, and an announcement of forthcoming meetings is also published. Mention is usually made of the planned program and the guest speaker's name. If the autograph collector-lecturer offers the local newspaper a few photographs of some especially choice items in his collection, the newspaper will generally follow up with a feature story on the hobby, thus providing some more free publicity. This same procedure can be followed when exhibiting autographs in a school or library display. A local radio or television station may be attracted by the picture or pictures and the write-up in the newspaper. The collector may then be invited to appear on a panel, variety, or hobby show. Only a few opportunities of this sort are necessary for a speaker to become widely known far beyond the confines of his or her hometown.

What, exactly, should an autograph lecture include? The possibilities are practically endless! They are limited largely by the speaker's background knowledge, collecting experience and the specific items in the autograph collection itself. The direction of a lecture will be determined by the age of the audience and the aspects of the hobby that the speaker feels they will find of greatest interest. Thus, for one audience a speaker needs to talk very little. The displays of his or her autographs arranged on tables at the front of the room will suffice. The collector-lecturer can simply conduct a question-and-answer session after the group has been permitted time to examine the displays, or specific autographic specimens can be selected, held up one at a time and discussed. The audience will be interested in knowing how the letter or photograph was obtained, and they'll also expect to hear some interesting facts about the notable. The item can be handed to someone in the front row, to be passed around throughout the audience.

There are certain advantages to this type of presentation. The collector avoids the difficult time consuming work of preparing and becoming comfortably familiar with a formal speech. He or she won't have to worry about being too inexperienced to carry on at length—extemporaneously—in front of an audience of strangers. This procedure also provides the novice speaker with something to hold in his or her hands and an opportunity to move around, picking up items from the displays and handing them to the listeners. This helps to smooth over possible rough spots that may occur when there is a lack of ease and awkward stiffness that so frequently characterizes people who are not used to being at center stage. Most audiences enjoy the opportunity to handle and study the autographs and to ask questions. This activity gives them a sense of participation, which is often more satisfying than plain listening.

There are also disadvantages. All the autographic material must be carefully framed or at least encased in plastic holders to protect the items from the ravages of so much handling. Passing material from person to person is also a distraction. It takes attention away from what the speaker has to say. Too many questions may be asked. The speaker may be unable to answer them all satisfactorily. It's certainly no disgrace to have to say occassionally, "I don't know". But a collector forced, again and again, to admit an inadequacy in knowledge fast loses the respect and confidence of an audience. All too often, even small groups have at least one member who is widely read on a great many subjects, and this person may delight in posing questions designed to rattle a speaker. Don't be misled into believing a question-and-answer session or a "show and tell" procedure is always the easiest for the beginner.

Some collector-lecturers prefer careful advance planning and the rehearsing of a relatively formal speech. Due thought must be given to the selection of anecdotes or personal experiences to be used for illustrating important points. However, this speech should be written only in outline form. Never try to do a word-for-word draft. Once the proposed content is satisfactory, write down the key words and phrases to identify the progression of topics and points in the outline. These should be copied on 3x5 cards. The speaker can hold these small cards inconspicuously in one hand and refer to them when necessary. Certainly this practice results in a more pleasing performance than merely reading from a written script. Lecturing without notes should be avoided, for it's easy to forget a good many important highlights and end up rambling. These small cards containing key word cues can probably be dispensed with after a collector has tested a particular lecture on two or three groups and gained some confidence.

A formal lecture or speech by an autograph expert can be fascinating, but audiences generally will enjoy an opportunity to inspect some of the autograph specimens mentioned in the discussion. Interesting items from the speaker's collection should always be displayed on tables or on a bulletin board. The audience should be invited to examine these *after* the lecture, and the speaker should be available to answer questions on an individual basis. This avoids interruptions during the lecture and does away with distractions caused by passing items from hand to hand in the audience.

The collector engaged to speak to a youth group will find they will want to know how he or she became interested in the hobby of collecting autographs. Most adult audiences also appreciate a certain amount of background narrative of this kind. Boys in particular pay rapt attention to all a speaker says about sports figures, astronauts, famous inventors and scientists. Young listeners of either sex are likely to be interested in the better-known current television and movie stars and the leading lights in the field of popular music.

Giants of literature and history, great composers and artists, generals and kings and queens can all be made equally appealing to teenagers, by the skilled speaker who has a rich storehouse of autograph anecdotes and collecting experiences. Never "talk down" to a young audience. Try to use, in beginning the lecture, some personality or notable of particular interest to them. Such a procedure helps a speaker establish an immediate rapport. Then the transition can be made to other categories of collecting, or the overall subject of collecting autographs as a hobby.

Take into consideration the stated purpose of the organization when adapting a lecture to fit the group. Is it a political club? A church sponsored social group? A professional organization? A community service group? A local civic organization? A high school French or Spanish club? A music appreciation society? A travel club? Any autographic material most in line with the obvious interests of the organization will make for an attention-grabbing opening subject.

The real secret of success in holding the attention of an audience lies not so much in whether the speaker talks about Marie Curie, Ty Cobb, Buffalo Bill, Margaret Mead, Albert Einstein or Babe Ruth, but whether or not the notables discussed are relevant for the occasion. The speaker can overcome many odds by communicating his or her own enthusiasm and expertise on the topic under discussion. To the outsider, any unfamiliar hobby is like a closed room. How is the door opened initially? What keys does the listener need? What are the costs involved? And what rewards can be realized upon entering the room? These are all questions a lecturer should consider in advance.

14. Proper Care of Autographs

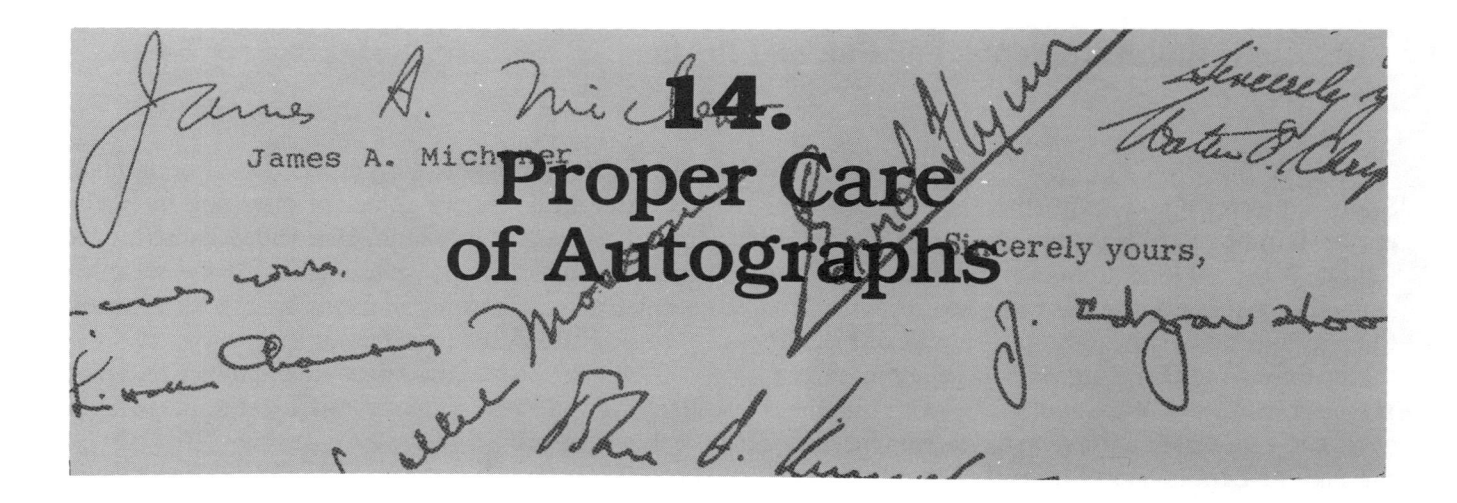

The most effective way to keep autographic specimens in prime condition is to store them in a warm, dry, safe place. The collector should refrain from handling them unnecessarily. This is the recommended procedure for dealing with extremely valuable and rare historical material costing hundreds, perhaps thousands of dollars. The same rules are advisable for the more unusual and potentially valuable modern items in a collection. The ideal storage place fulfilling these specifications would certainly be a safe-deposit box. They are readily available at any bank for a moderate fee, and provide a collector with a guaranteed safe repository for prized autographs.

However, for every collector who accumulates high-priced specimens largely as an investment, there are hundreds of others who collect less costly autographs purely as a hobby, for personal pleasure and diversion. If autographs are something to be enjoyed in solitude or shown off to interested friends and perhaps loaned to a club or library for exhibit, they still need to be protected or they will go downhill in value. Unprotected or carelessly stored autographic specimens soon become warped, wrinkled, torn, discolored, smudged or stained.

An album is a satisfactory means of storing signed photographs and letters as well as most other autographic materials. This is also the best possible way to show a collection to friends without subjecting the items to rough or undue handling. One good album for storing and displaying autographs has a perforated page interleaved between each of two permanent sheets of soft backing paper. Every time a new photograph or letter is added, the detachable perforated sheet is removed and thrown away. The end result is an album that doesn't bulge. Photographs should be mounted in the album with regular photograph corner mountings. Never use glue! Then, any desired photograph or other autograph can easily be removed at any time.

Photographs and various other autographic items can also be stored in a sturdy loose-leaf binder fitted with double, clear plastic sheets, inside which the specimens can be inserted. Certain sheets are made to fit 3x5 cards or 5x7 photographs, etc. Other sheets accomodate photographs and autographs up to 8x10 in size. Larger autographic materials are better mounted in the type of album suggested in the preceding paragraph. Material in a loose-leaf binder of plastic sheets can be safely passed around for viewing without the risk of fingerprints, smudging, or other damage. And any item can easily be removed and replaced at will.

A manila file folder or even an envelope of appropriate size offers protection for material not likely to be handled frequently. These should be stored flat, one on top of the other, in a cool, dry, protected place such as a roomy drawer or closet shelf. Use a large heavy book as a weight to prevent the photographs and other autographic material from curling.

For smaller items—whether these are photographs, cut signatures, or cards of various sorts—a metal or plastic box for filing 3x5 index cards is useful. Such a box offers protection against dust, dampness and rough handling. It also provides an easy system for keeping smaller specimens in alphabetical order, for handy reference.

Such file boxes come in larger sizes also. Some collectors prefer putting their folders of material in boxes rather than storing them flat on a shelf. When folders of photographs are frequently slipped in and out of the file box, the constant shuffling in and out of the box and in and out of the folder may rub off the signatures to some extent. A collector must take particular care with them and try not to cram such a file overfull as this increases the risk of bending photograph corners. Folders shouldn't be so loosely packed that the material will slide out of place or have room to curl. The extra care needed for the proper use of a metal file box for large material is the major reason flat storage is considered safer.

Overzealous in protecting autograph trophies, a novice may mistakenly attempt to preserve a signature by covering it with clear tape. This is a foolish practice! It deters from the value of the autograph. No one would even accept such a specimen in trade, for when an attempt is made to remove the covering tape, most of the signature is likely to be torn from a card or lifted from a photograph.

There are good plastic sprays on the market. To judge from their advertising claims, they guarantee lifetime protection to almost anything on which they are applied. Collectors take heed! If such a product is sprayed on your autographic specimens, the present and future value of the collection will be destroyed—even though you may have protected it from dust and dirt and some of the wear and tear of handling.

Picture frames are another effective means of protecting and displaying autographed photographs and other material of appropriate dimensions and content. Having everything in a sizable collection professionally mounted and framed is not economically feasible. The expense may be worthwhile only for a few especially interesting or valuable items for permanent display in the home. A collector can pick up inexpensive picture frames in any discount store, and find a variety of used frames at local flea markets. Collectors willing to devote a bit of time and effort to the task, however, can make suitable frames for autographed photographs and letters quite inexpensively and successfully. Do-it-yourself framing requires patience and care, but no great degree of skill. The necessary materials are as follows:

1. Poster paper. This can be obtained in plain white or in a variety of interesting colors.
2. Roll of cellophane. One roll will suffice for the framing of many specimens. Plastic wrap or similar products found in any store also work well.
3. Roll of transparent tape.
4. Cardboard cartons or sheets to use as a stiff backing material. Check your local supermarket or liquor store.
5. Rubber-base cement. This doesn't seep through to stain the poster-paper frame, nor will it tear the photograph if it must be removed from the frame for any reason.
6. Box of small gold stars. These can be used to denote rank when the autograph subject is an armed forces notable.
7. Flags cut from old encyclopedias or an atlas. These can be used to denote the nationality of a foreign celebrity.

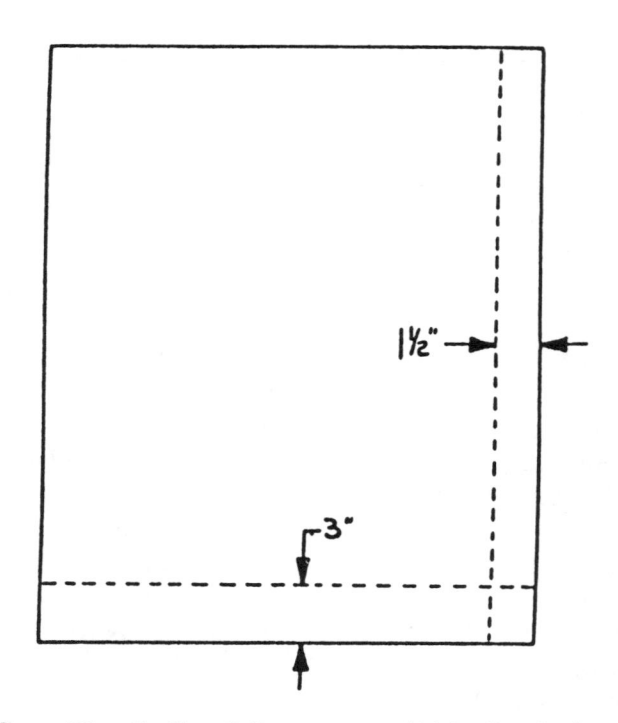

Step No. 1: Carefully measure 1½ inches in from the side and 3 inches up from the bottom of the poster paper. Draw a very light, but legible dotted line as shown here.

Proper Care of Autographs 141

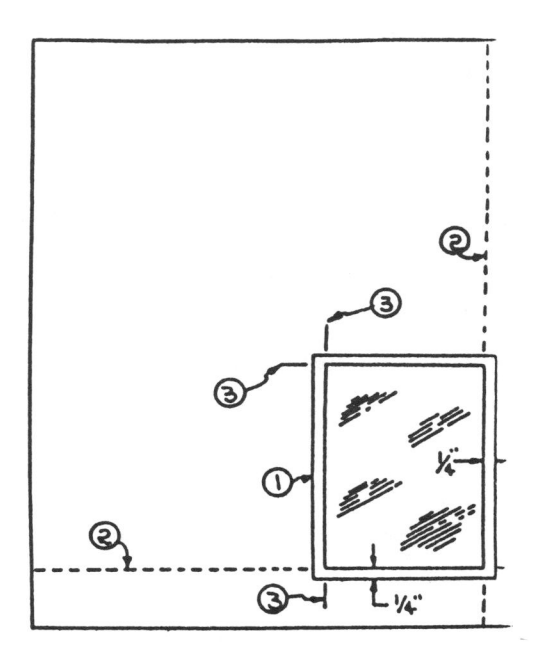

Step No. 2: Lay the photograph (1) on the poster paper. Let its edge overlap the dotted guidelines (2) by at least ¼ inch. Draw fine lines (3) just inside the outer edges of the picture. This will insure a proper fit when the frame is done.

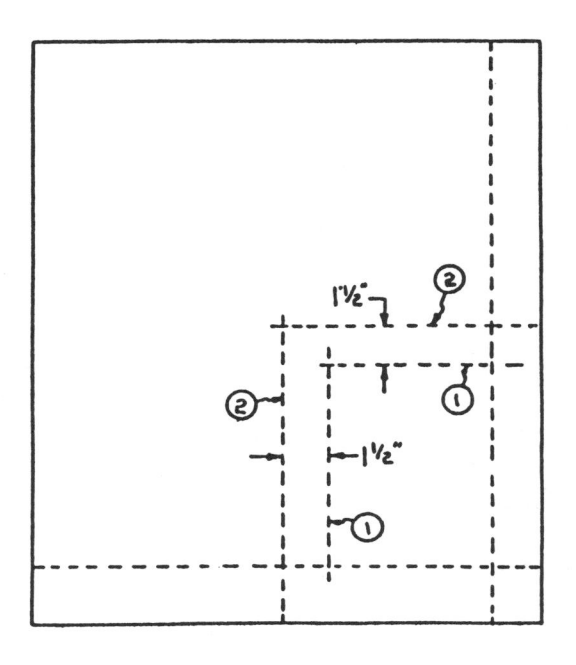

Step No. 3: Make dotted lines (1) to denote the inner border of the frame. Measure out from these lines as denoted. Then draw dotted lines (2) for the outer edges or border of the frame.

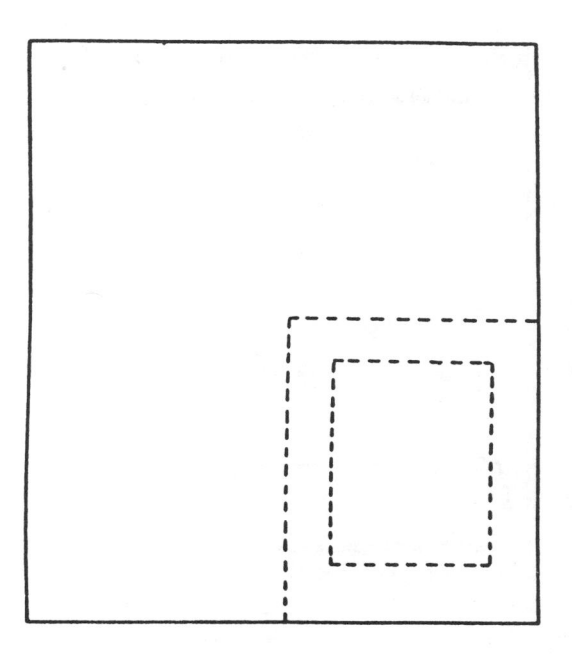

Step No. 4: Carefully cut the completed poster paper frame along the dotted lines.

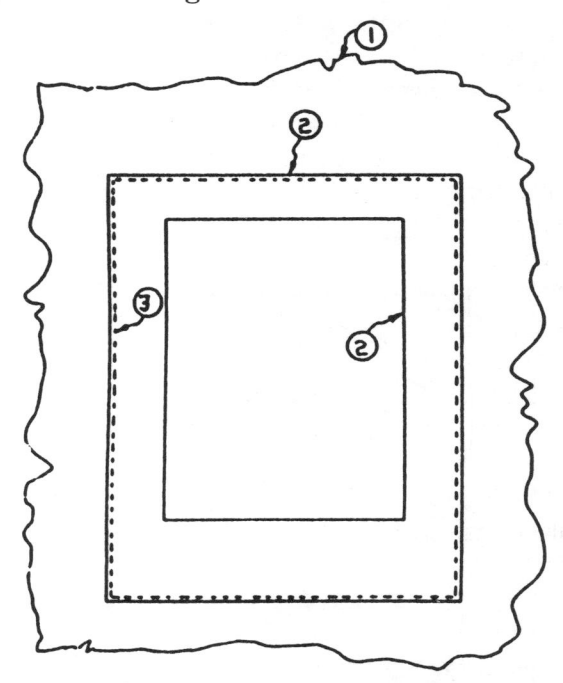

Step No. 5: Lay the completed basic frame on a piece of heavy cardboard (1). Draw a line around all four of the inner and outer (2) edges of the frame. Lift off the frame. Cut out the heavy cardboard about ¼ inch inside (3) the lines just drawn around the *outer* edges of the frame. Be sure to cut inside these lines so the cardboard backing will not show in the finished framed photograph.

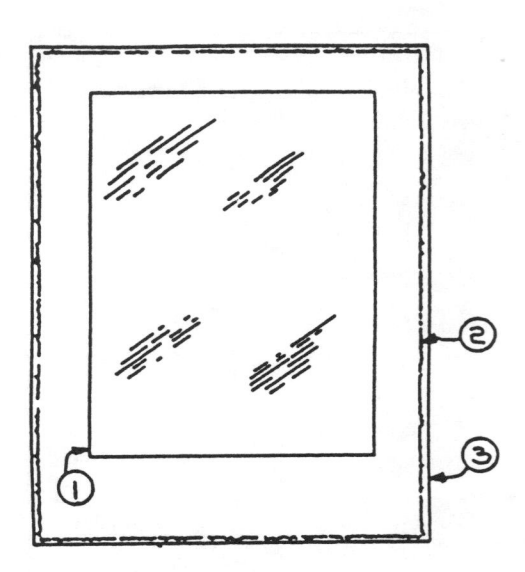

Step No. 6: Using rubber base cement, touch each of the four corners on the back of the autographed photograph (1). Now lay the picture, centered squarely, over the four guidelines marking the inner border of the frame. Spread cement in a fine line (2) all around the edge (3) of the cardboard backing, where it extends beyond the photograph. Put the poster-paper frame on top, again making sure to center precisely. Press all edges firmly.

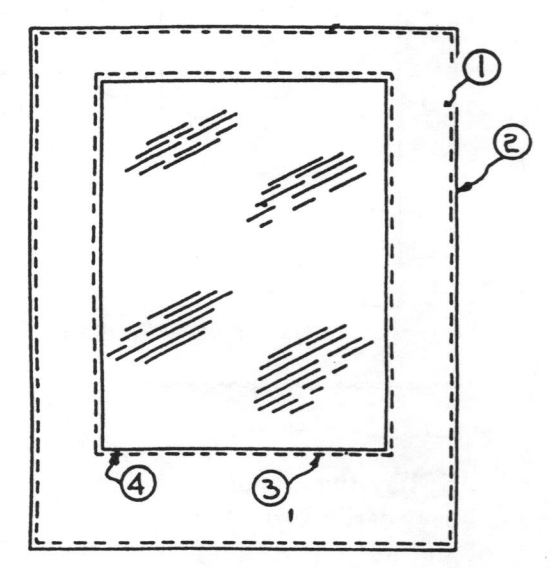

Step No. 7: The completed frame. The position of the cardboard backing is denoted by the dotted lines (1). The poster-paper frame is (2). The photograph can be seen as (3), and the inner frame line (4).

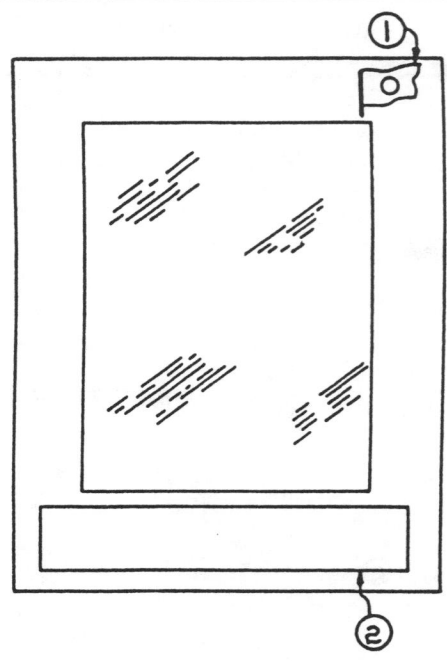

Step No. 8: Colorful decorative touches can be added to the framed photograph—gold stars to denote the rank of military leaders, for instance. A flag sticker (1) can be used to denote the nationality of a foreign notable. A typed thumbnail biography (2) of the celebrity can be neatly glued into place.

The caption suggested in the last illustration can consist of a thumbnail biographical sketch of the autographic subject. If the major facts of the notable's career are widely known—merely add a couple of highlights. The addition of a caption provides the collector with a handy source of quick reference details. It also makes it unnecessary to answer numerous questions about the subject when others view the photograph.

After the eight framing steps have been completed, it's time to add the protective cellophane wrapping. Unroll a sufficient amount of cellophane. Lay the framed autograph on this, face down. Cut the cellophane about 1½ inches longer and wider than the frame. Fold over the edge of the frame. Secure the cellophane to the cardboard backing at the center of one side with a small strip of tape. Then secure both corners of the same side. Pull the cellophane taut to insure a uniform, wrinkle-free covering before taping it to the cardboard backing on the opposite side. Repeat the procedure with the cellophane folded over at the top and at the bottom of the frame.

The initial few frames the collector makes will take more time than later ones. It takes a little practice to become used to the process. Frame-making can be speeded up further by first sorting all the autographic specimens according to size. Then cut the required number of frames of the same size at one time.

Letters and photographs from literary greats can be effectively displayed by adapting the framing instructions already given. Simply use a little ingenuity and make the poster-paper frame resemble a book. The only additional equipment that will be needed is an ordinary black felt tip pen and a beveled-edge ruler. The accompanying illustration shows the suggested format.

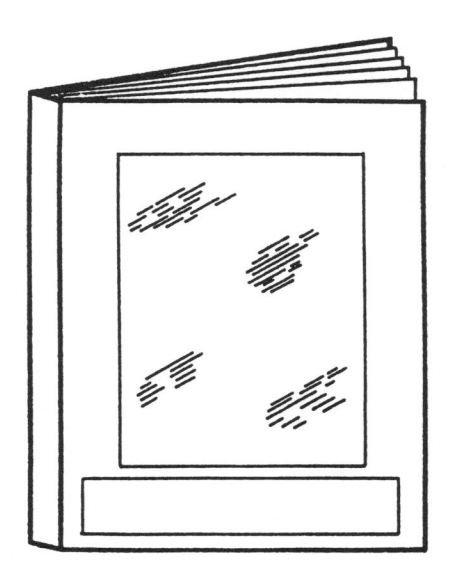

Sometimes a letter or a document is in such sad condition that the autograph may be ruined if some action isn't take immediately. The collector is justified in attempting whatever remedies are within his or her skill. However, unless training and experience have made you an expert in this field, never attempt a major restoration. Amateur efforts will all too often ruin what one is trying to save. Seek the assistance of a large library. In most cases they will have both the equipment and the trained personnel required for dealing with these problems. If the library staff can't do the job themselves, they can recommend a reliable restorer. Some libraries will make repairs for a fee, but most take care of only their own materials. The average autograph dealer ranks right along with the ordinary collector when it comes to restoration. He or she is generally not competent in this field, but through a vast knowledge of the autographic market, the dealer may be able to suggest qualified experts. No matter how terrible the condition of a specimen appears to the novice, there is always something that can be done to improve the state of disrepair.

If autographs get wet, separate them carefully. Place each specimen or sheet between two dry white blotters. When most of the excess moisture has been absorbed by the blotters, remove the autographic material. Lay the still-damp sheet on a fresh blotter. Place a clean sheet of paper on top. Press firmly with a warm iron until the specimen underneath is dry.

If an autograph is wrinkled or has deep creases from previous folding, lay it on the bathroom vanity. Run the hot water until the room is steamy. The paper will absorb enough moisture from the damp air to make it limp. Always lay the autographic material on a porcelain or glass surface to avoid discoloraton. Then place the specimen between two clean white blotters and weigh it down with heavy books until it is completely dry.

For stains on autographic material, the following solvents are recommended in "The Repair and Preservation of Records," Bulletin No. 5 of the National Archives. Usually, though, it's preferable to let an expert decide which cleaning methods should be employed on valuable historical material and whether or not cleaning should be attempted in the first place.

Stain	Solvent
Adhesive tape	Benzene or carbon tetrachloride
Duco cement	Acetone
Glue (linen or glassine tape)	Warm water
Lacquer	Acetone
Oil	Benzene or carbon tetrachloride
Paint	Mixture of benzene and alcohol
Paste	Water
Rubber cement	Mixture of toluene and benzene
Scotch tape	Mixture of toluene and benzene
Shellac	Ethyl alcohol
Wax	Mixture of toluene and be

A tear must be given temporary repair to prevent further damage to the autographic material. Use only white tissue paper as reinforcement or backing. Fasten this tissue with library paste on the back side of the sheet only. This paste will not leave a stain. The tissue can be removed easily by the expert who eventually makes the professional repair.

The following nine rules may be second nature to experienced collectors as most are simply common sense. They are listed here for the sake of the young beginner whose enthusiasm may sometimes outweigh good judgment:

1. Never glue autographic material in a scrapbook. Glue leaves stains and also helps deteriorate the items.

2. Never use plastic sprays, varnish or shellac to cover and preserve any kind of autographic specimens.

3. Never cut *anything* out of a letter or a document.

4. Never make marks or notations of any kind on a letter, document, photograph, or other kind of autographic material.

5. Never use paper clips or rubber bands on autographic specimens. Paper clips eventually rust and rubber bands rot. Both will leave unsightly stains.

6. Never store autographed photographs or other materials in a damp place. Mold forms quickly and will seriously discolor the item.

7. Never leave autographic material in direct sunlight. Don't do this even if the specimens are covered with glass. The sun will discolor the paper and fade the script.

8. Never fold letters or other autographic materials. Never store specimens in such a manner as to create wrinkles and creases.

9. Never undertake any but the most minor repairs without first consulting an expert. And on especially valuable autographic materials, leave all such measures in the hands of the experts.

15. Record-Keeping

As the new collector sends out his or her first dozen or so autograph requests, the necessity and importance of record-keeping seldom comes to mind. Some sort of system should be initiated early—and it should be updated constantly. The blithe beginner also is usually unconcerned about the methods and means of caring for and storing a growing collection. At the start it's difficult to realize how quickly the new hobby can expand, how much storage space it may soon require, and how easily certain autographic material can be misplaced or buried among other prizes.

Some kind of record-keeping is essential for every autograph collector. As the years pass and a collection expands, the hobbyist inevitably forgets or confuses at least some of the pertinent details about his or her acquisitions. No matter how good a collector's memory may be, signed photos, notes and letters can easily be lost and forgotten. Accurate records are also invaluable whenever a collection or a single item are to be traded or sold.

When starting to collect by using the mail service, a loose-leaf notebook will be adequate. Separate pages may be assigned to each category, and

Former prince and princess of Siam, now recognized as Thailand. These photos were sent to the author when the couple visited the Untied States duirng 1953.

145

additional pages can be inserted as the collection grows. Pages can be assigned to each personality, if the collector proposes to accumulate several types of autographic specimens from one source. The above illustration of sample entries from a "WORLD LEADERS" category shows a practical format. This can be varied according to the needs of the individual collector. When an autograph request is mailed, the date is written in the block provided. The results—when a reply is received—are recorded in the designated space. If no reply is forthcoming after a few months' wait, the earnest collector should write the notable again. Persistence usually pays off in the long run.

Another simple method of keeping decent records can be accomplished by using convenient 3x5 file cards and a sturdy metal file box. When a personality of interest is mentioned in a newspaper or magazine article, jot down the name on one of these cards. File the cards in the box alphabetically, by the person's last name. When time permits, look up his or her address in the reference section of your local library. (See chapter 3 for suggestions). When mailing off an autograph request, note the date on the card, and when a reply comes, fill in all the other details.

Either of these methods of record-keeping can also be employed when autographs are ordered from a dealer or traded to another collector. Of course, a line or column should be allotted for recording the price paid, and also one for noting the condition of the item.

NATION AND CAPITAL	HEAD OF STATE AND TITLE	PROGRESS
Afghanistan (Kabul)	Babrak Karmal, President	Date sent 6-8-81 Results 4"x5" S.P.
Albania	Haxhi Lleshi, President	Date sent 4-5-75 Results A.L.S. & 8"x10" S.P.
Algeria (Algiers)	Chadli Benedjedid, President	Date sent 2-7-82 Results A.N.S. & 5"x7" S.P.

Record-keeping 147

MAILED REQUESTS

NAME *Averill, Howard Earl*

ADDRESS *914-4th, #6, Snohomish, WA. 98290*

DATE REQUESTED *1-4-83* DATE RECEIVED *1-22-83*

WHAT RECEIVED *(2) 3"x5" Plaque Cards; (2) 2"x3" Photos*

APPROX. MARKET VALUE *Plaque Cards: $4-8; Photos: $3-5*

COMMENTS *Elected to Baseball Hall of Fame 1975. He died at 81 with pneumonia, Aug. 16, 1983 in Everett, Washington.*

Hall of Famer Earl Averill was always most generous in givin gout autographs to his many fans. Prior to his death on August 16, 1983, Earl signed two plaque cards sent to him by the author. Included with their return were two extra 2x3 photos.

                    PURCHASED FROM DEALER

NAME *Speer, Albert*   ITEM *5"x7" S.P.*

DEALER *Conway Barker*   PRICE *$35.00*

DATE ORDERED *5-23-83*   RECEIVED *5-30-83*

CONDITION *Excellent*   RARITY *Quite*

COMMENTS *Speer was Hitler's architect during the rise of Nazi Germany. He went to prison on war crimes charges*

16. Helpful Sources and Other Data

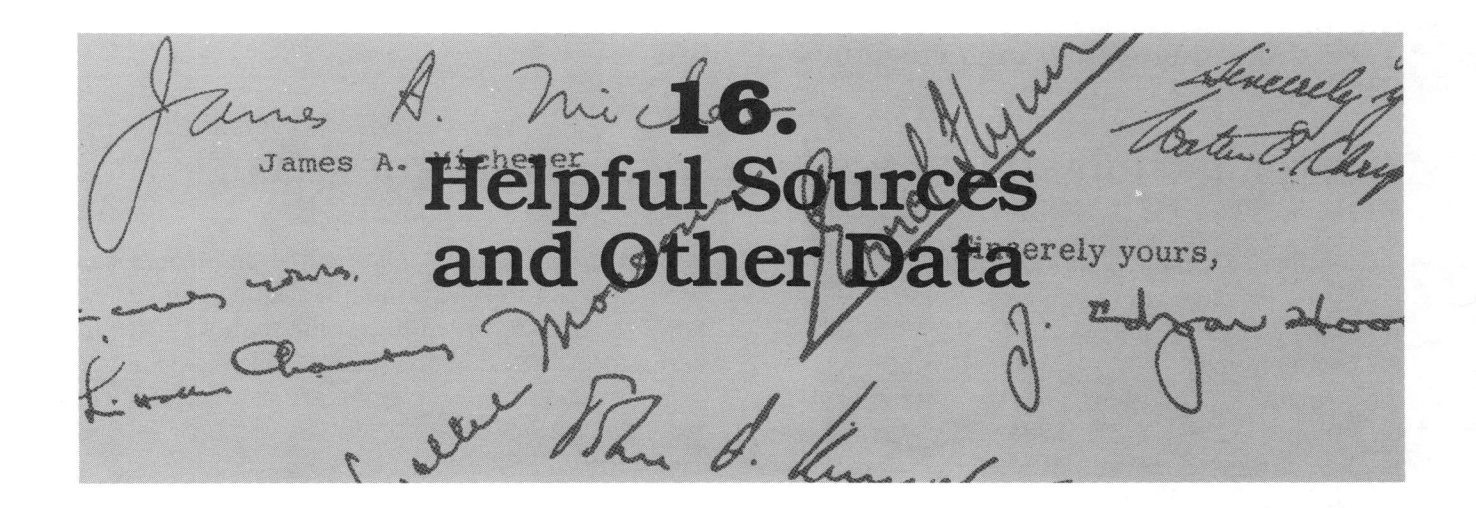

REPUTABLE DEALERS IN AUTOGRAPHIC MATERIALS

The dealers listed below sell, trade and purchase all types of autographs. They're always interested in signatures, old family papers, historical documents, signed photographs, manuscripts of all sorts, letters and other correspondence, ledgers, diaries, journals, and various other items of interest. Older historical items are of special interest, but contemporary artists, statesmen, military leaders, scientists, composers, authors, poets and the like will also be considered.

A reputable dealer will offer material to prospective buyers on an approval basis. They always guarantee any item sold through the mail. Such experts know current values and their experience and knowledge enable them to determine the rarity of the material they handle. They are able to recognize facsimiles and forgeries and they will offer assistance in locating excellent material at a fair price to build a nice collection.

Conway Barker, P.O. Box 30625, Dallas, TX 75203. (214-358-3786). Mr. Barker will send collectors a free regularly updated list of autographic items he has for sale.

Walter R. Benjamin Autographs, Inc., P.O. Box 255, Scribner Hollow Road, Hunter, NY 12442. (518-263-4133 or 4134). This large firm offers a subscription of six copies of *The Collector* for $10.00. The fee can be used as a credit toward a first purchase of $50.00 or more. Their publication contains valuable information on many areas of autograph collecting, and has a well-organized section describing current autographic material for sale.

Dana's House, P.O. Box 30370, Royal Lane Station, Dallas, TX 75230. (214-238-9933). Offers an excellent list, free, of current autographic material for sale.

Gallery of Champions, 504 South Beach Blvd, No. 116, Anaheim, CA 92804. (714-995-2229). Will send, on request, a current list of autographic items for sale. They specialize in sports.

National Pastime, The, 93 Iselin Drive, New Rochelle, NY 10804. (914-576-1755 or 212-224-1795). Call only between 4:00 PM and 8:00 PM (EST) as these are the hours designated for special telephone orders. They'll send their current list of available autographic sports material. Many deceased Hall of Famers as well as other baseball greats can be obtained at extremely reasonable prices.

P.M. Antiques & Collectibles, P.O. Box 224, Coffeyville, KS 67337. (316-251-5308). This firm will send a current list of available sports and other autographic material. They often offer seasonal specials on their materials. Here a collector can find many excellent autographs mostly at reasonable prices. Recent offerings included 8x10 signed photographs of Hall of Famer Luke Appling and Jocko Conlan at only $5.00 apiece and 20 different autographed Hall of Fame plaque cards for a $20.00 price tag. Also holds interesting through-the-mail autograph auctions quite regularly.

USEFUL REFERENCE BOOKS FOR THE COLLECTOR

Abbat, William. *The Colloquial Who's Who —1600-1924* (two volumes), New York: Publisher unknown, 1924-1925. An excellent reference book on psuedonyms.

Appleton's Cyclopaedia of American Biography (7 volumes), New York. 1886-1889. This set of books contains hundreds of signature specimens of American celebrities.

Benjamin, Mary A. *Autographs: A Key to collecting*. R.R. Bowker Co. 1946. A classic guide to autograph collecting.

Broadley, A.M. *Chats on Autographs*. London, 1910. This book contains excellent illustrative material and good basic information on the hobby of autograph collecting.

Flower, D. and A.N.L. Munby. *English Poetical Autographs*. London: Publisher unknown, 1938. This book contains reproductions of 46 manuscripts ranging from Sir Thomas Wyatt to Rupert Brooke.

Geigy, Charles. *Handbook of Famous Personages*. London: Basle, 1925. The most comprehensive single volume known. The scripts of over 1200 persons, eminent in every walk of life, are beautifully illustrated in this book.

Greg, W.W. *English Literary Autographs 1550-1650* (three volumes), London: Oxford, 1925-1932. This series of books is considered to be the classic in its field. Contains facsimile autographic material of over 130 British authors.

Hamilton, Charles. *collecting Autographs and Manuscripts*. University of Oklahoma Press, Norman, Oklahoma. 1961. Contains excellent facsimiles.

Madigan, Thomas F. *Word Shadows of the Great*. New York, 1930. Excellent introduction to autograph collecting as a hobby.

Scott, Henry T. *Autograph collecting*. London. 1894. Contains excellent autographic facsimiles and reveals numerous interesting details about collecting.

Stonehill, Charles A. Jr., Andrew Block and H. Winthrop Stonehill. *Anonyma and Pseudonyma* (four volumes). New York: R.R. Bowker Company, 1927. An excellent reference book on famous people who chose to use pseudonyms.

PERIODICALS OF VALUE TO THE COLLECTOR

Antique Trader, The. Billed as "America's Widest Used Publication on Antiques and Collector's Items." Many autographic materials are offered for sale in this publication's classified advertising section. Subscriptions are available. Write to: The Antique Trader Weekly, P.O. Box 1050, Dubuque, IA 52001.

Current Biography. A monthly publication that can be found in almost all libraries, or obtained through subscription. Check your local library.

PHOTOGRAPH AND BASEBALL CARD SOURCES

Den's Collectors Den, P.O. Box 606, Laurel, MD 20707. (301-792-0955 or 301-766-3900). Excellent color and black-and-white photographs of many old-time as well as current sports stars. They also sell various inexpensive card sets suitable for autographing, including "Baseball Immortals" and "All Time Greats."

National Baseball Hall of Fame, Cooperstown, NY 13326. (607-547-9988). They sell complete sets of official Hall of Fame plaque cards at reasonable prices. Single cards are also available.

Perez-Steele Galleries, P.O. Box 1776, Fort Washington, PA 19034. (215-836-1192). Write for information on their complete limited edition collection of Hall of Fame art postcards. These are by far the finest cards available for autographing.

SPECIAL ORGANIZATION FOR COLLECTORS

The Manuscript Society is an international organization of autograph collectors. Its purpose is described as follows: "To foster the greater use of original source manuscript material in the study, teaching and writing of history . . . To facilitate the exchange of information and knowledge among researchers, scholars and collectors . . . To encourage the meeting of autograph collectors and stimulate and aid them in their various collecting specialties." There is an annual membership fe Check your local library for the current ad

Appendix: A Collector's Glossary

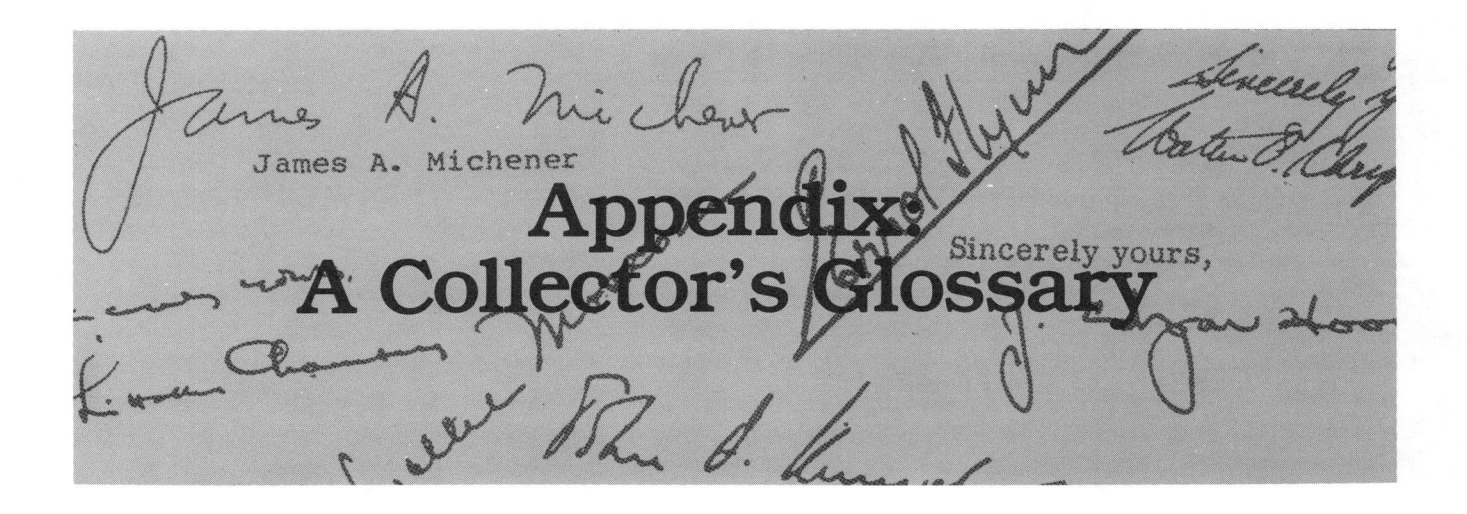

The catalogs, brochures and lists published by autograph dealers and auction houses in the United States, Canada and Great Britain use certain standard abbreviations and definitions in describing autographic material they have for sale. Every autograph collector should become familiar with the most common of these, for they're also used regularly by fellow hobbyists. Having knowledge of these terms will save much time and effort when placing an order through the mail or in other correspondence about autographs: it will also help you to avoid misunderstandings when purchasing autographs.

The word *autograph* is derived from two Greek words: *autos* (self) + *grapho* or *graphein* (to write). Used outside the collecting hobby, the word autograph signifies only a signature written in the person's own hand. Used by collectors, the term denotes any inscription made by hand, anything handwritten, or any writing in a person's own hand, as follows:

- A signature alone
- A page of handwriting
- An unsigned handwritten letter
- An artist's sketch
- Musical notation
- A printed or typed document signed by its originator
- Deeds, wills, or any other handwritten documents.

The word *holograph* is also derived from two Greek words: *holos* (whole) + *grapho* or *graphein* (to write). A holograph is precisely speaking, the correct term for a letter or a document written entirely in the signer's own hand. At one time it was the common British word for an autograph. In the United States, however, *autograph* has always been the word most commonly and widely used by collectors and dealers. The word *holograph* is considered somewhat pretentious, and today *autograph* takes precedence universally.

SPECIAL ABBREVIATIONS USED BY COLLECTORS

Each of these designations signify the entire letter, document, manuscript, card, quote, or note was handwritten by the signer. "A" or "Auto" may be used interchangeably. For example, A.Ms.S may also be found listed as Auto.Ms.S.

A.C.S.	Autograph card signed
A.D.S. or A.Doc.S.	Autograph document signed
A.L.S.	Autograph letter signed
A.Ms.S.	Autograph manuscript signed
A.Mss.S.	Autograph manuscripts signed
A.N.S.	Autograph note signed
A.Q.S.	Autograph quote signed

These abbreviations denote only the signature is in the handwriting of the author or signer. The body of the autographic specimen may be in the hand of another individual, a printed form, or typewritten.

C.S.	Card signed
D.S. or Doc.S.	Document signed
L.S.	Letter signed
Ms.S.	Manuscript signed

Sincerely,

[signature]

James C. Hagerty
Press Secretary to the President

[signature: George F. Kennan]

[signature: Helena Rubinstein]

Sincerely,

[signature]

John L. McClellan

[signature: Nelson A. Rockefeller]

[signature: W. S. Maugham]

THE WHITE HOUSE
WASHINGTON

[signature: Bette Davis]

with best wishes

[signature: Dwight D. Eisenhower]

[signature: Barry Goldwater]

[signature]

[signature: Maurice H. Stans]

[signature: Bobby Riggs]

[signature: Sargent Shriver]

[signature]
Hubert H. Humphrey

Sincerely,

[signature]
Governor

[signature: Chet Huntley]

Appendix: A Collector's Glossary   153

Mss.S. Manuscripts signed
N.S. Note signed
Q.S. Quote signed
T.L.S. Typed letter signed
T.Ms.S. Typed manuscript signed
T.Mss.S. Typed manuscripts signed

Other Standard Abbreviations Used by Collectors

d/w dust wrapper
g.e. gilt edged
mtd. mounted
n.d. no date
n.p. no place
n.y. no year
p. one page
pp. pages
port. portrait
pres. president
ptd. printed
sec. secretary
sig. signature
sgd. signed
sm. small
SP Signed photograph
sq. square
T.E.G. Top edge gilt
trans. translation
v.d. various dates
vol. one volume
vols. volumes
w.ad.sh. with address sheet (the back page of the last sheet, the location of the address before envelopes were in vogue).
w.env. with the original stamped envelope
wm. watermark

AUTOGRAPH SIZE DESIGNATIONS USED BY COLLECTORS

Duodecimo (commonly listed as 12mo): Equal to ½ octavo or about 3x4 in size.

Sextodecimo (commonly listed as 16mo): Equal to ¼ octavo or about 1½x2 in size.

Octavo (commonly listed as 8vo): 5x7 to 6x9 in size.

Quarto (commonly listed as 4to): 7x9 to 9x12 in size.

Folio (commonly listed as fol.): 12x16 in size. This would include anything the size of legal stationery.

Giant Folio: four to eight times as large as folio.

Elephant Folio: Used to denote enormous sheets or pages.

Atlas Folio: The same as Elephant folio.

Standard sizes of autographed photographs: 3x5; 4x6; 5x7; 8x10; and 11x14 in size.

DOCUMENTS, MANUSCRIPTS, LETTERS, AND NOTES—THEIR DIFFERENCES

Every collector should know the specific differences between a manuscript and a document and between a note and a letter. They are as follows:

Manuscript: Either handwritten or typed material for a book. This can be a collection of poems, songs, or speeches. Technically, letters are the most common form of manuscripts.

Document: An official paper of any type. An impersonal communication or correspondence. A record (diary, deed, etc.).

Note: An impersonal correspondence or communication in most cases, although it could be personal at times. Any message *not* beginning with a salutation and *not* ending with a subscription and a signature.

Letter: A personal correspondence or communication. This can be any message beginning with a salutation and ending with a subscription and a signature. This rule holds true regardless of the length of the material or on what it is written.

Other Important Definitions Used by Collectors

Contemporary Copy: A copy of the original material made at the same time the original was written, or within a short period thereafter.

Cut signature: A signature standing alone that was cut away from a letter, manuscript, document, card, book, etc.

Docketed: Bearing a notation made and signed or initialed by the recipient or his agent. This sometimes gives the origin of the material. It often explains the content. It may provide other information, such as the date the autographic material was received.

Fine: In autograph collecting, this word is used to denote the specific material's desirability as a collector's item in comparison with other items from the same source. For example, a handwritten copy of the Gettysburg Address would be described as "fine" to indicate it is more desirable than most other Lincoln items. "Fine" is *not* normally used to characterize the physical condition of the particular autograph.

M.C.: Designates all senators and representatives who have been in the United States Congress since 1787 when the Constitution was adopted.

M.O.C.: Designates any member of the Old Congress. This is better known as the Continental Congress, in session from September 1774, to March, 1789. This term is used when an A.L.S. or a L.S. by one of these men is offered for sale.

Modern: Any autographic material dating from the sixteenth century to the present.

Oblong (obl.): Long narrow sheets (no size limitations). The size of an oblong sheet is more clearly defined in catalog listings by specifying "oblong quarto" (obl. 4to) or "oblong folio" (obl. fol.).

Old: All autographic material dating from the fifteenth century or earlier. In the United States, however, all material preceding 1650 is considered "old."

Page: One side of a sheet. A letter advertised as three pages in length could have one sheet written on both sides and a second sheet written on only one side. Or the letter may consist of three sheets of paper, each of which is written on only one side.

Provenance: The historical background and previous ownership of certain autographic material. A buyer of real estate gets a thorough title search conducted to determine the previous owners of the property from deed to deed. So can the ownership and past history of autographic items be traced from generation to generation of owners, in order to prove authenticity.

Provenience: The same as above.

Signature: A person's name signed only by himself or herself. This is never a name signed by a secretary or a machine. The term *signature* always implies an original, not a photocopy or a photograph of the original.

SIGNER (or SIGNERS): Spelled in all capital letters in almost all cases, but sometimes only the first letter is capitalized. This denotes the men who signed the Declaration of Independence. *SIGNER* is also used to designate the men who signed the Constitution of the United States. In this case the phrase "of the Constitution" is always added. Lower case letters are always used *(signer)* to indicate the signer of *any* other document—the United Nations Charter or the League of Nations Charter, etc.

Sleeper: A valuable autograph, but one most collectors might overlook. Such an item is sometimes unappreciated simply through an oversight. Or its owner may not have recognized or noticed its unique features. For example, the author picked up a copy of Ulysses S. Grant's autobiography at a flea market auction for $20.00. The identical autographed book was listed at the time in a dealer's catalog for $250.

Special Punctuation Used by Collectors

Certain punctuation marks have special meanings in the listings found in autograph catalogs. *Parentheses* around a person's name always denote the individual didn't write or even sign the material in question. Instead, the autographic material contains something written about the person. Or it may only refer to the notable.

Brackets around a date [1856] indicate the author of the item didn't affix the date at the time of the writing. The date was added at a later time by a collector after he or she had determined the proper date through research. In essence, brackets can be safely taken to mean a probable date.

Index

A

A.L.S., 27
Aaron, Henry Louis "Hank", 105, 111, 112, 129
Abbreviations used by collectors, 151, 153
Acheson, Dean, 50
Actors, 61-2
Actresses, 61-2
Adams, Abigail, 66, 76
Adcock, Joe, 128, 132
Addresses, forms of: government officials, 31-3; foreign heads of state, 33-4; military leaders, 33; royalty, 33
Adenauer, Konrad, 47
Address sources for collectors, 34
Akers, Jack Delane, 122
Albertype plaque cards, 83
Albums, autograph, origin of, 14
Alexander, Grover Cleveland, 85
Alexandria, 14
Ali, Muhammad, 37
Allen, Ethan, 66
Allison, Bob, 128
Alston, Walter Emmons "Walt", 106
American Antiquarian, The 18
American History, 65-9
American League, 119, 124; teams, addresses, 117-8
American Men of Science, 34
American Revolution, 65
American writers, 58-61
Amherst College, 77
Amsterdam University Library, 18
Anderson, John, 44
Anderson, Marian, 38
Anonyma and Pseudonyma, 150
Antique stores, 50
Antique Trader, 150
Aparicio, Luis Ernest Aparicio, 109, 111, 160
Appleton's Cyclopaedia of American Biography, 150
Appling, Lucius Benjamin "Luke", 95, 111
Aquinas, St. Thomas, 18
Arabs, 13
Arbuckle, Fatty, 37
Archives, National, 50
Aristotle, 17
Armstrong, Neil, 16
Army Photographic Agency, U.S., 50
Arnold, Benedict, 18, 66
Arthur, Ellen, 66
Artvue plaque cards, 83
Ashburn, Don Richard, 120
Ashmead, Henry B., 18
Athletic teams, autograph requests of, 115-6
Atlanta Braves, 118
Auctions, 53
Audubon, John James, 60
Autobiography, Benjamin Franklin, 17
Autograph albums, origin, 14
Autograph collecting, 20, 150; commercialization, 18; history, 13, 14, 18; specializing, 35; research, 35;
Autograph collector organization, 150
Autograph dealers, 149-50
Autograph hobby, abuse of, 10
Autograph, collector's definition of, 151
Autographs: A Key to Collecting, 150
Autographs: address sources for collectors, 34; authenticity, 26, 54; care of, 139-40, 143-4; catalogs, 18, 19; definition, 13; exhibiting, 135-8; historic value, 16; lecturing about, 136-8; mounting, 140-4; obtaining, 21-5; of lasting interest, 56-7; photographic facsimile, 26; record-keeping of, 145-8; times to request, 24; trading, 10; value of, 53-70, 74, 77; written requests, 24-5
Autopen signatures, 72-3
Averill, Earl, 101, 147

B

Bagby, James Charles Jacob Jr., 127, 132
Bainbridge, William, 66
Baker, Floyd Wilson, 127, 132
Baker, George, 44
Baker, John Franklin "Homerun", 91
Bakker, Jim, 69
Baltimore Orioles, 117, 124, 128
Bancroft, David James, 97
Bancroft, George, 77
Banks, Ernest "Ernie", 102, 109, 111
Barker, Bob, 38
Barker, Conway, 149
Barney, Rex Edward, 128, 132
Barrow, Ed, 83, 90
Barrymore, John, 61
Bartell, Dick, 129, 132
Baruch, Bernard, 28-9
Baseball: autographs, value of, 83-106; card sources, 150; career leaders, addresses, 119-20; Hall of Fame, 83, 107, 109, 117, 119, 150; Most Valuable Players, addresses of, 123-6; old-timers, 127-34; players, addresses, 111-4; stars, 36-7; Writers' Association of America, 123
Baylor, Donald Eugene, 124
Bearden, Henry "Hank" Eugene, 130, 132
Beatles, The, 57
Beckley, Jacob Peter, 97
Beecher, Henry Ward, 66
Beethoven Ludwig, 54, 62
Begin, Menechem, 69
Behringer, Charles Leonard "Charlie", 90
Bell, Alexander Graham, 66
Bell, James "Cool Papa", 101, 109, 111
Bellomont, Lord, 68
Ben-Gurion, David, 69
Bench, John Lee, 119, 120
Bender, Charles Albert "Chief", 83, 90
Berger, Wally, 131, 132
Berkeley, Sir William, 68
Berle, Milton, 38
Berlin, Irving, 63
Bernard, Francis, 68
Bernhardt, Sarah, 61
Berra Lawrence Peter "Yogi", 99, 111
Betancourt, Romulo, 69
Bevins, Floyd Clifford, 129, 132
Bibliotheque Nationale, 16
Bill, Buffalo, 66
Bizet, 62
Black Hawk War discharges, 77, 79
Blackwell, Ewell "the Whip", 127, 132
Bliss, Col. Alexander, 77
Blount, William, 73
Blue, Vida Rochelle, 124
Blyleven, Rikalbert Bert, 120
Boccaccio, Giovanni, 18
Bodleian Library, 17
Bonaparte, Napoleon, 69, 74

Bonds, Bobby Lee, 119
Bonney, William (Billy the Kid), 66
Books, autographed, 50-1
Boone, Daniel, 66
Booth, Edwin, 77
Booth, John Wilkes, 77
Bordagaray, Frenchy, 128, 132
Boston Braves, 127, 131
Boston Public Library
Boston Red Sox, 117, 119, 124, 127, 128, 130, 131
Botha, Pieter Willem, 69
Bottomley, James Leroy, 101
Boudreau, Louis "Lou", 97
Bourguiba, Habib, 69
Boxing champions, 37
Boyer, Kenton Lloyd "Ken", 125
Braddock, Jim, 37
Bradford, William 73
Bradley, Joseph, 47, 50
Bradley, Omar N., 48
Brahms, Johannes, 53, 62
Branca, Ralph Theodore Joseph, 129, 132
Bresnahan, Roger Patrick, 86
Brett, George Howard, 124
Brissie, Leland "Lou" Victor, 132
British Museum, 16, 18
Brock, Lewis Clark "Lou", 111, 119, 120
Brooklyn Dodgers, 117, 125, 128, 129, 130
Brouthers, Dennis "Dan", 86
Brown, John, 73
Brown, Jr., Edmund, 44
Brown, Mordecai Peter Centennial, 90
Brown, William P., 19
Buck, Pearl S., 50
Buckeley, Morgan G., 84
Buffalo Bill, 53
Bunning, James Paul, 119, 120
Burdette, Lew, 127, 132, 132
Burgmeier, Thomas Henry, 120
Burkett, Jesse Cail, 83, 87
Burns, Charles F. 18
Burr, Aaron, 66
Burroughs, John, 53
Burton, Richard, 39
Bush, George, 44
Byrne, Thomas Joseph, 127, 132
Byrnes, James F., 50, 66

C

Cain, Robert Max, "Bob", 127, 132
Caldwell, Erskine, 38
California Angels, 117, 124
Camilli, Adolph Louis "Dolph", 121, 125, 131, 132
Campanella, Roy, 96. 109, 111, 117
Campaneris, Dagoberto "Bert", 119
Campbell, Bruce Douglas, 131, 132
Candelaria, John Robert, 121
Canterbury Tales, The, 17
Cantor, Eddie, 53
Capone, Al, 66
Care of autographs, materials needed, 139-40, 143-4
Carew, Rodney Cline, 124
Carey, Max George, 84, 94
Carlton, Steve Norman, 121
Carroll, Clay Palmer, 122
Carson, Johnny, 38

156 Index

Cartoonists, 39
Caruso, Enrico, 63
Casadesus, Robert, 38
Casey, Hugh, 130
Castro, Fidel, 29-30
Cavaretta, Philip Joseph, 125
Cedeno, Cesar Eugenito, 120
Celebrities: addresses, 31-4; television, 38; theater, 38-9
Celebrity Register, The, 34
Chaldeans, 13
Chamberlain, Richard, 39
Chamberlain, Wilt, 37
Chance, Frank Leroy, 87
Chance, Wilmer Dean, 122
Chandler, Albert Benjamin "Happy", 105, 107, 111
Chandler, Spurgeon Ferdinand "Spud", 124
Chanute, Octave, 17
Chaplin, Charlie, 62
Charleston, Oscar McKinley, 102
Chats on Autographs, 150
Chaucer, 17
Chesbro, John Dwight, 87
Chevalier, Maurice, 61
Chicago Cubs, 118, 125, 129, 130, 131
Chicago Historical Society, 7
Chicago White Sox, 115, 117, 130
China, 13, 14
Churchill, Winston, 69, 73
Cicero, 14, 18
Cid, El, 14
Cincinnati Reds, 118, 125, 127, 128, 129
Cist, L.J., 77
Civil War: generals, 55-6; letters & diaries, 55
Clap, Thomas, 70
Clark, Tom, 40
Clarke, Fred Clifford, 86
Clarkianus, 17
Clarkson, John Gibson, 94
Clay, Cassius (Muhammad Ali), 37
Clem, William J., 91
Clemens, Samuel Langhorne, 73
Clemente, Roberto Walker, 100
Cleveland Indians, 117, 124, 127, 131
Clinton, General George, 73, 75
Cobb, Ty, 37, 84
Cochrane, Gordon Stanley "Mickey", 83, 89
Codex Allexandrinus, 17
Colavito, Rocco "Rocky" Domenico, 128, 132
Colfax, Schuyler, 53
Collecting Autographs and Manuscripts, 150
Collector, The 18
Colleges, 77
Collins, Edward Trowbridge, 85
Collins, James Joseph, 87
Colloquial Who's Who, The—1620-1924, 150
Colt, Sam, 66
Comiskey, Charles Albert, 85
Composers and musicians, 62-3
Compton, Arthur H., 70
Conlon, John Bertrand "Jocko", 101, 109, 111
Connolly, John 44
Connolly, Thomas Henry, 91
Connor, Roger, 102
Constitution, 18
Contemporary Authors, 34
Contemporary Copy, definition, 153
Coolidge, Grace, 66
Coombs, Earl Bryan "Colonel", 97
Cooney, John Walter "Johnny", 127, 132

Cornell University, 77
Cotton, Robert, 17
Coveleski, Stanley Anthony "Stan", 96
Coward, Sir Noel, 61
Coxe, Tench, 68
Cramer, Roger Maxwell, 131, 132
Crawford, Samuel Earl "Wahoo Sam", 93
Crockett, David, 66
Cromwell, Oliver, 69
Cronin, Joseph Edward "Joe", 93
Crosetti, Frank Peter Joseph, 130, 132
Cuba, 29
Cummings, William Arthur "Candy", 85
Curiosity Cabinet, The, 19
Cushing, Thomas, 68
Custer, George, 66
Cut signature, definition, 153
Cuyler, Hazen Shirley "Kiki", 96

D

d'Estaing, Valery Giscard, 69
Daggett, Albert, 56
Dale, Sir Thomas, 68
Dali, Salvador, 42, 54
Dana's House, 149
Danforth, Elliott, 77
Dante, 18
Dark, Alvin Ralph, 129, 132
Darwin, Charles, 57
Davis, Jefferson, 53, 66, 80
Davis, Varna, 80
Day, J. Edward, 42-4
Dayan, Moshe, 53
Dealers, autograph, 149-50
Dean, Jay Hanna "Dizzy", 91
Dean, William F., 24
Decatur, Stephen, 66
Declaration of Independence, 16, 18, 53, 73; signers of, 77
Defense of Fort McHenry, 60
Definitions used by collectors, 153-4
DeGaulle, Charles, 69
Delahanty, Edward James, 87
DeLancey, James, 68
Demaret, Jimmy, 37
Dempsey, Jack, 37
Den's Collectors Den, 127, 150
Detroit Tigers, 117, 119, 124, 127, 128, 130, 131
Dewey, George, 66
Dewey, Thomas, 66
Dickens, Charles, 19, 73
Dickey, William Malcolm "Bill", 91, 111
Dihigo, Martin, 103
Dillinger, John, 66
DiMaggio, Dom, 130, 132
DiMaggio, Joseph Paul "Joe", 91, 111, 127, 130
DiMaggio, Vince, 130, 132
Directory of American Scholars, 34
Disney, Walt, 66
Doby, Lawrence Eugene "Larry", 131, 132
Docketed, definition, 154
Document, definition, 153
Documents: early American, 54-5; presidential, 54, 71
Dole, Robert, 44
Donohue, Peter Joseph "Pete", 127, 132
Dooley, Tom, 53, 66
Douglas, William O. 66

Drake, Nathan, 79
Dreiser, Theodore, 53
Dropo, Walt, 131, 132
Drysdale, Donald Scott "Don", 106, 111
Duffy, Hugh, 83, 87
Duke University, 16
Dumas, Alexander, 53
Durocher, Leo, 130, 132
Duvalier, Francois, 53

E

Earhart, Amelia, 66
Early American insurance policies, 55
Eastwood, Clint, 37
Eden, Anthony, 69, 73
Edison, Thomas, 66
Edward II, 14
Edward III, 14
Edward IV, 15
Edward VII, 15
Egypt, 13, 14
Einstein, Albert, 45
Eisenhower, Dwight D., 47, 50, 53, 72, 76
Eisenhower, Mamie, 10, 66
El-Khoury, Bechara, 47
Ellis, Havelock, 70
Ellsworth, Oliver, 73
Emancipation Proclamation, 68
Emerson, Ralph Waldo, 60
Emmet, Dr. Thomas Addis, 77
England, 13, 14, 17, 18
English Literary Autographs, 150
English Poetical Autographs, 150
English writers, 58
Erskine, Carl Daniel, 129, 132
Etten, Nichols Raymond Tom "Nick", 121
Euclid, 17
Evaluating war autographic material, 56-7
Evans, William George, 100
Evelyn, John, 17
Evers, John Joseph, 87
Ewing, William Buckinham "Buck", 85

F

Faber, Urban Charles "Red", 95
Fads, effect on autograph prices, 56
Fain, Ferris Roy, 131, 132
Farragut, David, 66
Faubus, Orville, 39
Faulkner, William, 55, 60
FBI, 81
Feller, Robert William Andrew "Bob", 94, 111
Ferrell, Richard Benjamin "Rick", 106, 111
Ferriss, Dave, 131
Fine, definition, 154
Fingers, Roland Glen "Rollie", 124
Fisher, Jack, 128
Fisher, Ray, 129, 132
Fitzgerald, F. Scott, 54
Flea markets, 50
Flick, Elmer Harrison, 94
Florence National Central Library, 18
Flynn, Errol, 62
Folger Shakespeare Memorial Library, 57
Ford, Doug, 37
Ford, Edward Charles "Whitey", 101, 111
Ford, Gerald, 44

Foreign heads of state, forms of address, 33
Foreign writers, 57-8
Forgery, 80-1
Foster, Andrew "Rube", 105
Foster, George Arthur, 120, 125
Fox, Margaret, 69
Foxx, James Emory "Jimmy", 83, 90
France, 18
Franco, Francisco, 69
Franking, 76
Franklin, Benjamin, 17, 53, 66; *Autobiography*, 17
Fraser, John Malcolm, 69
Frazier, Joe, 37
Frederick VIII, 53
French writers, 58
Frick, Ford Christopher, 97
Frisch, Frank Francis "Frankie", 89
Frost, Robert, 60
Fulton, Robert, 75

G

Galileo, 70
Gallery of Champions, 149
Galvin, James F. "Pud", 95
Gandhi, Indira, 69
Gandhi, Mahatma, 69
Garagiola, Joseph Henry "Joe", 130, 132
Garfield, Lucretia, 66
Garr, Ralph Allan, 120
Garvey, Steven Patrick, 125
Gaston, Nathaniel Milton "Milt", 130, 132
Gates, Thomas, 68
Gatling, Richard, 66
Gehrig, Henry Louis "Lou", 37, 85
Gehringer, Charles Leonard "Charlie", 111
Generals, Civil War, 55-6
Gentile, James Edward "Jim", 132
George II, 17
German writers, 58
Germany, 14; Nazi, World War II, 64-5
Gettysburg Address, 18, 53, 77, 78
Gibson, Joshua "Josh", 99
Gibson, Robert "Bob", 105, 109, 111
Giles, Warren Christopher, 103
Gish, Lillian, 62
Giusti, David John, 120
Gladstone, William, 53
Gleason's Pictorial, 18
Glenn, John, 16
Globetrotters, Harlem 39
Godfrey, Arthur, 38
Goldwater, Barry, 44, 73
Golf stars, 37
Gomez, Vernon Louis "Lefty", 99, 109, 111
Goodyear, Charles, 66
Gordon, Ruth, 39
Goslin, Leon Allen "Goose", 96
Gossage, Richard Allen "Goose", 122
Gould, Chester, 39
Government leaders, U.S., forms of address, 31-2
Goya, 75
Graham, Billy, 50, 69
Granger, Wayne Allen, 122
Grant, Ulysses S., 51, 68
Grate, Don, 131, 131
Gray, Pete, 127, 133
Gray, Thomas, 58

Greece, National Library of, 18
Greeley, Horace, 66
Greenberg, Henry Benjamin "Hank", 93, 111
Grey, Zane, 60
Griffith, Clark Calvin "Cal", 37, 83, 87
Grimes, Burleigh Arland, 95, 111, 129
Groat, Richard Morrow "Dick", 125
Grove, Robert Moses "Lefty", 89
Guide to Archives and Manuscripts in the United States, 18
Guidry, Ronald Ames, 121
Gwinnett, Button, 53

H

Haddix, Harvey "Kitten", 128, 133
Hafey, Charles James "Chick", 99
Hagen, Walter, 37
Haines, Jesse Joseph "Pop", 97
Hale, Nathan, 66, 73
Haliburton, Richard, 53
Hall of Fame, Baseball, 107
Hall, Monte, 38
Hamilton, Alexander, 17, 19, 71, 73
Hamilton, William Robert "Billy", 94
Hammerstein, Oscar, 63
Hancock, John, 55, 65
Handbook of Famous Personages, 150
Harding, Florence Kling, 66
Harlem Globetrotters, 39
Harridge, William "Will", 99
Harriman, Averill, 66
Harris, Stanley Raymond "Bucky", 101
Hartnett, Charles Leo "Gabby", 91
Hatlo, Jimmy, 39
Haverford College, 77
Hayes, Helen, 61
Hearns, Tommy, 37
Heilman, Harry Edwin, 90
Helf, Henry Hartz "Hank", 127, 133
Hemingway, Ernest M., 60
Henderson, Rickey Henley, 121
Henrich, Thomas David "Tommy", 130, 133
Henry Huntington Library, 77
Henry IV, 53
Henry, Patrick, 66
Herman, William Jennings "Billy", 101, 111
Hernandez, Keith, 125
Hiller, John Frederick, 122
Hiss, Alger, 50
Historical societies, 16, 77
Historical Society of Pennsylvania, 77
History, American, 65-9
Hitler, Adolph, 65
Hogan, Ben, 37, 53
Holloman, Alva Lee "Bobo", 127, 133
Holmes, Larry, 37
Holmes, Oliver Wendell, 66
Holmes, Thomas Francis "Tommy", 131, 133
Holograph, 151
Hooper, Harry Bartholomew, 99
Hoover, Herbert, 28, 50
Hoover, J. Edgar, 42, 66
Hoppe, Willie, 37
Hornsby, Rogers, 37, 86
Houghton Library, Harvard, 77
House, Edward M., 66
Houston Astros, 118
Houston, Sam, 66
Howe, Gordie, 37

Hoyt, Waite Charles, 97
Hubbard, Robert Cal, 102
Hubbell, Carl Owen, 89, 111
Huggins, Miller James, 95
Hughes, Charles Evans, 53
Humphrey, Hubert, 44, 45
Hunter, Robert, 68
Huntington, Henry, 17
Hussein, King of Jordan, 47
Hutchinson, Thomas, 68
Huxley, Julian S., 70
Huxley, Thomas, 53

I

Identical names, 72-3
Iliad, 17
Illinois Historical Society, 77
India, 23
Indiana, University of, 77
Insurance policies, early American, 55
International Who's Who, 34
International Yearbook and Statesmen's Who's Who, 34
Irvin, Monford "Monte", 100, 111

J

Jackson, Andrew, 54
Jackson, Henry, 73
Jackson, Michael, 37
Jackson, Reginald Martinez, 124
Jackson, Stonewall, 66
Jackson, Travis Calvin "Stonewall", 106, 109, 111, 113
Jefferson, Martha, 66
Jefferson, Thomas, 13, 17, 18, 55
Jeffries, Jim, 37
Jennings, Hugh Ambrose "Hughey", 87
Jensen, Forrest Docenus, 131, 133
Jensen, Jack Eugene, 124
John Rylands Library, 18
John Work Garrett Library, 77
John, Thomas Edward, 120
Johnson, Andrew, 71
Johnson, Byron Bancroft, 84
Johnson, Eliza, 66
Johnson, Jud, 109
Johnson, Lyndon B., 27, 44, 45, 53, 72, 76
Johnson, Walter Perry, 37, 84
Johnson, William Julius "Judy", 102, 111
Jones, Bobby, 37
Jones, John Paul, 66
Joost, Edwin David "Eddie", 133
Joss, Adrian "Addie", 103
Jurges, William Frederick "Billy", 133

K

Kaat, James Lee, 120
Kadar, Janos, 69
Kaishek, Chiang, 69
Kaline, Albert William "Al", 105, 111
Kansas City Royals, 117, 124
Karpis, Alvin, 66
Keefe, Timothy J., 95
Keeler, William Henry "Willie", 86
Kell, George Clyde, 106, 111

Keller, Charles, "King Kong", 130, 133
Keller, Helen, 67
Kelley, Joseph James, 99
Kelly, George Lange, 100
Kelly, Michael Joseph "King", 87
Kelly, Walt, 39
Keltner, Kenneth Frederick "Kenny", 133
Kemp, Jack, 37
Kennedy, Jacqueline, 72, 76
Kennedy, John F., 42-4, 57, 76
Kennedy, Robert, 44, 53
Kennedy, Ted, 44
Kerr, Bobby, 129
Kerr, John "Buddy" Joseph, 133
Ketchum, Hank, 39
Key, Francis Scott, 58-9
Kieft, Willem, 68
Killebrew, Harmon Clayton, 106, 111
Kiner, Ralph McPherran, 102, 111
King, Rufus, 73
Kingman, David Arthur, 119
Kings, queens, other royalty, 63-4
Klein, Charles Herbert "Chuck", 105
Kluszewski Theodore Bernard "Ted", 121
Knowles, Darold Duane, 120
Koenig, Mark Anthony, 129, 133
Koosman, Jerry Martin, 120
Korean War, letters, 56
Koufax, Sanford "Sandy", 100, 109, 111, 128

L

L.S., 27
Lafayette, Marquis de, 19, 65
Lajoie, Napoleon "Larry", 84
Landis, Kenesaw Mountain, 86
Langtry, Lillie, 61
LaRoche, David Eugene, 120
Larsen Donald James "Don", 128, 133
Lattimore, Owen, 67, 70
Lavagetto, Harry "Cookie" Arthur, 129, 133
Lawrence, Gertrude, 61
Leakey, Louis, 70
Lee, General Robert E., 56
Lee, Gypsy Rose, 38
Lee, Richard Henry, 53
LeFlore, Ronald, 120
Lemon, Robert Granville "Bob", 102, 111
Lenin State Library, 18
Lenin, Vladimir, 69
Leonard, Sugar Ray, 37
Leonard, Walter Fenner "Buck,", 100, 111
Letter, definition, 153
Letters & diaries: Civil War, 55; Revolutionary War, 55
Lewis, John L., 31
Lewis, Meriwether, 67
Libraries, 77: ancient, 14; national, 16-8; university, 16-7
Library of Congress, 17, 18, 77
Lincoln National Life Foundation, 56
Lincoln, Abraham, 17, 18, 53, , 56, 76, 68, 77, 78
Lincoln, Mary Todd, 17, 68, 76
Lindisfarne Gospels, 17
Lindstrom, Frederick Charles, 102
Lipmann, Fritz, 47
List of Manuscript Collections in the Library of Congress, 18
Lloyd, John Henry, 103

Lodge, Henry Cabot, 67
Lolich, Michael Stephen "Mickey", 120
Longfellow, Henry Wadsworth, 53, 60
Lopes, David Earl, 121
Lopez, Alfonso Ramon "Al", 103, 111
Los Angeles Dodgers, 118, 125
Louis, Joe, 37
Louis-Phillippe, 53
Loyola, Ignatius, 69
Luther, Martin, 18, 53, 70
Lyle, Albert Walter "Sparky", 120
Lynch, Jr., Thomas, 73
Lynn, Frederic Michael, 124
Lyons, Theodore Amar "Ted", 93, 107, 109, 111

M

M.C., definition, 154
M.O.C., definition, 154
MacArthur, Douglas, 47, 67
Mack, Connie, 83, 84, 85
MacPhail, Leland Stanford "Larry", 103
Madison, Dolly, 17, 76
Madison, James, 17, 73
Maglie, Salvatore Anthony "Sal", 133
Maine Historical Society, 77
Majeski, Hank, 131, 133
Mantle, Mickey Charles, 37, 101, 107, 111
Manuscript, definition, 153
Manuscript Society, 10, 150
Manush, Henry Emmett "Heinie", 95
Maranville, Walter James "Rabbit", 83, 91
Marciano, Rocky, 37
Marcos, Ferdinand, 69
Marcum, Johnny, 131, 133
Marichal, Juan Antonio, 106, 109, 111
Marion, Francis, 73
Marion, Martin Whiteford "Marty", 123, 125
Maris, Roger, 128
Markarios III, 69
Marquard, Richard William "Rube", 99
Martin, Mary 39
Maryland Historical Society, 60
Mason-Dixon diary, 18
Mathewson, Christopher, 84
Matthews, Edwin Lee "Eddie", 103, 111
Mays, Willie Howard, 37, 103, 107, 108, 113, 128
McCarthy, Joseph Vincent "Joe", 93
McCarthy, Thomas Francis, 87
McCormick, Frank Andrew, 125, 133
McCormick, Frank, 130
McCovey, Willie Lee, 125
McDaniel, Lyndall Dale, 120
McDougald, Gilbert James "Gil", 131, 133
McDowell, Samuel Edward, 121
McGinnity, Joseph Jerome "Iron Man", 87
McGraw, Frank Edwin "Tug", 120
McGraw, John Joseph, 85
McHenry, James, 71
McKechnie, William Boyd "Bill", 83, 94
McKinley, Ida, 66
McMahon, Donald John, 120
McNally, David Arthur, 122
Medwick, Joseph Michael "Ducky", 96
Mencken, H. L., 60
Mendes-France, 69
Menon, V.K. Krishna, 23
Michelangelo, 18

Mifflin, Thomas, 71
Military figures, 45-7
Military leaders, forms of address, 33
Miller, Edward Robert "Eddie", 133
Millikan, Robert A., 67
Milwaukee Brewers, 117, 124
Minnesota Twins, 117, 124
Minuit, Peter, 68
Mitchell, John, 55
Mitchell, Loren Dale, 120
Mitchell, Martha, 67
Mize, John Robert "Johnny", 105, 113
Modern, definition, 154
Mondale, Walter, 67
Monroe, Eliza, 66
Monroe, James, 17, 73
Monroe, Marilyn, 62
Montreal Expos, 118
Moody, William H., 67
Moore, Joe Gregg, 130, 133
Morgan, J. Pierpont, 17
Morris, Robert, 73
Mosby, John S., 67
Moses, Grandma, 38
Movie stars, 37, 62
Mozart, 62
Musial, Stanley Frank "Stan the Man", 97, 113
Musicians and composers, 62-3

N

Nash, Ogden, 53
National Archives, 50
National Central Library (Florence), 18
National leaders, 69
National League, 119, 125
  teams, addresses, 118
National Library of Greece, 18
National Pastime, 149
Nazi Germany, World War II, 64-5
Nehru, Jawaharlal, 69
Nelson, Lord, 69, 74
New Jersey Historical Society, 77
New Testaments, 17
New York Giants, 129, 130, 131
New York Mets, 118, 119
New York Public Library, 16, 77
New York State Library, 77
New York Yankees, 124, 128, 129, 130, 131
Newcombe, Don, 123, 125
Newhouser, Harold "Hal", 123, 124
Nicholas V, 18
Nichols, Charles Augustus "Kid", 37, 83, 90
Nixon, Richard, 44, 45
Nobel, Albert, 70
Nobel Prize winners, 45, 47
North, William Alex, 121
North Carolina, University of, 16
Note, definition, 153
Nuxhall, Joseph Henry "Joe", 133

O

O'Rourke, James Henry, 87
Oakland Athletics, 115, 118, 124
Oakley, Annie, 67
Oberth, Hermann, 70
Oblong, definition, 154
Odyssey, 17

Index   159

Oeschger, Joseph Carl "Joe", 133
Old Testaments, 17
Old, definiton, 154
On My Own, 66
On the Constitution of Athens, 17
Orta, Juan A., 29
Oswald, Lee Harvey, 67
Ott, Melvin Thomas "Mel", 37, 90
Owen, Arnold Malcolm "Mickey", 130,133
Owen, Marvin James, 130, 133
Oxford, 17

P

P.M. Antiques & Collectibles, 149
Paderewski, 75
Pafko, Andy, 131
Page, definition, 154
Page, Geraldine, 39
Paige, Leroy Robert "Satchel", 99
Paine, Thomas, 60, 73
Palmer, Arnold, 37
Palmer, James Alvin, 122
Paraph, as means of identification, 75
Parker, David Gene "Dave", 124
Passeau, Claude William, 129, 134
Pasteur, Louis, 53
Patterson, Floyd, 37
Pauling, Linus, 53, 70
Pawnee Bill, 67
Peale, Norman Vincent, 69
Peary, Robert E., 67
Penn, John, 53, 67, 73
Penn, Thomas, 67
Penn, William, 17, 18, 67
Pennock, Herbert Jeffers "Herb", 89
Pennsylvania: Historical Society of, 77; University of, 77
Perez-Steele Galleries, 107, 150
Pergamum, 14
Perranoski, Ronald Peter, 120
Perry, Gaylord Jackson, 119, 120
Perry, Oliver Hazard, 67
Perry, Richard E., 53
Pershing, John J., 67
Philadelphia Athletics, 124, 127, 131
Philadelphia Phillies, 118, 119, 125, 131
Photographs: autographed, 11, 20, 23, 25-6, 27-30, 42, 44-5, 47, 49-50;
enclosing with request, 11
Pickford, Mary, 61
Pickney, William, 67
Pierpont Morgan Library, 77
Piersall, James Anthony "Jimmy", 134
Pike, Bishop, 69
Pittsburg Pirates, 115, 117, 118, 125, 128, 131
Pizarro, 74
Plank, Edward Steward "Eddie", 37, 87
Plato, 17
Pliny the Younger, 14, 17
Poe, Edgar Allen, 17, 60, 75
Politicians, 39-45
Polk, Sarah, 66
Pony Express letters, 54
Poore, Benjamin Perley, 18-9
Porter, Cole, 63
Porter, David, D., 67
Portillo, Jose Lopez, 69
Powell, John Wesley "Boog", 124
Preble, George Henry, 67

Presidential documents, 71
Presley, Elvis, 56
Priced Catalogue of Autographs for Sale at the Great Central Fair for the U.S. Sanitary Commission, A 18
Prices of various autographic materials, 57-70
Provenance, definition, 154
Provenience, definition, 154
Pseudonyms, 73
Puccini, 62
Purvis, Melvin, 67
Putnam, Israel, 73

Q

Quarterly Journal, A (Library of Congress) 18
Queen Victoria, 53
Quisenberry, Daniel Raymond, 122

R

Race, Elroy Leon, 120
Radbourne, Charles G. "Old Hoss", 86
Rainier, Prince of Monaco, 47
Rakotomalala, Louis, 47
Raleigh, Sir Walter, 57
Rand, Sally, 67
Raschi, Victor John Angelo "Vic", 128-9, 134
Reagan, Ronald, 25, 37, 39, 44, 72
Reed, George C., 67
Reese, Harold Henry "Pee Wee", 106, 113, 117
Reese, James Herman "Jimmie", 131, 134
Reference sources for collectors, 150
Religious leaders, 69
Renaissance, 14, 17
Republic, 18
Revere, Paul, 67
Revolutionary War letters & diaries, 55
Reynolds, Allie Pierce, 127, 134
Rhee, Syngman, 69
Rice, Edgar Charles "Sam", 95
Rice, James Edward, 124
Richard, James Rodney, 121
Rickenbacker, Eddie, 67
Rickey, Welsey Branch, 96, 117
Rickover, Hyman, 67
Riley, James W., 60
Risher, John Howard, 132
Rixey, Eppa, 95
Rizzuto, Philip Francis, 124
Roberts, Oral, 69
Roberts, Robin Evan, 10, 1132
Robespierre, 19
Robinson, Brooks Calvert, 106, 113
Robinson, Frank, 106, 109, 113
Robinson, Jack Roosevelt "Jackie", 37, 94, 117
Robinson, Sugar Ray, 37
Robinson, Wilbert, 87
Rock stars, 37
Rockefeller, Nelson, 44
Rockwell, Norman, 53, 67
Rodgers, Richard, 53
Rodney, Caesar, 67, 73
Roe, Elwin Charles "Preacher", 122
Rogell, William George "Bill", 134
Rogers, Will, 67
Romans, 14
Romney, George, 44
Romulo, Carlos, 53

Roosevelt Library, 16
Roosevelt, Eleanor, 27, 66
Roosevelt, Franklin, 71
Roosevelt, Theodore, 71
Root, Charlie, 129
Rose, Peter Edward, 120
Rosen, Albert Leonard "Al", 124
Rousch, Edd J., 94, 113
Royalty, 63-4
Rudi, Joseph Owen, 120
Ruffing, Charles Herbert "Red", 96, 113
Rush, Robert Ransom, 134
Rusie, Amos Wilson, 103
Rusk, Dean, 53, 67
Russell, Bertrand, 50
Ruth, Babe, 37, 83, 84, 128, 129, 131
Rutherford B. Hayes Library, 16
Ryan, Lynn Nolan, 37, 121
Rylands, John, Library, 18

S

Sabin, Albert, 53, 70
Sadat, Anwar, 69
St. Augustine, 70
St. John's Seminary, 77
St. Louis Browns, 127
St. Louis Cardinals, 117, 118, 125, 128, 130
St. Mary's of the Lake Seminary,
Salazar, Antonio de Oliveira, 69
Salk, Jonas, 37, 53, 70
Salutations, to celebrities, 31-4
Samuelson, Paul A., 67
San Diego Padres, 118
San Francisco Giants, 115, 118, 125
Sauer, Henry John "Hank", 125
Schalk, Raymond "Ray", 93
Schlesinger, Arthur, 67
Schmeling, Max, 37
Schmidt, Helmut, 69
Schmidt, Michael Jack "Mike", 125
Schoendienst, Albert Fred "Red", 131, 134
Schulte, Fred William, 134
Schweitzer, Albert, 45, 46, 50
Scientists, autographs of, 70
Score, Herbert Jude "Herb", 134
Scott, Winfield, 67
Scranton, William, 44
Seattle Mariners, 118
Seaver, George Thomas, 120
Seerey, James Patrick "Pat", 128, 134
Selassie, Haile, 69
Seminick, Andrew Wasil "Andy", 131, 134
Seward, William H., 67
Sewell, Joseph Wheeler "Joe", 103, 109, 113
Shakespeare, William, 17, 57
Shantz, Robert Clayton "Bobby", 124
Shapley, Harlow, 70
Sharkey, Jack, 37
Shaw, George Bernard, 17
Sheen, Bishop Fulton, 69
Shelley, Percy, 58
Shepard, Alan, 16, 45
Sherman, General W. T., 56
Sherry, Norman Burt "Norm", 134
Shirley, William, 68
Shockley, William, 67, 70
Shulte, Freddie, 131
Sievers, Roy Edward, 121
Signature: definition, 154; facsimile, 71-2

Signatures, Autopen, 72-3
Signer, definition, 154
Simmons, Aloysius Harry "Al", 83, 84, 91
Sisler, George Harold, 86
Sitting Bull, 67
Slaughter, Enos Bradsher "Country", 107, 113
Sleeper, definition, 154
Smith, Edgar, 127, 134
Smith, John, 68
Snider, Edwin Donald "Duke", 105, 113, 117
Spahn, Warren Edward, 100, 113
Spalding, Albert Goodwill, 86
Spanish-American War, letters, 56
Speaker, Tristran E. "Tris", 85
Special Punctuation used by collectors, 154
Speed, Joshua Fry, 68
Speer, Albert, 16, 148
Spellman, Cardinal, 69
Sprague, William, 77
Sprinz, Joseph Conrad "Joe", 134
Stalin, Joseph, 69
Stallard, Evan Tracy, 128, 134
Stanky, Edward Raymond "Eddie", 129, 134
Star Spangled Banner, The, manuscript, 58-9
Stargell, Wilver Dornel "Willie", 125
Stars, golf, 37
Stars, rock, 37
Stars. movie, 37
State Historical Society of Wisconsin, 77
Staub, Rusty, 119
Stengel, Charles Dillon "Casey", 37, 95
Stephenson, Jackson Riggs, 134
Stephenson, Riggs, 130
Stewart, James, 127
Stooges, Three, 53
Stratton, Monte Franklin Pierce, 127, 134
Stuyvesant, Peter, 67, 68
Sullivan, Ed, 38
Sumerians, 13
Sunday, W.A. "Billy", 69
Supplies needed, 11, 21
Supply and demand, effect on autograph values, 57
Sutter, Howard Bruce, 122
Sutton, Donald Howard, 120
Swaggert, Jimmy, 69
Swanson, Gloria, 62

T

Taylor, Courtney Townsend, 81
Taylor, Margaret, 66
Tefft, Israel, 77
Tekulve, Kenton Charles, 120
Television celebrities, 38
Terry, William Harold "Bill", 91, 113
Texas Rangers, 118
Texas, University of, 16
Theatre celebrities, 38-9
Thomas, Lowell, 53
Thompson, Samuel L., 101
Thomson, Robert Brown "Bobby", 129, 134
Thoreau, Henry David, 61
Three Stooges, 53
Tiant, Luis Clemente, 120
Tinker, Joseph Bert, 87
Tito, Marshal, 69
Toronto Blue Jays, 118
Torporcer, George "Specs", 127, 134
Torre, Joseph Frank "Joe", 125

Toure, Ahmed Sekou, 48, 69
Traynor, Harold Joseph "Pie", 37, 89
Trucks, Virgil Oliver, 128, 134
Trudeau, Pierre, 69
Truman, Harry, 28-9, 50, 76
Tryon, William, 68
Tse-tung, Mao, 69
Tshombe, Moise, 69
Tunney, Gene, 37
Twain, Mark, 73
Twining, Nathan, 45

U

University of: Indiana, 77; North Carolina, 16; Pennsylvania, 77; Texas, 16; Virginia, 16

V

Valenzuela, Fernando, 11
Values of various autographic materials, 57-70
Van Allen, James A., 47, 70
Van Buren, Hannah, 66
Van Loon, Hendrik Willem, 53
Van Twiller, Wouter, 68
Vance, Clarence Arthur "Dazzy", 93
Vander Meer, John Samuel "Johnny", 134
Vatican Apostolic Library, 18
Verdi, Giuseppe, 75
Verrazano, 17
Victoria, Queen, 53
Vidal, Gore, 38
Vietnam conflict, letters, 56
Virgil, 18
Virginia, University of, 16
Von Braun, Wehrner, 16, 50

W

Waddell, George Edward "Rube", 89
Wagner, Honus, 83
Wagner, John Peter, 84
Wainwright, Jonathan, 68
Walcott, Jersey Joe, 37
Walker, Harry William "The Hat", 130, 134
Wallace, George, 39
Wallace, Henry, 53
Wallace, Roderick John "Bobby", 91
Walsh, Edward Augustin "Eddie", 89
Walter R. Benjamin Autographs, Inc., 149
Walter, Bruno, 53
Walyers, William Henry "Bucky", 125
Waner, Lloyd James "Little Poison", 37, 96
Waner, Paul Glee, 83, 90
War autographic material, evaluating, 56-7
Ward, John Montgomery, 95
Warren, Earl, 40-1
Wartime letters: Korean War, 56; Spanish-American War, 56; Vietnam, 56; World War I, 56; World War II, 56
Washington Senators, 129, 131
Washington, Booker T., 70
Washington, George, 17, 18, 19, 55, 71, 73
Washington, Martha, 55, 65
Waterman pen, 14
Wayne, Anthony, 73
Wayne, John, 62
Weaver, Earl Sidney, 120

Webster, Daniel, 53, 67
Webster, Noah, 67
Weiss, George Martin, 99
Welch, Michael Francis, 101
Welles, Gideon, 67
Wertz, Victor Woodrow "Vic", 128, 134
Wesley, John, 69
West Chester State College, 77
Western Reserve Historical Society, 77
Westrum, Wesley Noreen "Wes", 131, 134
Wheat, Zachariah Davis "Zack", 93
Whitman, Walt, 16,60, 61
Who's Who, 34
Who's Who in America, 34
Who's Who in American Art, 34
Who's Who in Music, 34
Who's Who in the Theater, 34
Who's Who of American Women, 34
Wilhelm, James Hoyt, 113,120
William the Conqueror, 74
Williams, Tennessee, 58
Williams, Theodore Samuel "Ted", 95, 110, 113
Wills, Maurice Morning, 121
Wilson, Harold, 69
Wilson, Lewis Robert "Hack", 103
Wilson, Woodrow, 71
Wisconsin State Historical Society, 16
Wise, Rabbi Stephen, 69
Wolcott, Oliver, 53
Wolcott, Roger, 68
Woodling, Eugene Richard "Gene", 134
Word Shadows of the Great, 150
Wordsworth, William, 53
World War I, letters, 56
World War II, letters, 56
World Who's Who in Commerce and Industry, 34
Wright brothers, 17
Wright, George, 83, 85
Wright, Orville, 67
Wright, Turbutt, 68
Wright, William Harry, 91
Writers: American, 58-61; English, 58; foreign, 57-8; French, 58; German, 58
Writing: history, 15; materials, 13-4
Wyatt, Sir Thomas, 18
Wynn, Early, 100, 109, 113
Wythe, George, 53

Y

Yale University, 16, 77
Yastrzemski, Carl Michael, 124
Yat-sen, Sun, 69
Yawkey, Thomas Austin "Tom", 105
Yellow plaque cards, 83
Yost, Edward Fred Joseph, 129, 134
Young, Brigham, 67
Young, Denton True "Cy", 83, 85
Youngs, Ross, Middlebrook, 100

Z

Zale, Tony, 9
Zernial, Gus Edward, 121